CHANGING CULTURES

The Traveller-Gypsies

CHANGING CULTURES
General Editor: Jack Goody

The aim of this series is to show how specific societies and cultures, including sub-groups within more complex societies, have developed and changed in response to conditions in the modern world. Each volume will draw on recent fieldwork to present a comprehensive analysis of a particular group, cast in a dynamic perspective that relates the present both to the past of the group and to the external forces that have impinged upon it. The range of volumes in the series reflects the developing interests and concerns of the social sciences, especially social anthropology and sociology.

Also in this series
The Nayars Today by Christopher J. Fuller
The Skolt Lapps Today by Tim Ingold
The Yoruba Today by J. S. Eades
The Western Isles Today by Judith Ennew
Tázlár: a Village in Hungary by C. M. Hann
The Nyamwezi Today by R. G. Abrahams
The Rwala Bedouin Today by William Lancaster
Ambiguous Ethnicity by Susan Benson

The Traveller-Gypsies

JUDITH OKELY

Lecturer in Social Anthropology and Sociology
University of Essex

CAMBRIDGE UNIVERSITY PRESS

CAMBRIDGE
LONDON   NEW YORK   NEW ROCHELLE
MELBOURNE   SYDNEY

Published by the Press Syndicate of the University of Cambridge
The Pitt Building, Trumpington Street, Cambridge CB2 1RP
32 East 57th Street, New York, NY 10022, USA
296 Beaconsfield Parade, Middle Park, Melbourne 3206, Australia

First published 1983

Printed in Great Britain at
the University Press, Cambridge

Library of Congress catalogue card number: 82–9478

British Library cataloguing in publication data
Okely, Judith
The traveller-gypsies.
1. Gypsies–Great Britain
I. Title
941'.00491497   DX211
ISBN 0 521 24641 5 hard covers
ISBN 0 521 28870 3 paperback

In the following pages I have endeavoured to describe a dream, partly of study, partly of adventure, in which will be found copious notices of books, and many descriptions of life and manners, some in a very unusual form.

The scenes of action lie in the British Islands; – pray be not displeased, gentle reader, if perchance thou hast imagined that I was about to conduct thee to distant lands, and didst promise thyself much instruction and entertainment from what I might tell thee of them. I do assure thee that thou hast no reason to be displeased, inasmuch as there are no countries in the world less known by the British than these selfsame British Islands, or where more strange things are every day occurring, whether in road or street, house or dingle.

George Borrow 1851. Preface to Lavengro (vii-viii)

Contents

Preface

While a postgraduate student of social anthropology, I learned of a people who believed that you could only go to heaven if your ears were pierced. Accordingly I had my ears pierced on New Year's Day 1970. It was a fortunate opening to the decade, for by the end of the year I was living with the Traveller-Gypsies who also pierce their ears, some say in order to improve their vision. But it was the Travellers who gave me a new vision and 'heaven sent moments'.

My research for this study began as a project financed by the Joseph Rowntree Memorial Trust at the Centre for Environmental Studies between 1970 and 1973. It was directed by Barbara Adams. I am grateful for her initiative, advice and collaboration. I also benefited from the collaboration with my colleagues the late David Morgan, David Smith, Cathy Dean and Marie Welch. My main period of fieldwork, living on Traveller camps, was between 1971 and 1973. Follow-up fieldwork was carried out through the rest of the 1970s. From 1973 to 1976 I was supported by a studentship for a D.Phil. from the Social Science Research Council at the Institute of Social Anthropology, Oxford. Drafts of this publication were revised and finalised while I was a Lecturer in the Department of Anthropology at the University of Durham where I was inspired by the many discussions with my colleague and friend, David Brooks.

A number of individuals have given me advice and assistance at various stages of my research: Malcolm McLeod, Edwin Ardener, Hood Saleh, Rodney Needham, Filomena Steady, Wendy James, Esther Goody, Helen Callaway, Shirley Ardener, Michael Banton, Peter Rivière, Alan Campbell, Marie Johnson, Jane Szurek and the members of the Oxford Women's Anthropology Group. Steven Lukes once threw me an intellectual lifeline. I have benefited a great deal from discussions with social anthropologists and sociologists who have done long-term field research with Gypsies or Travellers in Europe and elsewhere: Thomas Acton, Jacqueline Charlemagne, Jean Claude Guiraud, Sharon Gmelch, George Gmelch, Martti Grönfors, Willy Guy, Nabil Hanna, Marek Kaminski, Jean-Pierre Liégeois and Anne Sutherland. There were those who gave me hospitality, insights and assistance during fieldwork: Diana Allen, the late Don Byrne, Eadie Connelly, José Corrocher, Marie Lafranque, Norbett McCabe, Graham Rock and Penny Vinson.

Preface

I owe a great debt to my supervisor Godfrey Lienhardt for his guidance, brilliance and good humour. He gave me the confidence to pursue my own ideas and trusted me when I disappeared up the M1. James Hopkins has given me quiet encouragement and listened to my stories over the years. Bridget Okely, my mother, helped me through various stages of writing up. Her perspective as a sociologist and her rampant feminism have always influenced me.

I am indebted to Daphne Bartrum and Rita Hart for their enthusiasm and patient, meticulous typing of the preliminary and final drafts. Heinemann Educational Books and the Centre for Environmental Studies have kindly allowed me to amend and reprint parts of two of my chapters, 'Gypsy Identity' and 'Work and Travel', from Adams *et al.*, *Gypsies and Government Policy in England* (1975: chs. 2 and 5). Individual authorship was erased from the proofs, in accord with the wishes of some of my colleagues. Malaby and Dent have kindly permitted me to amend and reprint part of my article 'Gypsy Women' from Ardener, *Perceiving Women* (1975).

I am grateful especially to Homer Sykes and to Harold Turner and a number of newspapers, including *The Times* and the *Echo and Post*, for permission to use their photographs. In order to protect the identity of the Travellers, I have excluded photographs which I took of individuals during my fieldwork. Only the photograph on p. 55 comes into that category.

Then there are the Travellers – who gave me friendship, protection, laughter, wisdom and another life. I cannot name them since the majority would prefer anonymity. For some years now I have pondered their words and deeds and am still learning from them. I can name my favourite Traveller children who at the time were still regarded as innocent by the dominant society, since they were not yet adults: Jane, Marina, Caroline, Elvie, Minny, Billy-boy, Jeanie, Lias, Billy, John-boy, Mathais, Toey, Creamy, Dave, Vicky and Leena. They were also my teachers. In so far as they can choose to continue to be Traveller-Gypsies their future fills me with optimism.

November 1981 Judith Melita Okely
May Street,
Durham

1   Historical categories and representations

The Gypsies or Travellers have scarcely written their own history. Theirs is a non-literate tradition, so their history is found fragmented in documents of the dominant non-Gypsy or Gorgio society. (Gorgio is the word Gypsies use to describe non-Gypsies and means outsider or stranger. It is often pejorative.) The history of the Gypsies is marked by attempts to exoticise, disperse, control, assimilate or destroy them. The larger society's ways of treating and identifying Gypsies are fundamental constraints on if not determinants of the Gypsies' actions. Persons who live under the shadow of the title 'Gypsy' or its equivalent will make the appropriate adjustments to the larger Gorgio society in which they are embedded.

Some introductory remarks concerning the complexity of locating the persons called Gypsies or Travellers come as a warning. The Gypsies' history cannot be a simple chronology of non-Gypsy written records; these can only provide clues for interpretation. Nor can the complexity be resolved by looking for the 'real' Gypsies, who are usually those who fit best the stereotypes of the observer. The very notion of the 'real' Gypsy raises more questions than answers.

Long-term participant observation among persons called or calling themselves Gypsies or Travellers can however be informative for both the present and the past. In this study, I shall be drawing on the various records and writings concerned with Gypsies or Travellers[1] mainly in Britain, in order to put my own fieldwork among Gypsies in southern England in the 1970s into context. In turn, such fieldwork should also throw light on the historical records.

The different ways in which Gypsies have been identified and recorded, whether the document be a legal order or a folklorist's piece, have depended on the wider context. The Gypsies' first appearance in the British Isles is defined and fixed by the first written records in the early sixteenth century of a category of persons called 'Egyptians'. The word 'Gypsy' derives from 'Egyptian'. Records of Gypsies are of two broad types: first, the legal definitions, public statutes and later government reports; secondly, by the nineteenth century, the literary and folklore sources.

The legal and government records are witness to the struggles between the state and the minority group. The state has attempted to control

1

and exercise force against Gypsies, partly because they avoid wage-labour, are of no fixed abode, and because they seek intermittent access to land. Those who confront the prevailing order, be it in small ways, those who demonstrate alternative possibilities in economic spheres, in ways of being and thinking, those who appear as powerful symbols, must, it seems, be contained and controlled. Although in fact the Gypsies' threat is trivial, their presence exposes profound dissatisfactions in the dominant system.

Folklore and exotic literature often convey the ideological and symbolic disorder which the Gypsies appear to represent. The Gypsies are shown in either positive or negative form. Their apparent differences from non-Gypsies are elaborated or simply imagined, for example the beliefs that the Gypsies are 'closer to nature' and 'wild and free' (see Okely 1981a).

Whether legalistic or exotic, all of the non-Gypsy records and representations can be treated as artefacts to decipher. Even when the information appears to be obtained directly from the Gypsies it also requires interpretation. The Gypsies acquire maximum manoeuvrability if they give the outsider that which pleases him or her and resembles his or her presuppositions. The Gypsies appear to conform, while retaining a certain independence. Yet they are never free of the dominant system. For instance, since a travelling people are seen to defy the state's demand for a 'fixed abode', they are seen as both lawless and fascinating. In turn it may suit the Gypsies to *be* fascinating, while concealing their own way of ordering their lives. Thus stereotypes of Gypsies and accounts from them, whether 'lies' or 'truths', may be inversions or mystifications rather than reflections of 'reality'. Images of and information transmitted by Gypsies to Gorgios may speak more of Gorgios than of Gypsies.

It has been claimed that literate people have history, while non-literate people have myth, but in the case of Gypsy–Gorgio history there is a fusion of the two. The literate tradition of the dominant society has assisted in myth making, especially with regard to the myths of the Gypsies' origins. A number of places of origin have been attributed to Gypsies in the British Isles, as elsewhere in Europe. Gypsies in Britain were at first said to have come from Egypt. Perhaps the Gypsies played along with this. By the nineteenth century, the theory of an Indian origin emerged, thanks to diffusionist ideas and to studies of the dialects or 'secret' languages used by Gypsies mainly among themselves. Whether all those persons calling themselves and called Egyptians from the sixteenth century on were from overseas is a matter of considerable conjecture and controversy. Today, the extent to which Indian origin is emphasised depends on the extent to which the groups or individuals are exoticised and, paradoxically, considered acceptable to the dominant society.

Foreigners and counterfeits

The 'Egyptians' were first recorded in the British Isles in Scotland in 1505 in the accounts of the Lord High Treasurer. They presented themselves to James IV as pilgrims, their leader being lord of 'little Egypt' (Vesey-Fitzgerald 1973: 21). In England, this category of persons was first recorded in 1514 in the form of an 'Egyptian' woman who could 'tell marvellous things by looking into one's hands' (Vesey-Fitzgerald 1973: 28). One origin for this Egyptian label, both in the British Isles and elsewhere in Europe, is, according to Clébert, that well before Gypsies or 'Tsiganes' were publicly recorded in western Europe (in the fourteenth century) 'all mountebanks and travelling showmen found themselves dubbed "Egyptians"' (1967:27). Persons believed by many Gypsiologists to be the first Gypsies arriving in western Europe presented themselves as pilgrims, some from 'little Egypt', understood to represent the Middle East (Vesey-Fitzgerald 1973:13; de Vaux de Foletier 1970: 20-1). Acton, who supports the theory of the Gypsies' Indian migration, nonetheless gives an explanation as to why such 'Egyptians' might be encouraged to feign exotic origins, namely that at the period the stereotype image of an 'Egyptian' apparently fleeing from pagan persecution would have been 'favourable' (1974:61).

The Egyptian connection was further elaborated. It was said that Gypsies had to leave with Joseph and Mary in the flight from Egypt, or that Gypsies learnt their magical arts from a country renowned for such skills. These early 'Egyptians' in the British Isles were associated with exotic occupations, for example fortune telling, which they exercised 'with crafte and subtyltie' (Statute Henry VIII 1530), and James V paid 'Egyptians' who danced for him at Holyrood House in 1530.

Within a few decades, 'Egyptians' were ordered to leave the country, and deportations were carried out. A similar treatment had been imposed upon the indigenous mad in the fifteenth century (Foucault 1971). If not deported, Egyptians were imprisoned and their goods forfeited. By 1554, Egyptians who did not depart were to be judged felons and executed. But the problem for the authorities was that these Egyptians then asserted that they had been born in England and Scotland. In 1562, an order 'for the avoiding of all Doubts and Ambiguities' was introduced so that 'all such sturdy and false vagabonds of that sort living only upon the spoil of the simple people' might be punished, and the death penalty was extended not only to those 'in any company or Fellowship of Vagabonds, commonly called or calling themselves Egyptians', but also to those 'counterfeiting, transforming or disguising themselves by their Apparel, Speech or other Behaviour' (Thompson 1923a). This suggests that the Egyptian title was nothing but an assumed identity for many persons with no foreign origin. Since, in many instances, vagrants were subject to the same harsh

3

treatment as so-called Egyptians, there was no advantage in dropping the assumed title merely in order to escape the authorities. Moreover, money could be earned from the 'simple people', as well as from royalty, by presenting an exotic identity as fortune teller and dancer. The term 'Egyptian' or later 'Gypsy' could have been useful as a means of self-identification and it was not likely to be just a stigmatic label imposed by persecuting outsiders.

Further evidence collected by Thompson appears to support my suggestion that the foreign origin of many 'Egyptians' is questionable. Thompson's examination of constables' accounts and other sources reveals specific examples of persons recorded as vagabonds but convicted of felony for calling themselves by the name of an 'Egiptian', e.g. Robert Hylton of Denver, Norfolk in 1591 (Thompson 1928:37). Here self-ascription is acknowledged. Earlier in 1549 a John Roland was recorded in County Durham as 'oon of that sorte of people callinge themselves Egyptians' (1928:40). Around 1610 a pamphleteer declared that 'they goe alwais never under an hundred men or women, *causing their faces to be made blacke, as if they were Egyptians*' (Thompson 1928:34, my emphasis).

Thus the popular view that the early Gypsies were inherently different in physiognomy or so-called 'racial origin' should be treated with scepticism. It seems that persons calling themselves Eygptians found it useful to adopt not only a foreign title but also a foreign appearance.

Nonetheless, Thompson supported the notion of 'true-blooded' Gypsies who were entirely of foreign origin. He found many convictions of vagabonds recorded under names later recognised by 'experts' or Gypsiologists as 'true gypsy', e.g. Heron, White, Smith, Brown, Wilson and Young. These he suggests were really persons with 'a dash of Gypsy blood' or more, but disguised as vagabonds. Thompson does not consider the possibility that many Gypsy families may have emerged from the indigenous vagrant population as an ethnic group using the principle of descent and other self-defining features.[2]

Vagrants: an alternative category

The death penalty for Gypsies remained until 1783. However, Gypsies were not so easily eliminated: other measures had to be taken against them. The Gypsies' prosecution as 'vagrants' rather than as foreigners became clearer in the seventeenth century. Special orders were given to parish constables to chase Gypsies from their area, but with minimum success (Thompson 1928). In 1622, for example, the Bishop of Lincoln wrote to the Earl of Shaftesbury and other J.P.s in southern England, near my fieldwork area in the 1970s: 'His majestie is justly offended at you who ... do suffer your countrey to swarme with whole troupes of rogues, beggars, Aegiptians and idle persons.' The J.P.s were ordered to enforce 'these lawes for ye punishing, imploying, chasetising and rooting out of these idle people, symptomes of Popery and blynde superstition'. On 30 September an order was made for the provision of a marshal 'for the better clearing the county of rogues', and with authority to 'punish and chase away all rogues and vagrant persons'. It was also declared that 'All such persons as shall harbour such rogues and vagabonds shall be prosecuted' (Sessions Rolls 1581-1698:vol. I).

One focus was on the Gypsies' apparent idleness which, throughout Europe in the seventeenth century, was condemned by both Catholic and Protestant ideology and equated with rebellion (Foucault 1971: 56-7). As an alternative to execution, some Gypsies were to be put to 'honest service or to exercise some lawful work, Trade or Occupation' (Thompson 1923a). Those deemed idle were to be sent to the House of Correction established in the mid seventeenth century, and later to workhouses. There are examples of Gypsies being arrested and so punished in 1655, near my subsequent fieldwork area: 'George Brugman late of little Malvern Co. Worcester, Henry Hall born at Fairfield Co. Derby, Edward Morrell, William Morrell and Alexander Morrell born at Calne Co. Wilts were taken as "Egyptians" and sent to the House of Correction at [—], in order that they shall be "well whipped" and after sent by pass to the places aforesaid' (Sessions Rolls 1619-1657). A non-Gypsy was also punished for associating with Gypsies: 'Recognisance for the appearance of John Bourne at the next quarter sessions, to answer for "entertaining and harbouring several Egyptians in his House"' (Sessions Rolls 1619-1657). In March 1703 there is a further record of Gypsies: 'Warrant to the keeper of the county gaol to receive Thomas Ingroom, Margaret his wife, Easter Joanes and Susan Wood, the Head of a gang of about 50 gypsies travelling about telling fortunes and calling themselves Egyptians' (Sessions Rolls 1699-1850).

In contrast to isolated individuals, it seems likely that the Gypsies were (as they are today) a self-reproducing ethnic group with an ideology of travelling (the 1554 Statute describes how they go 'from place to place in great companies' (Thompson 1923a)), a preference for self-employment and a wide range of economic activities. It was however expedient for the state to deal with them as workless vagrants. In 1786, for example, in a special order to constables in my subsequent fieldwork area, Gypsies were classed with other persons also appearing to have lucrative occupations, and likewise condemned for their unconventional or 'unlicensed' form. Those deemed 'vagrants' included: 'Persons going about as Bear wards, or exhibiting shews, or players of Interludes, Comedies, Operas or Farces without authority, or Minstrels, Jugglers or Gypsies wandering in Form or Habit of Egyptians or Persons telling Fortunes ... and all Petty Chapmen and Pedlars not licensed ...' (Sessions Rolls 1752-1799). If such persons were found returning they were to be treated as 'incorrigible Rogues and Vagabonds'.

'Depraved' and ripe for conversion

In the nineteenth century, divergent approaches to Gypsies emerge in the literature. Some European scholars had begun to suggest that the various forms of 'language' or dialects found among Gypsies and sometimes labelled Romanes could be traced to a language of Aryan origin connected with early Sanskrit. This was publicised by the German author Grellmann (translated in 1787). In 1816 John Hoyland published the first English survey of Gypsies, using much of Grellmann, together with the results of written enquiries around England and just one visit to a Gypsy encampment.

Hoyland, a Quaker, alongside the Reverend J. Crabb and the M.P. George Smith, supported alternative forms of control to the policies of deportation or dispersal, namely conversion and assimilation into the prevailing order. 'The period in which banishments were generally pronounced on this people was too unphilosophical for any preferable mode of punishment to be suggested' (Hoyland 1816:195). Hoyland considered Gypsies to be 'depraved' (1816:158), and for them philanthropy and education should be the new policies. According to him, their wandering life originated 'in a scrupulous regard to the institutions of their ancestors' (1816:233). Here foreign origin was beginning to be used in the Gypsies' favour in a plea to the state. Since Gypsies had no parochial settlement, Hoyland demanded that they be treated as a special exception under the Vagrancy Acts, but only temporarily; Gypsies who had been introduced to the 'comforts of social order' and acquired 'mechanical professions which would render them useful and respectable' but who still 'indulged' in wandering would deserve maximum punishment (1816:233-4). Meanwhile, Hoyland declared: 'It is worse than useless and unavailing to harass them from place to place when no retreat or shelter is provided' (1816:161).

Hoyland's reprint of correspondence from the *Christian Observer* (1816:199) indicated the popular concern for the 'conversion' of Gypsies. J. Crabb referred to Gypsies as 'these poor English heathens' (1832:ix). Mission schools were established by the mid nineteenth century with uncertain success (see Acton 1974:104, Windstedt 1908:319). Crabb was one of the first to use pseudo-genetical theories to account for the Gypsies' alleged moral decline:

> Gypseys which originally came to this country, have been on the decrease in number and are gradually becoming less distinguishable as a peculiar race of people ... A description of vagabonds and itinerant tinkers, repairers of umbrellas and vagrants of the worst character have of late found admission among the Gipsies ... the standard of morals ... is of course much lowered by such intermixtures.
>
> (1830:9, quoted by Acton 1974:89)

Here 'real' Gypsies are distinguished from vagrants and even Tinkers, but due to alleged miscegenation, the categories were no longer distinct sets of people. Elsewhere, Crabb claimed that 'fifty years ago they were considered useful by the peasantry and small farmers ... their outrages and depredations were very few' (1832:23). The theme so familiar today, that in their 'proud' past Gypsies were once tolerated (see the Hampshire Association of Parish Councils 1961, and Okely 1975a:31), had already emerged by the 1830s.

In the 1870s and 1880s the M.P. George Smith chose to deprecate Gypsies, and partly because of their alleged Indian origins (Smith 1880). Dismissing the early charitable efforts of the missionaries, he believed legislation was necessary to transform radically the Gypsies' way of life (Acton 1974:108-9). Smith failed in parliament to ensure compulsory schooling and the registration of vans. The latter reflected most poignantly the problem for a sedentary society. Although Gallichan, a Gypsiologist, argued much later, 'The Gypsy is not dangerous simply because he has no fixed dwelling place' (1908:358), this appeared to be precisely the point of friction. Perhaps the dominant society's attempts to give Gypsies a single place of origin also reflects this problem.

Cultural differentiation

In contrast to the reformists who tended to deny exoticism in contemporary Gypsies, but who instead wanted them to be converted and assimilated either by charitable institutions or by direct state intervention, other writers elaborated the Gypsies' exotic potential. The full romance of exoticism, combined with the detail and authenticity that comes from first hand experience, are found in the celebrated works of George Borrow, e.g. *Lavengro* (1851) and *The Romany Rye* (1857). His first publication, *The Zincali: Gypsies in Spain* (1841), helped fix the favourable English stereotype of the 'real' Gypsy as Spanish, later assisted by Merimée's *Carmen* (1845) and Bizet's opera of 1875. Borrow also affirmed and publicised an Indian origin for persons who were in some cases referred to as Romanies in England and Wales. Other 'Gypsiologists' who were interested in Gypsies in England and elsewhere included Leland (1882, 1891 and 1893); and Hindes Groome (1880). Smart and Crofton compiled the first dictionary of Anglo-Romany, published in 1875. All contributed to the *Journal of the Gypsy Lore Society (J.G.L.S.)* founded in 1880, the year of Borrow's death. This offers a rich store of Gypsy material, randomly presented – folklore, rituals, details of parish records, first hand accounts, examples of the Romany 'language', genealogies and comparisons with Gypsies beyond the British Isles. The journal also contains some of the fantasy writings by persons who had rarely if ever met Gypsies.

Some of this literature which emerged in the nineteenth century, whether its authors were concerned with Gypsy 'culture' as a means of differentiation, or whether they were concerned with greater external control in order to eliminate difference, should be viewed as a record of collective misrepresentations. The production of these misrepresentations has sometimes required the Gypsies' collaboration. Some of the descriptions of meetings with Gypsies are important because they reveal the gullibility of the authors and the Gypsies' well-developed skills in defending themselves against outsiders.

The Indian connection

Diffusionism underlies the claim that within the British Isles the 'real' Gypsies found in England and Wales, and strangely not in Scotland and Ireland, are the descendants of migrants from India around 1000 A.D. Studies of the language or dialects of Gypsies in Europe in the late eighteenth and early nineteenth centuries revealed a connection with a form of Sanskrit said to have evolved around or before 1000 A.D. The different forms of 'Romany' found throughout Europe have also many words from Persian, modern and Byzantine Greek, Slavic and Rumanian. These other ingredients have been perceived by scholars as 'corruptions' of a once 'pure' Indian Gypsy language.

Scholastic weight was given later to the alleged Indian origin of some Gypsies in Wales thanks to the etymological work of John Sampson (1926), who believed that migration routes could be reconstructed according to vocabulary content (1923). The number of loan words in English Romanes, Sampson claims, 'even furnishes some indication of the length of their stay in any particular region' (1926:411). Although Sampson recognises that one group or nationality may simply take over words from others, for example 'in the Balkan provinces we find so many floating loan words borrowed by one race from another' (1926:411), yet he cannot consider that the same could have happened to a form of Indian vocabulary or language encountered on the well trodden trade routes between East and West.

Language has been equated by the Gypsiologists with 'race'. It has been implied by some that those Gypsies who use the most Romani words (whether or not these have traceable Sanskrit 'roots') have the closest genetic links with India. The underlying assumption is that language is transmitted or learnt only through biological descent. Edmund Leach, in a commentary on my scepticism concerning the Gypsies' alleged single Indian origin (Okely 1979b), presents in my support a convincing parallel: 'Forms of English are spoken in all parts of the world ... We do not on that account try to argue that the native speakers of true and creolised and pidgin English must all be descendants of fifth-century migrants from Jutland!' (1979:121).

It is not clear how many of the first recorded 'Egyptians' used a second 'secret' language that was nothing more than an indigenous slang, an underworld back slang or in some cases a version of Gaelic (later identified as Shelta among Irish Tinkers). There is one early record of some Romani phrases mistakenly called Egyptian collected by Borde (1547), who also travelled in France. It is not known from whom he collected this vocabulary, but the Romani links in his list were only generally recognised in 1874 (Sampson 1930:351). Otherwise Smart and Crofton give records of some Romani vocabulary from the 1780s (1875:1-2). The single case before the late eighteenth century is not sufficient to indicate the speech of all the early 'Egyptians'.

More recently Ian Hancock (1970) has suggested that Anglo-Romany may be a creole. But he still supports the notion of a 'pure' Indian language existing in slightly modified form, perhaps on the other side of the English channel:

> Certainly the wave of Romanichals to arrive in the British Isles during the mid-fifteenth century spoke their language in its most conservative form, allowing for the considerable amount of lexical and structural influence which had been affecting it during the three or four centuries of development outside of India; that this was so is indicated by the existence of 'pure' Romanes in North Wales today. (1970:42)

I suggest that the so-called 'pure' Anglo-Romany recorded by Sampson among some families in Wales at the beginning of the twentieth century could also have been imported by Gypsies who migrated from Europe more recently than the sixteenth century. In any case, Hancock's suggestion that Anglo-Romany is a creole could be extended beyond the British Isles. Further research is needed here. Perhaps many forms of Romanes might be classified as creole or pidgins which developed between merchants and other travelling groups along the trade routes. These served as a means of communication between so-called Gypsy groups.

Given the special economic niche of all Gypsies who can never approximate to economic self-sufficiency, but must always trade with outsiders in the surrounding society, their language usages have to be consistent with this position. In order to earn their living, the Gypsies need to be fluent in the languages of non-Gypsies. It would be of little use for Gypsies to tell fortunes in Romanes to non-Gypsies, their major clients. Thus, any forms of Romanes used between Gypsy groups cannot and can never have been the sole nor necessarily the dominant language of a Gypsy group. In the British Isles, for example, English is the dominant language.

The Gypsiologists make the same mistakes as the nineteenth-century anthropologists in the general study of languages and racial distribution. Some believed in the notion of a united Indo-European race with a 'real' language of which many European and Asian forms were considered to be mere fragmentations. Similarly, Gypsy language and the 'original culture' have been located as things once intact in India. It is assumed that Gypsies existed in India many centuries back as a 'pure' group or separate society with language, customs and genetic structure hermetically sealed, until some 'mysterious event' caused their departure from their mythical homeland. From then on they are said to have been 'corrupted' in the course of migration and during contact with non-Gypsies. Thus any custom which seems strange to the Gorgio observer is explained not in terms of its contemporary meaning to the group, but according to some 'survival' from mythical ancient Indian days, or even the contemporary caste system. Any cultural similarity between Gypsy and Gorgio is explained away and denigrated as 'contamination'.

There are similar problems and claims in discussing the origins of Gypsies elsewhere in Europe. The use of some form of vocabulary, dialect or 'language' identified as Romanes is found in varying degrees among some groups classified as Gypsies. Some 'dialects' are mutually unintelligible. Some groups, whether or not they are acquainted with such dialects or vocabulary, are credited with no Indian origins. For instance, the Yeniches travelling through Belgium and France are attributed with German origins. A group to be found in Rumania, often considered to be the location of the 'real Gypsy', is said to have been formed from members of the indigenous population (Beck and Gheorghe 1981:19). The Woonwagenbewoners in the Netherlands and the Landfahrer in Germany are attributed an indigenous origin, and since they are not identified as 'Rom' or by any of the other 'foreign' tribal titles used by some Gypsy groups, and presumably since they do not appear to have any visibly exotic customs, they have been denied status as an ethnic group by a number of social scientists reporting to the European Commission (Okely 1980:79). This was asserted without any apparent investigation into whether any of the Travellers themselves used specific criteria for membership based on descent.

Similarly, the Tattares of Sweden are said to have little or no foreign, exotic ancestry. In his study of the genealogies of the Tattares, who prefer to call themselves Resande, Heymowski (1969) found a high proportion of ancestors of Swedish nationality. These included a few peasants, but were mainly persons with itinerant occupations and also German mercenary soldiers. Heymowski therefore suggests that the Tattares are not really an ethnic Gypsy group. He gives proper status as 'real Gypsies' to those Travellers or Gypsies who identify themselves as Kalderash, allegedly from eastern Europe (see Acton 1974:22). Yet Heymowski admits that the Tattares appear to use the principle of descent to identify themselves in contrast to anyone vaguely called 'Tattare' by the surrounding sedentary population. A later study of Gypsies in Sweden reveals the considerable flexibility in the Gypsies' choice of labels presented to outsiders. For instance, Gypsies originating from Poland, without any previous claims to being

Kalderash, adopt Kalderash names upon arrival in Sweden because such persons are given exotic and favourable status by the dominant society (Kaminski, personal communication 1975). Indeed Tattares were excluded from lucrative welfare programmes (see Acton 1974:22). Elsewhere in Europe, e.g. in Belgium, France, the Netherlands and Germany, it also seems that groups or 'tribes' who refer to themselves as Rom, Kalderash or Lovari are most likely to be credited with eastern, Indian origins and given 'real' status, if only by Gorgio scholars and political representatives.

Those observers who seek to prove Indian origin will sometimes attempt to identify traces of Indian 'culture' among European Gypsies. Thus Irving Brown, in trying to prove the links between the Rom and an Indian group called the Dom, whom he visited in the 1920s, naively produced such evidence as; the similar 'musical propensities of the race' (1928:173); ancestor worship; consumption of pork and liquor on all ceremonial occasions; eating of horse-flesh (actually the opposite to European Gypsy beliefs, see chapter 6); bride price (1928:174); 'greater vivacity' than the surrounding population; and their use of a council (1928:176)![3] This highly respected Gypsiologist could not even in this case point to a potentially more plausible trait like language:

> The words used by Dom are different from those of other Indian Gypsy tribes and ... are not found in European Romani. [This is] no proof either of a lack of relationship between these tribes or with the Gypsies in the outside world. Like most thieves' cant, such vocabularies are purely artificial, and spring up and die like mushrooms. (1928:175)

Thus the original search for Indian links based on language links is turned on its head when it suits the Gypsiologist!

The theories of race and those concerning both Romanes and Indo-European non-Gypsy languages all rest on the presumption of a single origin in space and time. The Gypsiologists were probably influenced by the more general theory concerning the origin of non-Gypsy Europeans, but although the latter has been discredited, the single 'birth place' for 'real' Gypsies is today still upheld by Gypsiologists, government administrators and some members of Gypsy organisations. Indian origin was used in the 1970s by the World Romani Congress, based in Europe, when requesting special ethnic status within the United Nations.

This uniting theme was exploited in the British television programme 'Romany Trail' (B.B.C. 2, The World About Us, November 1981). The extremely varied religious practices and occupations of the groups, who were all identified by the researchers as 'Gypsies' and filmed in Egypt, Europe and India, were given a common eastern and Indian origin. This was asserted despite the fact that aspects of their allegedly shared yet 'isolated' culture indicated many more marked

11

resemblances to aspects of the culture of the surrounding non-Gypsy population; for example, specific healing practices and dances, and the use of certain musical instruments. Their culture was more visibly syncretic than one which could be explained as random 'survivals' from India.

It was even claimed in the television programme that the Gypsies had brought the 'Punch and Judy' puppet show from India centuries ago. The programme opened with scenes of English Gypsies at Appleby Fair. Viewers were informed that the original Rom who had allegedly migrated to the British Isles were few and far between, having intermarried with the surrounding population. The implication was that the majority of Gypsies in Britain were therefore not authentic. There was little or no attempt to explore the similarities likely to be found between any mobile, non-wage-labour, non-peasant, ethnic groups, *regardless* of their real or mythical origins from a single location.

Paradoxically, there is very little evidence that Indian origin had been indicated or used by Gypsies until it was first given to them by Gorgio scholars (see Vesey-Fitzgerald 1973:16). Even today the title 'Romany' is not generally interpreted at the local level as of Indian origin. The most frequent explanation which I was given by Gypsies was: 'We're Romanies 'cos we always roam.' A nomadic travelling identity was thus given priority over any exotic point of departure. But for nineteenth-century scholars and still today in the ideology of the dominant non-Gypsy society, exotic origin, safely many centuries ago (as opposed to more recent immigration by other persons from India), has become a mythical charter for selective acceptance of members, usually a minority, of a potentially threatening group.

Less interest has been shown in the capacity of a sedentary economy or in the western case a capitalist mode of production to generate and sustain its own nomads. It seems more than coincidence that throughout Europe 'Egyptians', 'Saracens' later called Tsiganes or Gitanes, 'Bohemians' and 'Tattares', and other wandering bands variously named and later identified by Gypsiologists, were officially recorded and were thus made visible at the time of the collapse of feudalism, in the fifteenth and sixteenth centuries. So far this appearance has only been explained in terms of waves of nomads migrating in linear fashion from a single eastern locality. My own suggestions can only be conjectural and abbreviated in this study, and will be controversial to the *aficionados* of Gypsiology. My scepticism about some of the conclusions from the etymological evidence is shared in part by Vesey-Fitzgerald (1973:4-11) who nonetheless supports the Indian origin.

It may be the case that groups of people brought or appropriated some linguistic forms, creole or pidgin related to some earlier Sanskrit in the movements along the trade routes between East and West, but it does not follow that all 'real' Gypsies or Travellers are the genealogical descendants of specific groups of persons allegedly in India nearly a thousand years ago. It is of course exciting that such linguistic links can be made between some Gypsies and 'magical' Asia. The Gypsiologists have thus given exotic status to persons who labour also under negative and banal images.

A common Indian origin has also been seen, especially by Gorgio members of the World Romani Congress, as a strategy for international solidarity among Gypsies. There are major advantages to be derived from international solidarity among Gypsy groups who face common problems of persecution, but an appeal to non-Gypsy governments in terms of common exotic origins might have negative results. The already existing hierarchy of 'real' and 'counterfeit' Gypsies might be further exaggerated. As already indicated in the case of Sweden and the Netherlands, travelling Gypsy groups without claims to exotic origins risk losing their rights as ethnic groups and may be more vulnerable to assimilation programmes. Moreover, even those groups attributed with 'real' Indian origins might find themselves dismissed as 'inauthentic' or 'corrupted' whenever non-Gypsy observers fail to find sufficiently alluring signs of exotic 'culture' among the persons they actually encounter. The Gypsiologists' emphasis has already led to fictitious divisions in Britain between the 'true-blooded' Romany and the rest, including the counterfeit or drop-out, 'half-blood' or mere 'Traveller'. (The Gypsies have themselves played along with this and indeed those I encountered in fieldwork entertained some ideology of 'pure' blood, but this was not connected with alleged Indian origin.)

In the long run it would seem to be more productive for international Gypsy pressure groups to emphasise the common rights and contribution of all Gypsy groups, regardless of their alleged geographical and 'racial' origins. A sentimental appeal to Gorgio tastes for exotica and based on very speculative evidence is likely to be counter-productive. Moreover, a focus by non-Gypsies on the Gypsies' alleged foreignness and exoticism usually ignores the groups' own criteria for membership and as likely or not neglects the full history of the different groups' appearance and survival within the countries they inhabit.

The following section is concerned mainly with the case of Gypsies in Britain, but some aspects may be applicable to a discussion of the origin of Gypsies elsewhere in Europe.

Some indigenous origins?

It is not clear whether the first recorded 'Egyptians' in the British Isles, nor indeed many of their equivalent on the European continent, were all foreign immigrants. Within the British Isles in the fourteenth century, there is plenty of evidence of large numbers of 'wayfarers' or 'rovers' (Jusserand 1889). These included performers, pedlars, peasants out of bond, preachers, mendicant friars, and pilgrims. The Gypsiologists acknowledge the presence of 'Tinkers' (not necessarily from Ireland) before the first records of Egyptians (Vesey-Fitzgerald 1973; Acton 1974:66; McCormick 1907:394). Shakespeare's Henry IV refers to Tinkers and their 'language'. 'Tinker' and 'Tinkler' were recorded as trade names or surnames as early as the twelfth century(*Oxford English Dictionary*). But the first mention of 'Tinkers' as a group appears in a statute in the mid sixteenth century (Jusserand 1889:128).

What does seem clear is that there were plenty of indigenous recruits for nomadic groups who could have chosen to organise themselves to exploit economic opportunities on the road. In addition to earning a living as pedlars and performers, and as casual agricultural labourers, 'Egyptians', seemingly from a mysterious foreign land, could present themselves most successfully as exotic fortune tellers and gain freedom of movement as pilgrims and penitents. There were more likely to be opportunities of this kind for groups of persons who were brought up as nomads within kin based groups using the principle of descent than for isolated individuals and families. The most successful would be self-producing and able to use kinship connections for group cooperation, mutual aid, and protection against rivals or the persecuting authorities.

Already in the fourteenth century, there were increasing numbers of 'rovers' who had fled the village or the farm to which they belonged. Escaped villeins or serfs provided the 'wandering class' with most of its numerous recruits. If not practising a 'definite craft, nor having wherewith to live', they were vulnerable to conscription of labour (Statute of Labourers 1351). At the same time as state legislation was initiated to prohibit any persons going out of their 'own district', labourers were actually sought out by landowners who paid them by the day and at wages other than those of the tariff (Jusserand 1889: 144-8).

Later, in the fifteenth and sixteenth centuries, throughout Europe the uprooted population of the middle ages was considerable. This population has been counted among the ancestors of the modern proletariat. I am suggesting that some might also be considered as ancestors of many Gypsies; for instance, those who were neither bound as serfs, nor absorbed into the trades and guilds, and who, like the rovers or escaped villeins found in the fourteenth century, were selling their labour on an hourly or daily basis (see Mandel 1969:34).

Marx gives another origin of the modern proletariat, which might also suggest the origin of some Gypsies; a group which chose to reject wage-labour rather than be proletarianised: 'The prelude of the revolution that laid the foundation of the capitalist mode of production, was played in the last third of the 15th and the first decade of the 16th century. A mass of free proletarians was hurled on the labour-market by the breaking-up of the bands of feudal retainers' (1887:718). Thus, former servants and clerks to the feudal nobles became wanderers and beggars. A third origin of the proletariat, and possibly of Gypsy groups, was from dispossessed peasants, after their land had been changed from agricultural cultivation to grazing for sheep, during the development of the wool industry (Mandel 1969:35).

It seems not impossible that this mass of potential free labourers, the majority of whose descendants were to become wage-labourers, might also have provided the majority of recruits, through association and incorporation by marriage, into groups who were identified and who identified themselves as 'Egyptians'. Elsewhere in Europe, for example in France, historians have noted that 'the arrival of some "Bohemians" coincided with the establishment of the "corporations de gueuserie", or "guilds of beggars"' (Clébert 1967:63). Although it is argued by Clébert that the beggars, pedlars and 'Bohemians' remained distinct (1967:65), it does not necessarily follow that all these peoples were of entirely different origins. Moreover, people could still cross the boundaries of each group without weakening the organisational and ascribed boundaries (see Barth 1969).

Since beggars and others banded together for survival, it may be the case that groups of so-called 'Egyptians' were composed also largely of disenfranchised and indigenous persons. In this case they may have adopted an exotic nomenclature, parts of a second secret 'language' – either a creole or pidgin which had crossed many national frontiers of Europe; and exploited certain occupations, such as fortune telling and entertainment which were consistent with a magical, mysterious nomenclature. In so far as there may have been some foreign immigrant families it would have needed only a few to introduce some 'Romany' creole into the argot and thus consolidate this novel identity. The newcomers would in any case have been compelled to make close liaisons with the indigenous population, including wandering vagrants, and learn the dominant non-Gypsy language in order to tell fortunes and to earn their living in other ways within the larger economy.

My suggestions will appear controversial. Obviously more research would be necessary to confirm the sources of recruitment to various Gypsy groups. At this stage I remain sceptical concerning some of the exotic criteria for identifying the 'real' Gypsies. I question the implicit assumptions that an ethnic group needs to be defined on the basis of its claims to foreign origins and claims to any vestiges of exotic 'culture'. An ethnic group's right to self-determination should not have to rest on that kind of romance. The following sections show the confusions concerning the identification of the 'real' Gypsy by even those persons who considered themselves to be the Gypsies' supporters in the British Isles.

Romanies or half-castes

Both in the nineteenth century and after, the Gypsiologists claimed the existence of a 'pure-blooded' minority who had almost never married

Gorgios. It was no accident, and indeed part of the logic of Gypsy–Gorgio interaction, that the Gypsies who chose to befriend the Gypsiologists were classed as 'real Romanies' while others who perhaps chose to avoid them or who offended them in some way were rejected and branded 'didikois' or some other pejorative term.

In the 1870s, Smart and Crofton first recorded the word 'didikois', referring to a group allegedly consisting of 'half-breed' Gypsies who were said to mispronounce a Romany word (1875:51). Their racial mixture was by implication the cause of their misuse of the 'traditional' language. The Gypsiologists appeared to believe that 'racial purity' and knowledge of the most archaic Romany were closely connected. In the 1920s, John Sampson also presumed a similar relationship (1926:xi). Racial 'outbreeding' was believed to bring proportional cultural decline.

The Gypsiologists' racial theories conflicted with their own evidence; the 'pure-blooded Romany' was nothing more than a category. Hindes Groome was to some extent aware of these problems. While he supported the notion of 'full-bloods' and 'half-bloods' (1880:249) and classified 'Gypsies' by 'the Romani look, language, habits and modes of thought' (1880:252), at the same time he noted the difficulties in equating specific physical or 'racial' attributes with knowledge of the Romany language and traditions. Moreover, he recognised that Gypsies married outsiders (1880:250), and drew attention to the pedigrees of the Romany families recorded by Smart and Crofton. In one, marriages with Gorgios actually outnumbered those with Romanies (1880:251). The pages of the *J.G.L.S.* also give frequent examples of Gypsy–Gorgio marriages. Nevertheless the majority of Gypsiologists used the category 'pure-blooded' or 'true Romany' as if empirical fact. As recently as the 1960s, Duff classified British Gypsies into four social groups on the basis of their alleged genetic inheritance (1963:260-1). Paradoxically, the least sociable group in his Gorgio terms were considered to have the least Romany 'blood'.

The beliefs in a mythical minority of 'real Romanies' and a genetic explanation for culture were recorded in government documents through the 1950s and 1960s. For example, the first government survey of Gypsies in Kent in 1952 considered that only 10% of its eleven hundred Gypsies appeared to be 'members of the Romany families' (Adams 1952). The Gypsiologist Vesey-Fitzgerald was brought in for advice, thus making a direct link between the concerns of government and those of Gypsiology literature. He affirmed the distinction between 'Romanies' and 'Travellers', using the traditional but unscientific category 'full-blooded' to describe the Romanies for whom he advocated preferential political support. He argued that 'any attempt to abolish nomadism in Romany families (I am not of course referring to Travellers) would have disastrous consequences both in health and morals' (Adams 1952: Appendix III).

This survey set the tone for other local authorities. The fiction of the 'full-blooded' Romany was used to condemn the majority, if not all of the Gypsies in the locality, and even to justify making no site provision when the 1968 ruling required it (see Okely 1975a:33). In practice of course it has been impossible to identify 'Romanies' by their physical or 'racial' features. The physiognomy of the majority of Gypsies is very

English Gypsy men and boys. *Evening Post-Echo Ltd*

much like that of the average English Gorgio. Although the occasional individuals with dark hair and brown eyes might attract attention, the favoured 'real Romanies' are just as likely to have blue eyes and fair hair. But these facts are not 'seen' by the Gorgio observers for whom the racial theory offers a pseudo-scientific basis for social selection. 'Real Romanies' are those families who reflect best the observers' preferences (Okely 1975a:32).

Travellers, Tinkers, Gypsies and exotic origins

In the sub-classification of groups of Gypsies or Travellers within the British Isles and Ireland, a mythical Indian origin has been invoked to discriminate between the 'real Romanies' or 'Gypsies', and the 'Tinkers'. The English and especially the Welsh Gypsies are given the exotic Indian or Romany origin, while it is said that the Irish and Scottish Travellers or Tinkers are 'merely' descendants of vagrants and victims of the Great Famine or the Highland Clearances. It is conveniently forgotten that the first 'Egyptians' were recorded in neither England nor Wales, but in Scotland.

Sometimes, the evidence presented for this classification is linguistic. The Tinkers frequenting Ireland and Scotland have their own Cant or 'secret language' including 'Shelta' and 'Gammon', which linguists have sometimes contrasted with 'Romany' or 'Anglo-Romany'. But whenever Romani words are found in these other 'languages' or dialects, they are dismissed as the result of English influence. My own evidence indicates that the use of Romani vocabulary varies *within* each group, and that there is both short- and long-term movement of all Travellers or Gypsies between territories within the British Isles and Ireland. This was especially the case during the two world wars.

There is considerable inter-marriage between groups. Moreover the incorporation of Gorgios or 'Flatties' occurs in all groups. The Travellers or Gypsies do tend to identify themselves according to one of the four national divisions of the British Isles, but this does not mean that one is more 'Indian' or Romany than the other. National labels are manipulated according to context, as is the 'real Romany' identity.

The term 'Traveller' does not imply a drop-out from the sedentary society, as is so often supposed by outsiders, but full membership of an ethnic group using the principle of descent (see chapter 5). The term emphasises a travelling, nomadic identity. Those Travellers who associate themselves with Ireland or Scotland tend not to adopt the nomenclature 'Gypsy'. They are labelled 'Tinkers' and, although they may use this among themselves, they frequently use the less pejorative term 'Traveller', especially in communications with outsiders. McCormick employed the term 'Tinkler-Gypsies' to refer to Travellers in Scotland (1907).

Generally the term 'Gypsy' is more frequently given to and adopted today by Travellers associated with England and Wales. Gypsies may use this title privately, but, like the Tinkers, often prefer the less stigmatised term Traveller, again especially when relating to outsiders.

During the 1960s, among some authorities, the label 'Tinker' completely replaced the 'didikois' or alleged half-breed as one of contempt (see Acton 1974:206-11). As with any Gypsies, the Irish Tinkers of the present were unfavourably juxtaposed with 'authentic' ones of the past. Worcester County Council reported that the 'Irish Tinkers' in their area bore 'little resemblance to the tinker of Irish legend who seems to have been something of a character and as such regarded with affection' (Worcester County Council 1966). In practice, the Irish label was conveniently attached to *any* Travellers coming up against the authorities (Okely 1975a:33). The Tinker became synonymous with every unpopular or stigmatised aspect of any Gypsy groups: scrap work, travelling, urban proximity, law breaking, elusiveness and independent life style.

This view of the Tinker appeared in the Ministry of Housing and Local Government (M.H.L.G.) report on Travellers in England and Wales. Whereas the English-born Gypsies were defined in terms of 'racial' types (revealing the familiar conceptual muddles), the Irish Tinkers were defined in terms of their alleged living patterns which, by no coincidence, were those most offensive to the sedentary authorities. The author(s) moved from merely recording others' allegations to presenting them as objective description (M.H.L.G. 1967:3, quoted also in Acton 1974:202).

The policies of deportation and banishment of Gypsies prevalent in the sixteenth century also reappeared in the twentieth century. Enoch Powell, calling for the abolition of the 1968 Act, suggested that 'alien' Gypsies or Travellers should be dealt with 'through the laws of nationality and immigration' (*The Times*, 12 December 1970). Given the limited movement of Gypsies from the continent, it is unclear what 'foreign' Gypsies Powell was concerned about. Here the romance of foreign origin was used against Gypsies.

Non-ethnic, 'universalistic' categories

In the 1960s, liberal 'universalistic' categories competed with the racial and genetic ones. This cannot be explained by any greater enlightenment about the 'chimera of race' (Bohannan 1963:185). Certainly Dominic Reeve had repudiated the Gorgio discussion of 'didikois' as 'just racial nonsense' (1960:ix-x), but reviews in the *J.G.L.S.* reaffirmed the Romany myth. Moreover, Reeve still gave credence to the terminology associated with racial theories. 'Many of the "flash" travellers are of the deepest and most pure-bred Romani blood in the country' (1960:104).

At a public health inspectors' conference on Gypsies in 1968, a lec-

19

turer in education reaffirmed the existence of three racial categories: pure-blooded, mixed and housedweller drop-outs, but at the same time emphasised the educational 'disadvantages' of all and suggested no discrimination in new government measures towards them (Wade 1968:117). The honorary assistant editor of the *J.G.L.S.* endorsed the differentiation between groups, but regretted that this led to a 'kind of inverted racialism' when local authorities justified the closing of stopping places (Wade 1968:120).

The shift towards an all-embracing category rather than the repudiation of the theoretical foundation of racial categories coincided with renewed interest in integration or assimilation programmes for Gypsies. Here recognition of the Gypsies as an independent ethnic group would be under-played. The advisers to the Plowden Committee on primary school children asserted that Gypsy children 'are probably the most severely deprived ... in the country' (1967:vol.2, Appendix). The category 'deprived' had replaced Hoyland's early-nineteenth-century 'depraved', and both were associated with rather similar policies of assimilation, once called conversion. Sartre provides a useful parallel to the case of the Gypsies in his *Reflexions sur la question juive*, where he discussed the 'bad faith' of the democrat who wishes to universalise and humanise all groups:

> There may not be so much difference between the anti-semite and the democrat. The former wishes to destroy him as a man and leave nothing in him but the Jew, the pariah, the untouchable; the latter wishes to destroy him as a Jew and leave nothing in him but the man, the abstract and universal subject of the rights of man. (1973:57)

Interest in policies of integration, if not complete assimilation, coincided paradoxically with increasing awareness of the rights of 'racial' minorities as embodied in the 1965 Race Relations Act which hardly benefited Gypsies; they were merely redefined. The 1959 Highways Act section 127 had stated: 'If without lawful authority or excuse ... a hawker or other itinerant trader or gypsy ... encamps on a highway, he shall be guilty of an offence.' This could clearly be challenged on the grounds of racial discrimination. Therefore, in 1967 three High Court judges ruled that a 'Gypsy' is 'a person leading a nomadic life with no fixed employment and with no fixed abode' (Mills v. Cooper, Queen's Bench Division, 9 March 1967).

The non-ethnic definition of a Gypsy as a person of no fixed abode was merely the old category 'vagrant' in a new guise. Although Gypsies and their supporters were able to take action with the Race Relations Board against publicans who banned entry to Gypsies, they were not able to challenge the Highways Act, and later the discriminatory clauses in the 1968 Caravan Sites Act.

The link between Gypsies and vagrants took a peculiar turn at a meeting of an urban council in 1967. It revealed that even a demand for concentration camps was not considered illegal under the Race Relations Act, so long as Gypsies were given a non-ethnic label. A councillor vigorously opposed provision for a permanent Gypsy site and was reported as follows:

> 'It's not gypsies we are talking about. We are taking about vagrants – relatively and basically worthless people' ... When he was a young man, he said gypsies were hardly ever seen throughout the country 'But today, you will see many thousands of vagrants ... They are beatniks of the worst possible type ... If you had to ask not just a German, but any other national in Europe today, as to what he would do with these people, he would give you one answer. He would say a concentration camp until they had mended their ways.'
>
> (*Hitchin and Letchworth Pictorial*, 28 April 1967)

When the Secretary of the National Council of Civil Liberties complained to the Race Relations Board, the Attorney General rejected any prosecution: 'No matter how inflammatory and intemperate words are used they must be directed against an ethnic or national group ... the words used in this context were directed against "vagrants, worthless people and beatniks" ... the problem did not involve gypsies' (Letter from the Greater London Conciliation Board, 20 October 1967).

The non-ethnic definition was sustained in the 1967 Ministry of Housing and Local Government census and report on Gypsies. The racial categories were not discredited by the Ministry, but they were considered 'of little practical importance: information was needed about the entire traveller population ... who in large measure follow a common way of life, *making the same demands on land*' (M.H.L.G. 1967:3, my emphasis). The last phrase reveals one of the major concerns of the sedentary society and of the state, and which was masked by the general theme of the Gypsies' 'deprivation', thus echoing the Plowden Report. The Ministry suggested that improved 'amenities' might 'exert a growing pull on the persistent travellers so that they will choose gradually to settle down, first on a site, and eventually in a house' (M.H.L.G. 1967:67). Thus the non-ethnic definition of Gypsies was associated with a policy of assimilation at Whitehall, while at local authority level, it was used to justify non-provision, if not dispersal and harassment.

Laws and policy in the twentieth century

In the first half of the twentieth century, attempts to pass legislation concerned specifically with the control of Gypsies, namely George Smith's revived Moveable Dwellings Bill, failed on several occasions.

21

However, there were a number of Acts not specifically addressed to Gypsies, which offered a potential means of control. These included Planning and Public Health Acts in the 1930s. Emphasis was on living space and sanitation. Acton states that these had 'very little effect on the Gypsies' (1974:120). After the Second World War, however, such legislation was often used against Gypsies or Travellers, as a means of dispersing them (see chapter 7 and Acton 1974:133). Earlier, thanks to the informal intervention of a member of the Gypsy Lore Society, Dora Yates, the 1908 Children's Act excused Gypsy children from compulsory school attendance during the summer term, if their parents were travelling (Acton 1974:121).

From the late 1940s, coinciding but contrasting with the nostalgic rural literature on the 'real Romanies' (see below), the M.P. Norman Dodds showed an interest in the living and working conditions of Gypsies, and in conjunction with Gypsy representatives, and some evangelists, formed a 'Gypsy Committee' with a Gypsy Charter (Dodds 1966:39-40). In 1951, the new Conservative government agreed to a pilot survey in the single county of Kent.

The 1959 Highways Act had specifically singled out the Gypsies for prosecution for camping on the roadside. The 1960 Caravan Sites and Control of Development Act, although not specifically addressed to Gypsies, radically affected them. Tighter controls were introduced for private sites, all of which now required planning permission. As a consequence, many Gypsy encampments, used for either short- or long-term stays, were closed (Adams *et al.* 1975: 9-10).

The same year, planning permission was given for the first official site for Gypsies run by a district authority in West Ashford, Kent. By 1962, the Ministry of Housing and Local Government had begun to recognise the Gypsies' problems in finding legal sites. A Ministry circular of 1962 encouraged local authorities to conduct surveys and provide sites. It was even acknowledged that Gypsies had 'the right to follow their traditional way of life' (quoted in M.H.L.G. 1967), although only those whom the Ministry labelled the 'true gypsies and romanies'. A few sites were opened, but prosecutions against Gypsies continued on a large scale (Adams *et al.* 1975:11).

Partly in response to Dodd's persistence, the Labour government of 1964 agreed to the first national census of Gypsies in England and Wales. Questionnaires were administered by local officials and sometimes the police. The total count revealed about 15,000 individuals. Given that the survey was conducted often by persons responsible for dispersing Gypsies, it was not surprising that this was considered an under-count. The main findings were publicised in the 1966 Ministry circular which again encouraged official site provision. In the same year the Gypsy Council was founded. It affirmed 'the essential unity of travelling people, irrespective of group and origin', and their right to 'self-determination ... their traditional mode of life ... and a legitimate need for camp sites' (Gypsy Council 1967).

The report based on the census, *Gypsies and other Travellers* (M.H.L.G. 1967), emphasised the Gypsies' absence of legal sites and public health facilities, and gave momentum to the second part of Lubbock's 1968 Caravan Sites Act which for the first time required local authorities to provide sites for Gypsies. In exchange, the local authorities would, after specified provision, obtain 'designation' which relieved the authority of any further provision and gave it new 'control powers' to ensure the eviction of any person 'being a Gypsy' stationing a caravan on unauthorised land. Although the Act was ostensibly that of a private member, the sections concerning Gypsies originated from the Labour government in exchange for free drafting (Adams *et al.* 1975:16-22). This new 'welfare' intervention marked a major shift in national policy towards Gypsies. Some of its implications and effects are explored in chapter 7.

Literature and social science

The literature on Gypsies in Britain[4] in the twentieth century shows something of the earlier contrasting concerns; either to control or to exoticise Gypsies. Policy questions and the legal categories of the state were placed gradually in the setting of detailed (although not always well informed) official reports, for example, the Kent survey (Adams 1952); the Plowden Report (1967); the M.H.L.G. Report (1967); the report on Scottish Travellers (Gentleman and Swift 1971); and the Cripps Report (1976). Both the exotic and folklore tradition, as well as the controlling or reformist traditions, were affected by the growth of social science, especially sociology and to some extent social anthropology.

From a social science perspective, one of the most brilliant contributions to the study and history of Gypsies is that of T.W. Thompson, a member of the Gypsy Lore Society, whose articles appeared in its journal mainly in the 1920s. He made close contact with a number of Gypsy families over a period of time and painstakingly sifted parish records and other historical and contemporary sources to present a systematic and ethnographic approach to aspects of the English Gypsies' social organisation, beliefs and ritual. His references to Frazer, Rivers and Malinowski indicate a varied social anthropological influence (1913, 1922, 1926, 1930b). His articles have since been much plagiarised.

In addition to the literature by Gorgios, there are now a number of autobiographies and contributions from mainly literate Gypsies, some of whom have found a place as special individuals within the Gorgio world. The evangelist Gipsey Smith (1901), for example, gives a detailed account of his Gypsy upbringing and his later work among both non-Gypsies and Gypsies. While keen to exploit and elaborate his Gypsy origins, he disassociates himself from them (1901:363). 'Gipsey' Smith was fully incorporated into the social reformist perspective of non-Gypsies found in the nineteenth century. Indeed, there are several other Gypsy autobiographical accounts of childhood in the travelling community which the authors have later left, e.g. Petulengro (1935), Wood (1973) and Whyte (1979). In some there are insights into the authors' dilemma as to whether to exoticise or denigrate Gypsy identity for the dominant Gorgio readership. All are informative documents; some more than others, and notably the accounts from Boswell (1970), and Connors (1973), which transcend the problems of authenticity. Dominic Reeve, who claims Gypsy descent though not upbringing, depicts the travelling life in narrative form, but is not explicitly autobiographical (1958, 1960). Although each detail is ethnographically accurate, the content is limited compared to Boswell and Connors.

Given the difficulties in gaining an inside view of the Travellers' way of life, it is not surprising that this is largely absent from most of the Gorgio literature, including much of that with some social science research pretensions. Some authors have synthesised and popularised the existing material, and supplemented this by a few descriptions of personal encounters (Vesey-Fitzgerald 1973; Duff 1963). In the period immediately after the Second World War, a number of popular writers linked Gypsies with a 'vanishing' rural England. These writers, often with gentrified names (Vesey-Fitzgerald 1973; Croft-Cooke 1948; de Baraclai Levy 1958), and living in the home counties, described a few Gypsies they met on their country rambles. There is always the danger of generalising from a few incidents and conversations, especially when Gypsies must be adept at confusing strangers. Much of Sandford's collection records what Travellers say on first encounter (1973). Long-term acquaintance and day to day immersion in the group(s) are really the only ways of getting near an inner perspective of the Travellers. This will also help to make sense of their relationship with the dominant society.

Viewed only casually, Travellers may find themselves described in patronising ways even by well-meaning liberals. For instance it has seemed to be complimentary to place Gypsies in terms of a theory of social Darwinism. Thus Sandford claims: 'Their nomadic life-style goes back further than our settled one. They represent our remote past in human form' (1973:5). He implicitly draws upon an evolutionary typology which places nomads lower down a single ladder of progress. Nomads are seen sentimentally or negatively as 'hangovers' from some hypothetical linear development in which sedentary living is considered to be the single superior future.

One of the first social scientists to apply the social anthropologist's method of long-term participant observation among the Gypsies in the British Isles, and indeed in Europe, was Farnham Rehfisch, whose study of the Scottish Tinkers (1958) remains largely unpublished. A portion appears in his 1975 collection *Gypsies, Tinkers and other Travellers*. Rehfisch drew attention to the Tinkers' criteria for membership, their contempt for wage-labour and their tradition of misleading outsiders (1958). Barth had given an imaginative account of the Tattares or Gypsies in Norway and of the functional adaptability of large sibling groups scattered over a wide area (1955). He discussed the question of recruitment and 'passing'. However, his description of the Travellers as a 'typical parasite group' or 'typical pariah section of the population' (1955:286) lacks any major consideration of the Travellers' economic contribution.

The work of social anthropologists who use a small sample to be studied in depth contrasts with the quantitative pretensions of surveys, including that of the 1965 government census. In the latter, the chances of gaining accurate quantitative information were slight. Moreover, the researchers writing up the report had to interpret the census returns largely without direct contact and acquaintance with the Travellers. Some of this difficulty was handled by discussions with a few non-Gypsies who knew Travellers. As with the earlier writings of Gypsiologists, generalisations are made about Gypsies on the basis of a few observations. In the case of the Ministry, the generalisations are stretched over England and Wales and given scientific status by appearing on pages decorated with numerical charts and tables (M.H.L.G. 1967). Nevertheless, this first census stands as an invaluable information source for the Travellers' geographical distribution, family size, locations, etc. The subsequent report on Travellers in Scotland is also an important reference book (Gentleman and Swift 1971).

A sociologist's perspective is provided by Acton (1974) in his study of activities and policies at government and national level in England. He moves from the 1880s through to the post-war developments and the formation of Gypsy pressure groups. An historical chronology of events is presented with the aid of considerable and careful library research, as well as the use of local government literature and the files of the Gypsy Council as major sources. There is an excellent classification and critique of the phantom of the 'true' Gypsy, showing how the labels 'didikois' and 'Tinker' were misused by the Gorgio authorities. Acton admits to some participant observation among Gypsies at grass root level, but states that his argument rests 'as much as possible on documentation rather than merely on personal observation' (1974:3). The latter has been used in his account of the Gypsy Council. This account comes over largely as the personal biography of its first secretary, a Gorgio, Grattan Puxon. It is unfortunate that the day by day descriptions of individuals and factions who are given status by the metropolis should masquerade as the research into the 'wider issues' which sociologists are keen to accuse anthropologists of neglecting.

Acton felt that the 'great need was not for another detailed study of some small group of South Essex Gypsies' (1974:3), as if any such studies ever existed. When obliged to make observations concerning the Gypsies' local social organisation, recruitment, marriage patterns and economic activities, he has to depend heavily on published material, which in other contexts he recognises as inadequate. He is correct in insisting that 'a sociology of minorities must also be one of majorities' (1974:2), and his study is mainly about the powers and policies of the dominant Gorgio authorities through their own written sources. Acton would also surely accept that there is a need for the voices of the minority at the grass roots to be transmitted through the printed word; if only initially via a Gorgio participant observer and mediator. There is of course a similar need for participant observation among the Gorgio authorities (Okely 1980).

There are examples elsewhere in Europe of studies of the Gorgio authorities' documents, which piece together the Gypsies' recent history. Kenrick and Puxon (1972) have investigated the Nazi policies which led to the extermination of over a quarter of a million Gypsies, and the outrageous legal loophole which enabled the German government to deny reparation to many of the survivors. A detailed study of Gypsies in German-occupied Netherlands has also, like those of Kenrick and Puxon (1972) and Puxon (1976), suggested that post-Nazi policy and legislation 'have not risen very much above the tenor of what the Germans imposed ... in their decree of 1944' (Sijes 1979:173). A brilliant study has been made by Guy of the shifts in the Communist government's policies and practices towards Gypsies in Czechoslovakia and the refusal to accord the Gypsies the rights of an ethnic minority (1975, 1978). Liégeois' work mainly in France ranges from the investigation of state policies (1978b) to Gypsy national leadership (1976), and the attitudes of social workers, local officials and the general public towards Gypsies (1977; *Études Tsiganes* 1980; see also Okely 1980). Beck and Gheorghe have embarked on a study of the history of the Gypsies in Rumania (1981).

The research by Adams *et al.* on Gypsies in England (1975) included participant observation with Gypsies, Gorgio officials and supporters at local level in two regions. There were interviews with every council providing a Gypsy site, studies of local authority policies and circumstances in three areas, and an account of the national political manoeuvres leading to the 1968 legislation.

From the mid 1970s there emerged a number of publications mainly by social anthropologists and based on long-term participant observation with Gypsies. Sutherland's monograph is on Gypsies in California (1975; for a review see Okely 1975g). Gropper (or Cotten) focuses on Gypsies in New York (1975); Sharon and George Gmelch have each completed studies among the Travellers in Eire (1975 and 1977). George Gmelch especially supports the theory that the 'rapid modernization of rural Ireland resulted in the obsolescence of most of the Travellers' traditional skills and services' (1977:157). Gmelch considers that if Travellers were able to obtain wage–labour employment 'many of the problems which currently confront them would be eradicated or minimised' (1977:161). Studies of Gypsies elsewhere imply some scepticism of this type of analysis (Sutherland 1975, Gropper 1975, Okely 1975c and chapters 2 and 4 below).

Significant research based on long-term fieldwork has emerged from Scandinavia. Grönfors has published rare details of feuding patterns among Finnish Gypsies (1977). Kaminski combined his experience of Gypsies in Sweden, Poland, and Czechoslovakia to examine the ways in which they manipulate their ethnic and national identity (1980). A number of articles and papers provide further comparisons: Barnes on Irish Tinkers (1975), Liégeois (1971a) and San Roman (1975) on Gypsies in Spain, Rao on the Manus in Alsace (1975), Miller on the Rom in the U.S.A. (1975), Viljanen Saira on the cultural symbols of Gypsies in Finland (1978) and Reyniers and Gilain on Gypsies in Belgium (1979). The association, Les Amitiés Tsiganes de Toulouse, has produced a joint report for the European Commission on its action work among the Gypsies in the area (summarised in *Études Tsiganes* 1980 and Okely 1980). Detailed anthropological studies of Gypsies in Afghanistan and Egypt by Rao and Nabil Hanna respectively have not as yet been published.

Some common aspects emerge from many of these studies of Gypsies on several continents. Invariably the Travellers or Gypsies differentiate themselves from Gorgios, Gajés, payos, 'country people' or Flatties. Many are found to have pollution beliefs which express and strengthen this separation. There is usually an ideology and practice of self-employment and occupational flexibility. Many groups exploit geographical mobility, although not all could be labelled nomads. Indeed nomadism is officially banned in the Communist countries of eastern Europe. Perhaps one aspect common to all groups is that they have had to survive hostility and periods of persecution from the dominant society. They have also been the objects of fantasy and romance. The form which either persecution or exoticism takes changes with historical context.

2 Modern misrepresentations[1]

The Gypsies and Travellers decorate their homes with mirrors and dazzling chrome. Gypsies are reached by way of mirrors, through which they pass and where non-Gypsies see only reflections of themselves. Alternative glimpses are carefully deflected. In Gorgio print, distorted views repeat themselves. Contrary evidence must needs be overlooked. Plain facts are real illusions. On each side of these reflections there is vested interest in distortion.

Alleged isolation

Common misrepresentations of Gypsies have tended to include assumptions that the 'real' Gypsies were formerly or ideally in a state of isolation, with unique, self-contained 'traditions'. The 'true' Gypsies are also depicted in only rural settings, despite the industrial revolution. Croft-Cooke presents the stereotyped view of English Gypsies as historical fact: 'In Stuart times they split into smaller convoys but remained isolated from the housedwellers and spoke English imperfectly if at all ... in the last century they were much as Borrow found them, a secret people, choosing lonely places, respecting their own laws and customs' (1955:113). According to Croft-Cooke, in the nineteenth century the Gypsies became 'far more dependent on trade' with housedwellers 'than they had been heretofore' (1955:113).

Gypsies today are portrayed as victims of cultural disintegration and as helpless in the face of industrialisation, modern technology and urban advance. Trigg, for example, has written of English Gypsies: 'such isolation caused partly by the need for protection and partly out of desire to preserve cultural integrity has kept the gypsy ignorant of the outside world' (1967:43). Similarly, the sociologists Goulet and Walshok, describing Spanish Gypsies as 'under-developed marginals', consider that their contact with 'modern sectors' has been largely through coercive and formal institutions like the police and school (1971:456). As recently as 1973, Vesey-Fitzgerald asserted that 'mass communications have removed the barriers ... Education, economic pressures and, in due course, miscegenation will do the rest. The long, long history of the Gypsies of Britain is coming to an end' (1973:254).

The isolation model persistently ignores the Gypsies' dependence, as always, on the larger economy and the necessity for continuous rela-

Reflections. *Evening Post-Echo Ltd*

tions with outsiders, based on detailed knowledge and flexibility in the face of change. The notion of isolation gives credence to a separate and complete 'culture'. Signs of change are interpreted as loss of independence, and development is described as disintegration. The Travellers' strategies of survival, only recently closely observed, are interpreted solely as the desperate measures of a dying group. The fictive, hermetically sealed group has also been perceived as biologically distinct, indeed a separate 'race'. Marriage outside or into the group, bringing offspring of 'mixed origin', has been thought to bring cultural change, along with genetic variation, and in equal proportions.

The notions of economic, cultural and 'racial' isolation of the Gypsies or Travellers within western capitalism seem hardly plausible. The Gypsies, when first identified in Europe, and indeed their equivalent anywhere else, have never been self-sufficient. They are dependent on the larger economy, within which they took possession of or created their distinct niche. The Gypsies can only survive as a group within the context of a larger economy and society, within which they circulate supplying occasional goods and services, and exploiting geographical mobility and a multiplicity of occupations. Instead of elaborating their alleged 'Indian' origin, it is more relevant to examine the economic and political circumstances of the Gypsies' appearance and continuity within the different countries where they now exist. Indeed, as I have suggested in chapter 1, it is likely that their first 'appearance' as persons called 'Egyptians' in the written records was as much a response to changes within Europe as to some monocausal and linear migration from beyond Europe.

A common 'explanation' for some of the so-called 'traditional' occupations associated with the Gypsies and Travellers throughout Europe and elsewhere is that they were 'those which were cursed or prohibited to upper castes in ancient India' (e.g. M.H.L.G. 1967:2). But any explanation for the Gypsies' appropriation of fortune telling, horse-dealing, tinsmithery and entertainment lies less in the Gypsies' alleged origins than in the structural similarity which these occupations possess when seen in relation to a larger, usually sedentary economy.

Given the Gypsies' interdependence with non-Gypsies, they have always had to develop and change in accordance with changes in the dominant economic and social order. Adaptation to modern conditions merely demonstrates a continuity of adaptation. The Gypsy group cannot be presented as once self-contained within Europe and then suddenly impinged upon by outside forces, since persons called 'Gypsies' emerged in Europe at the end of feudalism and flourished with industrialisation and within capitalism. (Indeed, even the Indian caste model cannot posit a theory of isolation.)

The rural image

Recent fixed images of Gypsy rural crafts and leafy locations conflict with evidence of Gypsies or Travellers residing and working in urban areas from the earliest times. The 'traditional' Gypsy was not exclusively rural. Indeed, in the early nineteenth century, Hoyland recorded the opinions of a lawyer acquainted with Gypsies north of London. He described how even then they were being forced out of urban areas by the authorities:

> The situation of this people daily becomes increasingly de-
> plorable ... the fear of apprehension as vagrants and the pro-
> gressive inclosures near towns and villages had a tendency to
> drive them to a greater distance from the habitations of man
> ... [as they] were expelled from Township after Township
> without any provision being made for their refuge. (1816:iv)

Far from the Gypsies choosing rural 'isolation', it was often imposed
upon them. Elsewhere, we find a continual traffic of Gypsies in towns.
Borrow wrote of the 'Metropolitan Gypsyries' in Wandsworth in 1864
(1874:207), Leland of Gypsies in London in the 1870s (1893:36-7) and
other towns (1882; see also Smith 1880). Smart and Crofton asserted:
'Most of our gypsies cease their roving habits during the colder months
of the year and take up their abode in or near our larger towns'
(1875:xiv). They recorded urban groups both in London and Birming-
ham (1875:xi). Depending on whether the local economy is mainly
agricultural or industrial, the Travellers or Gypsies make the necessary
adjustment in the goods and services offered, and may move between
rural and urban-based work, according to season.

The close connection between the Travellers and the wider economy
is confirmed by their choice of location. The 1965 census of Gypsies living in caravans in England and Wales indicated certain concentrations
in the more industrialised or heavily populated zones: 43% in the south
east and 17% in the west midlands, with only 8% in the northern Yorkshire and Humberside regions. There were also a few concentrations
of Gypsies in less industrialised and less populated areas, for example,
the Vale of Evesham, where there were regular opportunities in casual
farm work (M.H.L.G. 1967:8). The majority of Gypsies were located
within easy access of industrial and residential areas, on the urban–
rural fringes, where encampment was less restricted by the non-Gypsy
authorities. Later, in 1980, the Department of the Environment's regular counts indicated that 60% of the caravan dwelling population of
Gypsies in England and Wales was concentrated in the south east (including East Anglia).

The decline in some 'traditional rural' occupations does not mean
the inevitable shattering of the Gypsy or Traveller 'culture' and
economy, as has been too often suggested. Moreover, the extent of
Gypsy rural 'handicrafts' and rural 'skills' has been grossly exaggerated. Too often, only the exotic and easily visible 'Gypsy occupations'
have been recorded. Those occupations where it has suited the Gypsies to conceal their identity have more often been overlooked (Okely
1979a).

Horse-drawn caravans

Another recent stereotype of 'real' but defunct Gypsies is of inhabitants of ornately decorated horse-drawn caravans. But these belong

31

only to a passing phase in the Gypsies' history. The Gypsies in England and Wales used horse-drawn caravans for only about a hundred years of their history. Previously they travelled with pack-horses and tents, resorting to tilted carts as the road surfaces improved. Carts were gradually modified to the enclosed living waggon with stove and bed. These do not predate 1800, and few Gypsies used them before 1850 (Ward-Jackson and Harvey 1972:28). Moreover, the Gypsies' appearance with such vehicles was hardly heralded with enthusiasm. On 11 July 1833 *The Times* reprinted an extract from the *Devonshire Chronicle* as follows:

> Gypsies, impelled by the march of intellect, seem resolved no longer to march a-foot, and now travel the country in capacious machines larger than a Paddington omnibus, drawn by two or more horses. A numerous gang of these itinerant thieves located themselves a few nights ago in Stoke Lane, near Taunton, having no less than 17 horses among them.
> (Quoted in *J.G.L.S.* 1908:96)

During the 1950s, the majority of Gypsies and Travellers opted for modern caravans which they called 'trailers', drawn by motor lorries. Some Gypsies, mainly in Humberside, retained their horse-drawn bow top waggons, and were to be found in considerable numbers in the 1970s. But they were not given a friendly reception by the local population as has been alleged for the Gypsies of the past. The switch to motorisation meant that the Gypsies' nomadism was enhanced, not diminished. They could travel faster and greater distances. Technology was harnessed to their needs. Thus modern capitalism generates nomads, it does not simply inherit them.

The notion of a separate culture and economy

Evidence of the persistent adjustments by Gypsies to changes in the larger society confronts those who uphold the images of a 'traditional' and isolated Gypsy culture. Those of the exoticist tradition have tended to construct a minority remnant of 'real' Gypsies from the past and disown the others, perhaps the majority, who also call themselves Gypsies or Travellers. One such stereotype, for instance, is that of the 'real Romany' who is alleged to live in rural Wales. Other observers, often using social workers as their main informants, explain the apparent loss of clearly recognised 'traditions' in terms of 'acculturation' or assimilation by the dominant society. An intact culture is projected on to the past. In this way the notion is not discredited.

The term 'acculturation' is used to describe what happens when groups of different cultures are believed to come into continuous first hand contact, and when there are subsequent changes in the original cultural patterns of either or both groups. This term has been adopted as an explanatory principle for example by Marta (1979) in a study of Gypsies in Italy and Sweden. It is especially inappropriate, since it rests on the premises that Gypsies once existed independently of the dominant culture and society. Thus industrialisation is seen as one of the mechanisms for acculturation and the destruction of the Gypsies' alleged autonomy. Marta writes: 'Industrial society has irretrievably jeopardised the Gypsies' economy. Activities such as the Lovara's [a group of Gypsies] cannot subsist within a capitalist mode of production' (1979,1:10). This perspective which fixes, for example, the Lovara's identity as redundant horse traders overlooks both the Gypsies' history of adaptation and their continuing potential for adapting. Some of the so-called 'traditional' Gypsy occupations include horse-trading, fortune telling and casual farm work. Some may be less important today, but fortune telling is not necessarily jeopardised. The vicissitudes of life in a capitalist system continue to encourage people to resort to fortune telling. New occupations have replaced the old ones, e.g. tarmac laying, car dealing, scrap metal salvage and antique dealing (see chapter 4).

The Travellers' skills and 'traditions' in occupations lie not in the content of their occupations, but in their form. Some of the key factors which are overlooked include the Gypsies' preference for and successful practice of self-employment and occupational flexibility. This way of earning a living is consciously chosen, and cannot be explained merely as the result of 'prejudice' against Gypsies and their unjust exclusion from the 'opportunities' of the wage-labour market. The Gypsies' use of the 'informal economy' provides the material context for their cultural identity, which is bound up with their rejection of wage-labour (see chapter 4).

The Travellers' skills have been underestimated or overlooked because too much emphasis has been put on illiteracy and their lack of formal schooling. Thus the Gypsies have often been seen by educationalists, who use their own ethnocentric criteria for education and training, as handicapped. Scant attention is paid to the alternative education and training which the Gypsy children receive, precisely because they do not attend school. Moreover, absence of or infrequent schooling does not necessarily mean ignorance of the wider society. The children accompany their parents and other adults on their work rounds. They are also witness to the visits to the camp sites by non-Gypsies who wish either to evict the Gypsies or do trade with them (see chapter 9).

The word 'culture' can be variously defined to cover the totality of the Gypsies' social and economic organisation or be restricted to beliefs and rituals. In either case, the group's culture is not self-contained. The Travellers' economy is directly dependent on the wider economy, even though self-employment gives a measure of freedom from non-Gypsies, mobility and flexibility. The group's beliefs and rituals are not an abstract totality floating separately from the material circumstances and relations of production with non-Gypsies. Moreover the Gypsies' beliefs and rituals should also be seen in the context of their ideological relations with the wider society. Since Gypsies are not a separate society, they can hardly be attributed with an autonomous culture. This absence of autonomy should not preclude the understanding that the group's beliefs and practices have coherence and form a meaningful whole. The coherence comes also as a response to the dominant society and ideology.

In order to protect themselves as a distinct group within a society which is always trying to assimilate or destroy them, the Gypsies uphold specific ethnic boundaries. These are based on the principle of descent, the practice of self-employment, a commitment to certain values, an ideology of travelling and pollution taboos. Their ethnic identity and beliefs are neither a passive nor a random construct, but a coherent system which when affirmed as daily practice both reflects and reinforces the boundaries between Gypsy and Gorgio. Unfortunately, some beliefs and practices, for example ideas of good luck associated with specific animals, have been labelled as mere 'superstitions'.

Beliefs and symbolic ideas should not be explained merely as examples of 'culture lag', nor as passive reflections of the ideology of the dominant society. There is systematic selection and rejection. Some symbols may parallel those of non-Gypsies, but their meaning may be transformed. To suggest that some of the Travellers' beliefs are senseless leftover flotsam and jetsam from the 'advanced' and literate society is an insult to the minority group's mode of thinking. One task of the social anthropologist is to make sense of the ways of other peoples, and to dispose of ethnocentric and paternalist judgements of others' systems of thought (see chapters 6 and 12).

Thus 'culture contact' between Gypsies and non-Gypsies does not operate as if the allegedly untouched and isolated Gypsy group is helplessly changed by the dominant culture. Even a subordinate group must make sense of its position and use symbols which are meaningful. Such symbols can be rationalisations of subordination, or they may be a potential source of power and inspiration for overcoming oppression.

The notion of a 'pure-blooded race'

The notion of a bounded 'race' mistakenly fixes Gypsy identity in biology. The evidence of mixed marriages and the passage of personnel across the ethnic boundary, just like the notion of a 'traditional and independent culture', has been used to discredit the existence of a contemporary Gypsy group, and to reify the former existence of some 'pure-blooded race'. Race in any case is no more than a social category, it is not a physical reality for any group (Bohannan 1963:185). The Gypsies

Modern misrepresentations

or Travellers can maintain an ethnic boundary which manipulates or ignores biological descent. They use 'blood' as a metaphor for ethnic continuity. Evidence from this study (chapter 5) and elsewhere (Rehfisch 1958; Okely 1975a) reveals the Gypsies' manipulation of genealogies, their regular practice of 'passing' into the dominant society through marriage and the relinquishment of Gypsy identity. Similarly there is the practice in all groups of the absorption through marriage of Gorgios whose offspring may then claim the right to Gypsy identity. Thus the Traveller groups are as much a social construction as a genetic or biological entity. While not a separate race (and no such entity exists) they are still an ethnic group (see chapter 5).

The myth of land scarcity

The Gypsies appeared and survived largely because of the possibilities available to an occupationally and geographically mobile group who were self-employed and who used kinship and descent to transmit a certain monopoly. Their survival problem has been not so much that of securing trade from the larger economy, as of gaining legal access to

A temporary site. *Harold Turner*

35

land for intermittent residence and work purposes. As already indicated, the Gypsies were prosecuted from early times for apparent 'idleness' and for having no 'lawful work, Trade or Occupation' (Thompson 1923a), i.e. they rejected wage-labour and those occupations approved by the state. Nonetheless, they were able to find individuals and groups who paid for their goods and services. Legal controls against them as self-employed workers within the 'informal economy' have been less effective than the increasing controls during this century over their use of land. In so far as they are nomads, they are freed from the burden of tenure, rent, land ownership, rates and identification which comes from a fixed abode. But they have a continuing and varying need for access to land which is controlled by laws reflecting the concerns of the dominant housedwelling society. The Travellers' special land requirements are a hidden factor in their relations of production. The main threat to the Travellers is less that of adjustment to providing goods and services within an advanced industrial economy, as has been so frequently suggested, but the state's increasing controls over land occupation and usage (see chapter 7).

Thus the economic advantages of mobility and self-employment are counter-balanced by the political and legal constraints on caravan dwelling and movement. Fixed notions of land ownership and usage make no accommodation for the occasional and variable use by irregular visitors. The Travellers' use of land for living space and, for example, for scrap metal sorting conflicts with such basic planning laws as the separation between residential and industrial zones. There are additional official controls even where no scrap metal work messes up the planners' maps. Travellers may often obtain the consent of the non-Gypsy owner to reside on his or her land, or they may purchase their own land as a base from which to travel at times, and yet in either case they can be prosecuted for residing there. In terms of a sedentary society, caravans suggest no fixed abode and a potential evasion of state control. In terms of a housedwelling ideology, caravans are defined as makeshift, transient eyesores; either temporary holiday accommodation or proof of inadequate municipal housing provision. The stigma of the caravan is not inevitably visual, since planning permission to *park* an empty caravan is not required. However, decades of public health and now planning laws prohibit caravan dwellers from *living* in them. Thus there are added frictions in the Travellers' relations of production. The Gypsies may find work in an area and Gorgios willing to pay them for it, but simultaneously they may have no legal place either to reside or to complete the work.

Even when it is acknowledged that Travellers have adapted their occupations to changes in an industrial economy, it is sometimes claimed that there is no urban land available to ensure such adaptation. Here the rural image restricts the Gypsies to the countryside and woodlands where it is alleged there was both space and convenient invisibility.

36

Modern misrepresentations

The alleged absence of urban land is merely a rationale for the stigma of the mobile caravan and modern nomad. There are in fact ample plots of urban land suitable for encampments either in the long or short term, and frequently owned by central and local government (Okely 1976). The problem is not that of available space, but that of permanent and official acceptance of the presence of this minority of caravan dwellers or nomads who comply with neither the work nor the residence patterns of the dominant system.

Deviants from the dominant system and self-ascribed minorities are not, as the functionalists would claim, exceptions which merely reinforce the general rule. They can be seen as images of opposing systems. In practice, Gypsies or Travellers, who are dependent for their livelihood on non-Gypsies who are the majority, can remain only a minority. But such reasoning does not suffice. The Gypsies' symbolic work is seen as subversive, although their number is small.

3 Methods of approach

The circumstances for research

Social anthropologists have usually selected as their object of study people geographically distant from their home country or institute of learning. The more apparently isolated from western industrialisation, the more apparently appropriate. In practice, the majority of these islands, villages and tribes were under colonial rule, and experienced trading relations with outsiders, but such influences were usually peripheral to the analysis. The people in this study are within the geography of the anthropologist's own society and western industrialisation. Exotic quality cannot be measured in mileage, since Gypsies so close to 'home' are a subject of exotic image and stereotype. In every continent there are people classed as, or similar to Gypsies.[1] In every continent non-Gypsies have notions about them and encounters with them.

Some space will be devoted to the methodology and background to this research, both because it is still relatively rare for anthropologists to do fieldwork in their own country, and because such information should be regarded as integral to the final presentation.[2] The context and funding were not, until a later stage, those of the conventional postgraduate, but initially as part of a 'policy-oriented' project in a team which included a social administrator and an educationalist. The circumstances affected the methods and content. Constraints could sometimes be turned to creative advantage.

The political implications of the research could not be easily avoided. The appearance of a social anthropologist in the midst of Gypsies coincided with a change in the Gypsies' relationship with the state, namely the implementation of the 1968 Caravan Sites Act. The unprecedented legal obligation to provide sites rested on the assumption that Gypsies wanted conventional education and employment, settlement and ultimate absorption. The research was set up to examine this assumption, and independent of direct government supervision. An anthropological approach would be an important way of understanding the Travellers' perspective. But the initial assumptions and aims of the research organisation were ambivalent and the proposed methods somewhat different from those of anthropologists investigating a group from the inside by long-term participant observation. To liberal-minded outsiders, the Gypsies appeared as a 'problem' group, apparently deprived in terms of the larger society, although likely to be badly treated by the recent legislation. Unless an inside view of the Travellers' needs and interests could be attained, they might continue to be assessed solely in the terms of the dominant order.

The government had been either indifferent or hostile to research on Gypsies.[3] My employers were keen to produce a document with a format considered likely to influence the minds of administrators and policy makers. Greater credence was given to quantitative data, judged 'representative', to be obtained by a questionnaire administered to a large number of Gypsies throughout parts of England and Wales; i.e. the two countries covered by the 1968 Act. Questionnaires and large samples were trusted as 'scientific' despite the fact that the information acquired might be entirely unreliable. Qualitative methodology, depending mainly on participant observation for an intensive period in a single area, was at first distrusted as 'impressionistic' and fruitless for generalisations. Thus my early stages of fieldwork were governed by the need to demonstrate the viability of the methods adopted by social anthropologists.

My difficulties can be illustrated: after only two weeks' acquaintance with Gypsies in one camp, it was proposed that I administer a massive questionnaire before moving on, rather like a mobile X-ray unit, to the next camp. I put most of these weighty documents into a suitcase under my bunk bed and gave others to one of the council employees to administer. The Gypsies proved brilliantly inconsistent. It was recognised that their answers could not be 'coded'. Moreover the council employee found the questionnaire too burdensome to administer. Plans to dispatch these questionnaires to other persons claiming to 'know' Gypsies were abandoned. After a while it could be demonstrated that much of the information in the questionnaire could be obtained informally and that single stranded answers to questions of opinion were not only unreliable but also simplistic and dubious, whatever the 'democratic' and scientistic intentions behind a mass survey. Staying in a single area actually facilitated contact with a large number of families. But in accord with policy-oriented research which often mistakenly demands quantity regardless of quality, there were pressures to abandon my 'biased sample'.

Despite the preliminary difficulties, I was able to live for periods amounting to ten months in a caravan on four Gypsy camps and two months in nearby lodgings in south-east England between 1970 and 1972. In addition, I spent several weeks in northern England visiting Gypsies, many of whom lived in horse-drawn waggons. The main period of fieldwork was supplemented in 1974-5 by several months living near the camps, being visited by or visiting Travellers. A caravan on Gypsy camps was no longer available. After these periods of fieldwork, I continued to visit Gypsy families, some of whom had become close friends. I periodically contacted non-Gypsies associated with the Travellers, and spent considerable time examining local authority records. Only after long-term acquaintance with Travellers at a local level did I attempt to contact the 'national' Gypsy organisation. I have since made the acquaintance of Gypsies in Sweden, Ireland, Holland, Finland and France, and have found some useful comparisons.

Ways of entering

In addition to the challenge of expounding the advantages of social anthropology, there was that of entering Gypsy society. One local area had set up temporary sites with makeshift facilities on land already occupied by the Travellers. A local officer was sympathetic to the local volunteers, teachers and students who had made cordial relations with the Gypsy families. The resident warden of one site had adopted a non-authoritarian and unpretentious role with the Travellers. This locality seemed the most appropriate for establishing contact. I arrived in an atmosphere of minimum hostility and with a ready category as 'student helper'. By good fortune, the warden appreciated my interests. At first I visited the camp daily from nearby lodgings, asking many questions of the warden and other Gorgio 'helpers' rather than of the Gypsies. By feeling my way first with these intermediaries I was able to build up a general picture from their information based on many months' close contact. I sometimes arrived at alternative interpretations of events. The warden agreed to vacate his caravan for a two week trial period and I moved onto the site.

Soon I was offered my own caravan on various sites by the local officer, also sympathetic to my interests. Eventually I needed only to appear as a student, without any of the duties of a rent collector etc. This role first as a student helper or warden was the only possible opening, and available only during the short life of the temporary sites. Months if not years of day visits could have been spent in the vain hope that the Travellers might spontaneously invite me to join them. Attempts to divert me to other localities failed partly because the opportunity to live alongside Gypsies after such a brief acquaintance existed nowhere else. Within eighteen months the temporary sites or camps were replaced by 'permanent' sites with greater supervision by 'professional' council employees, arousing new hostility among the Gypsy tenants. Residence as a student helper became virtually impossible. On one of the new sites I was able to live for a few weeks as guest with a woman tenant whose husband was in prison. No other opportunity occurred.

My earlier residence on the temporary sites was achieved without the prior knowledge of senior county officials who later expressed alarm for my safety. The various responses by Gypsy and Gorgio to my presence on a temporary Gypsy camp are revealed as follows:

> The week that I a single woman moved into my caravan on the site, a councillor stated that every warden of a Gypsy site should be armed with a gun. The Gypsies were equally concerned for my welfare. But whereas the councillor saw the threat coming from *inside* the site, the Gypsies saw it coming from *outside* the site. They said 'If anyone comes to your door at night, don't open it, just holler and we'll come over. You'll be all right with us around to look after you.'[4]

At the beginning I made myself available for any odd jobs: reading letters, arranging for the rubbish skip to be emptied and placing liquidiser in the elsan lavatories after the sewage lorry's departure. I looked busy clearing up bits of rubbish and befriended the children who, unlike the adults, invaded my trailer at all times. One family had suffered a tragic death a month before my arrival. They were very welcoming and I spent many evenings talking, especially with the wife, sometimes until 2 a.m. after everyone else in the camp was asleep. My presence was, I hope, therapeutic. In this charged atmosphere, the young women also spoke about the travelling life, conveying truths never to be repeated. Thanks to her friendship, I established easy relations with other Travellers, and a new confidence.

Soon I dropped all pretence at being a warden, and a council employee assumed all the necessary duties. Rent collection which I undertook for four weeks had predictably become an embarrassment. From then on, I explained that I was a student wanting to know more about the Travellers' way of life. However, many who did not ask assumed that I was always a council employee. I could not avoid being seen to occupy a council caravan rent free. The local officer refused any offer of rent lest he be accused of providing for non-Gypsy tenants. There were other suspicions: that I was a journalist, a police collaborator, a foot-loose heiress, a girl friend of the warden, a drug addict and hippy, or someone on the run from the police. I discouraged all these images except the last. The journalist rumour had been inflated by another warden, a classic 'gate keeper' possessive of 'his' Travellers and apparently threatened by 'academics', especially female ones. The day before my visit to his site, he told the Travellers that I would be writing about their sex lives for the local newspapers.

In the long run, the warden's description of me did not fit what the Travellers saw. They judged me by observed behaviour and the personal interaction with them which never entailed a barrage of questions. Any mention of 'writing' produced a defensive reaction among all Travellers. Taking the advice of those long acquainted with Travellers, I did not emphasise this aspect.

Thus from the outset I was obliged to minimise my identity as a researcher. At the time I justified my actions by a perhaps naive conviction that I would never betray the Travellers and would reveal nothing

41

harmful, neither to individuals nor to the group. There are certain details and aspects of Traveller life which are disguised or will never be published. All the Travellers' names have been changed in this book. At the beginning of fieldwork the immediate concern was for some form of acceptance and the need to be disassociated from journalists, persons doing 'quickie' surveys and dissertations based on 'one-off' encounters. At the end of fieldwork some of my closest Gypsy friends guessed I was 'writing a book'; 'I bet old Julie's keeping a diary. She's all craft.' Others suggested I write one. One family remarked on my obvious interests in Gypsy customs: 'Every time we talk of those things your ears come right out.' They saw it as respect and contrasted this favourably with people who 'try to change us'. Other Travellers seemed completely indifferent, but some would probably never have approved, however anonymous the quotes and disguised the details. The fact that I stayed around, that I made friends, lived as they did, and went out to work with them, eventually discredited any rumour that I was a journalist or police collaborator, and won some respect. I tried to reciprocate for the hospitality, friendship, protection and wisdom I was given.

Any suggestion that the anthropologist merely be 'natural' or 'herself/himself' is unrealistic. There are inevitable difficulties in relying on intuition and the self formed in another culture. The following incident occurred in the first few months of fieldwork:

> Early Sunday morning a policeman drove in, came to my caravan and asked if I knew the whereabouts of a named person. Already children clustered around me listening. (The wanted man I later discovered had escaped from Borstal and was the younger brother of one of the site occupants.) I was able to say truthfully I didn't know of the man. The policeman went over to one of the Gypsy trailers and talked to the young wife outside. Another police car rolled in, blue light flashing. I became increasingly anxious; I should be acting the warden. The police entered the Gypsy trailer. Middle class conviction told me that I should challenge them for a search warrant. The children in my caravan were saying: 'It's all right miss, he's got out and he's run round the site.' Later I recognised that every trailer door was open, so the hunted man could enter. The police had unnerved me, if not the Travellers, and I told the children I would challenge the police. A couple of children came out with me, but 'instinctively' believing that children should be protected from conflict, I told them to wait inside. I got short shrift from the police.
>
> When I returned to my caravan the children declared that I had informed on the Gypsy Borstal boy and they dispersed to their parents. On their return I was told I would not be allowed in their trailers. Nevertheless, I went to the trailer of my

closest acquaintance and asserted my innocence. One of the 'proofs' of my treachery was that I hadn't taken a child as witness. Thus what I had 'felt' to be right was exactly wrong with the Gypsies. Another family then told everyone that I had 'confessed' my guilt. I was treated coldly for days but refused to be intimidated. A year later a family said they recognised my innocence, but explained it was always safest to suspect an outsider.

It is usually considered essential that the social anthropologist should learn and converse in the indigenous language. The Travellers did not, as some Gypsiologists claim, speak 'inflected' Romany, although they regularly used certain Romany words. The use of an alternative to English was an important clue to specifically Gypsy concepts, for example the word *mochadi* meaning ritually unclean. Romany words were also used in an English sounding sentence when Gypsies wanted to convey information to each other in the presence of non-Gypsies, but without arousing suspicion. The non-Gypsies or Gorgios would simply think they had misheard. Romany words used by Travellers or Gypsies cannot be explained functionally as just the need for secrecy; they are part of what it means to be a Gypsy. As I became closely involved with Gypsies or Travellers, more Romany words featured in our conversations, as if to emphasise our complicity. In contrast to the circumstances of some anthropologists, it was no compliment to the Gypsies to use Romany words on first acquaintance; this would have been threatening (see also Sutherland 1975:25).

Rather than drawing attention to myself as an outsider incongruously uttering Romany, it was important to become inconspicuous. My 'middle class' accent was jarring. The Gypsies have a category for a middle class lady – a *rauni* – and they called me one. One Gypsy woman appeared to flatter me: 'You must have had special training to speak like you do. I wish I could talk like that.' Sceptical of such comments I learnt as much as possible to imitate their enunciation. I threw in swear words and adopted their alternative English phrases and vocabulary such as 'trailer' for 'caravan'. The Gypsy woman who had previously flattered me said some months later: 'Judith, your speech *has* improved!' I made comparable adjustments in clothing: wearing modest longer skirts, loose, high necked sweaters. My gestures and stance changed unconsciously, as the alternative way of being came upon me. A social worker accused me of 'hypocrisy' and 'deceit' in my change of appearance, as if the self is morally bound to a single cultural identity. The Travellers responded favourably to these adjustments to their rules and ways, recognising them as respect. On occasions, being obliged to break from the field for the London research centre or an Oxford seminar, I would switch persona, as well as clothing, in a layby en route. Such transformation in my own, the same land, was the more bizarre.

Being a single woman of an age when most Traveller women would be married with several children added to the anomaly. I concealed some years and acted innocent; an honorary virgin. Since women had to be my major allies and informants, I avoided any affront to the segregation of the sexes. One flirtation, or merely a conversation alone with a man, risked public ostracism by men as well as women (see Okely 1975d). I aimed to talk to men in the company of their wives. The Traveller women commented approvingly on my cautious behaviour. During follow-up fieldwork I was able to go out with a man in his lorry during his work rounds, but both he and his wife's attitudes were exceptional. Awareness of this restriction in fieldwork increased attempts to elicit and record accurately information from men whenever possible.

A major break in my ambiguous role as benevolent student came when I participated in production. I acquired a 15 cwt van and went 'Calling' for scrap with two Traveller women. The first day we returned loaded with cast iron, to the astonishment of other camp members who regretted they had not asked me first. My van was an exploitable item. Some threatened to report me to the council, and were angry and confused. There was similar rivalry over my allegiance in the small gangs of potato pickers. Eventually the Travellers accepted the new image in contrast to that of council employee. My reputation as someone who could 'call for scrap as good as any of us' outlived the reality of my incompetence. Such abilities, including the use of 'bad language' and my much publicised acquaintance with Yorkshire Travellers with waggons, were all mentioned by Traveller friends when I first met their associates. I was told 'You can muck in with us.' Ultimately, shared experiences and prolonged companionship were more relevant to the Travellers than any visible interest in writing about them.

Participant observation

Observation has sometimes, even in social anthropology, been emphasised at the expense of participation. The material for this study did not come from 'feeding' tobacco to a handful of informants severed from their daily routine and activities in a formalised question and answer interview. This mode of communication risks an unequal exchange. Invariably the questioner assumes an authoritarian role, and in any case little opportunity is given for volunteered information and insights unpredictable to the observer. Although Gypsies may be an extreme case for the inappropriateness of questions, caution should be exercised in fieldwork anywhere. Beliefs and explanations for actions may only be made explicit among the actors in certain contexts, and not as answers to questions. Some of the explanations given may be mystifications. Ultimately the total meaning may never be articulated by the group participants, but instead be the work of the anthropologist to unravel.

Methods of approach

The Gypsies' experience of direct questions is partly formed by outsiders who would harass, prosecute or convert. The Gypsies assess the needs of the questioner and give the appropriate answer, thus disposing of the intruder, his ignorance intact. Alternatively, the Gypsies may be deliberately inconsistent. Other studies of Gypsies using structured interviews and questionnaires have demonstrated their inefficacy (see Goulet and Walshok 1971:459-61). I found the very act of questioning elicited either an evasive and incorrect answer or a glazed look. It was more informative to merge into the surroundings than alter them as inquisitor. I participated in order to observe. Towards the end of fieldwork I pushed myself to ask questions, but invariably the response was unproductive, except among a few close associates. Even then, answers dried up, once it appeared that my questions no longer arose from spontaneous puzzlement and that I was making other forms of discussion impossible.

Since I did not and could not select just a few individuals for intensive questioning I relied on unstructured and random information from a wide range of Travellers; all spontaneous informants. Implicit explanations were as significant as explicit ones. Verbalisation is only one among other sources of meaning. I perceived gestures, positionings and silences in their contexts, all clues for a composite understanding. Ideals and conventions became public and explicit when I unwittingly broke them. Then I was rebuked and properly instructed. Direct participation in 'Calling' with Gypsies, weighing in at scrapyards, picking potatoes and months of co-residence gave unique insights otherwise concealed. Housedwellers, shopkeepers and soon the police took me for a Gypsy. I learnt the Gorgios' responses to Gypsies by becoming the object of their fear or fantasy.

Participant observation in the work process had its instrumental rewards for greater acceptance. Even more significant was the access to information about the Gypsy economy. The relatively limited incidents experienced by the participant observer as worker, calling for scrap and rags at houses, coming face to face as stranger to persons normally known from the other side; these experiences helped explain more and beyond. The view was as an insider; a Gypsy being treated as such by Gorgios, the outsiders from which I came. As a fellow worker, I was told many anecdotes about similar or contrasting ways of earning a living. Being an accomplice and encountering stigma first hand, I was given statements, attitudes and explanations by the Gypsies in context and otherwise unavailable.

There are also unconscious ways in which the fieldworker adapts and more fully participates. You learn through the senses and in the body. Posture and movement synchronise with those around. There is a photograph of me standing with a Traveller, both of us posing for a Gorgio cameraman. I have assumed unconsciously the exact stance of my companion: arms folded, making a defensive barrier.

45

The kind of empathetic understanding required if participation is taken seriously has been too easily discredited as naive romanticism. It may be that the longing for an alternative identity, another life has been the unconscious compulsion to become an anthropologist in quest of distant lands. Such yearnings may have attracted certain sociologists towards minorities and deviants. But this romanticism is quickly transformed, if the research involves more than transitory visits. Fantasies become tainted by concrete knowledge. It is a hard labour to become another person and of another class and culture. The initial falsified identification has to confront a lived-in reality. Pains and problems may be harsher than those the romanticist would escape.

Participation in Gypsy life may seem suspect. There is a romantic tradition of individuals who have gone off with the 'raggle taggles'. When not simply fiction, such persons have tended merely to live out their fantasies of the wild and free. They selected certain aspects such as living in horse-drawn waggons, or even supposed that becoming a Gypsy meant sporting nudity, as in the case of Augustus John. A later generation of hippies have imagined themselves Gypsies. Actually this fantasy life has been sustained by minimising participation with persons born or brought up as Gypsies. The anthropologist participant observer must do better than that.

What and how to record

From the outset, I kept an alternative record to questionnaires, without premeditated criteria for relevance. Obviously my perception and memory of events had their own subjective filters, but material was not self-consciously eliminated from the beginning. Specific categories and topics emerged, maybe months after fieldwork. It could be demonstrated that even for a restricted 'policy-oriented' topic an understanding of the total context of travelling Gypsy life was necessary. The questions 'Do you want to travel?', 'Do you want to settle in a house?' were relevant, but too complex to quantify or reduce to one of five preordained answers. Worse, they revealed nothing of the viability of travelling or settlement. Qualitative methodology was seen to be valuable. Without direct recording, many of the quotations have lost the original dialect and exact expression, so my notes are usually a paraphrase or 'translation'.

Analysis

The commitment to participant observation as opposed to a questionnaire in the long run produced detailed and reliable information and quantifiable data for 73 families living in trailer units. These 73 formed part of the total 125 families in Adams *et al.* 1975. Additional insights and less complete information were gleaned from a further 30 families in trailers. Contact was made with a small number of families in houses, often relatives of those encountered on the road. Information on wealth, travelling patterns, choices in occupations, earnings, schooling, literacy, housing experience, Gorgio parentage, divorce, and genealogies were rarely obtained in answer to questions, but observed or volunteered in conversation. Since many of the families were known in depth for periods of at least twelve months, and despite gaps in between when they travelled elsewhere, it was possible to build up a composite record of 'hard' data. Shifts in occupations, income, camp membership, work partnerships and political clusterings could be observed over time. Alternative perspectives and information from local records, and from participant observation among Gorgio officials, voluntary workers and local residents were also crucial.

Since this 'hard' data had been cross-checked in so many contexts, its reliability was greater than any answers to formal surveys. More important than the mere accumulation of information is its interpretation. This is best achieved by the experience and understanding of context. A holistic and open approach to recording gives the stream of events, anecdotes, dialogue, the commonplace as well as the bizarre. Attitudes volunteered or surmised, contradictory statements; all this is the stuff for analysis, aided by the experience of participant observation both inside and outside the Traveller group.

The analysis of rules, ideals, taboos and categories is of a different order from quantifiable data. Aspects became apparent in repetitive patterns or in special incidents. Perception of meaning transcends the statement of the actors. The anthropologist is immersed week after week, and thus slowly acquires an alternative intuition. This understanding is not the spectator's stance and, although originating in field experience, long survives it. Retrospective analysis guided by this culturally acquired comprehension can transcend the information mechanically fixed in field notes. There is also a new coherence to be found in contemporary and historical records.

The mass of historical and folklorist data I found confusing before fieldwork. But direct participation in Gypsy life and prolonged co-residence helped to 'crack the code', bringing a new consistency in the otherwise disjointed data, and despite the gullibility or outmoded explanations of the Gorgio writers. I have tried to make sense of and incorporate these sources in analysing, for instance, pollution taboos, animal categories and Gorgio stereotypes. Fragments of earlier travelling, occupations and even names from churchyards restore history to the Travellers. In this way, the study intends to be more than one person's ethnography, time encapsulated. Documentation is restricted mainly to Travellers or Gypsies in England, but some stereotypes are international and some conclusions may be applicable to Gypsies elsewhere. None of these sources are treated *in vacuo*, divorced from ethnographic context, but are grounded in my own evidence. This

47

method contrasts with that of Trigg (1975) in his neo *Golden Bough* of Gypsiology. Rituals, beliefs from any country, any century, are torn from context and assembled without plausible explanation. Trigg's fieldwork seems thin and there are few insights from experience.

Method of presentation

Where relevant, some quantitative assessment has been made (see also Adams *et al.* 1975; Okely 1977), but since the study rests on intensive observation of the limited area accessible to one observer, qualitative material is paramount. Rather than lose the evidence in generalisation, case studies and extracts from field notes have been liberally inserted in the text. Each retains its specificity while illustrating a wider theme. The detail of fieldwork is too often absent from monographs for fear it be decried 'anecdotal'. Its judicious selection can be compared to mythical thought which, according to Lévi-Strauss, 'can be capable of generalising and so be scientific, even though it is still entangled in imagery. It too works by analogies and comparisons' (1966:20). The anthropologist works through images and anecdotes. No detail, no person can be total fiction. The leap from the specific to the general and symbolic is explicit. The single carefully chosen example offers generality through its very specificity.

Units

It would be misleading to label the 100 or more families I encountered as Gypsies of a single area, since the majority frequented many parts of the British Isles. The geographical edges and specific locations for observation were dictated by the limitations of the one observer. The most detailed information was available from those Travellers who occupied or regularly frequented the various places where I lived, or which I visited. Attempts to travel with one family were unsuccessful and would have had mixed advantages, as continuity in observing other families with whom I had established relations would have been lost. In studying Travellers, I could not select a single 'village', nor was it feasible to restrict myself to one 'group', even if it were possible to isolate such an entity. Vital observations on inter-group relations would have been lost. Thus I only observed the Travellers when they entered my location (see also Sutherland 1975). The method is similar to that advocated by N. Dyson-Hudson for the study of nomads: 'Our analytic units need not be population aggregates of some sort: they can as well (and sometimes more revealingly) be segments of time or action, points of contact or separation' (1972:10). Of course, the problems of 'analytic units', 'population aggregates' and the notions of a 'real' or artificially bounded 'community' confront any researcher, whether or not the subject includes nomads.

4 Economic niche[1]

Dependence and independence

The Gypsies or Travellers are dependent on a wider economy within which they circulate supplying goods, services and occasional labour. Unlike migrant workers moving from a single locality to another for 'settled' and wage-labour jobs, Gypsies operate largely independently of wage-labour. Some of the features of occupations adopted by caravan dwelling Gypsies are also applicable to some housedwelling Gypsies, some of whom may travel at certain times of the year (see Sutherland 1975). The Gypsies' greatest opportunities lie in those occupations which others are less able or less willing to undertake. This is true also of migrant workers in industrialised countries, but they tend either to take up wage-labour employment or to operate a small fixed business. The caravan dwelling Gypsy family is both self-employed and

A family visiting a dump to collect scrap metal. *Harold Turner*

geographically mobile as a domestic and productive unit with lorry, trailer-home and minimum overheads. With these advantages, Gypsies or Travellers can cater for occasional needs, where there are gaps in demand and supply, and where any large-scale, capital intensive, fixed and specialised business involving wage-labour employment would be uneconomic or insecure. Their occupations can be generalised as 'the occasional supply of goods, services and labour where demand and supply are irregular in time and place' (Okely 1975c:114; see also Cotten 1954,1955).

Table 1 groups almost all the occupations encountered during fieldwork. Occupations are grouped as (a) Sale of goods; (b) Services; (c) Seasonal labour, and (d) Specialised 'Gypsy' goods and services. It is important to consider aspects common to all of them, for example, self-employment, flexibility and mobility. All the occupations are consistent with the small scale on which each individual or family operates and with minimum capital equipment; a scrap collector needs a sledge-hammer and spanners, the tarmaccer uses a shovel, rake and garden roller or a mechanical vibrator. The lorry for loading scrap or tarmac is multi-purpose, being used also for towing the Traveller's home and transporting the family. Goods selected for hawking are easily portable. The occupations tend to be labour intensive.

Each occupation should be viewed as part of a combination of occupations commonly pursued by one family or individual over a given period of time. The Travellers' new emphasis on some occupations and shift away from others has not been as clear cut as any occupational change for members of the sedentary society, who usually pursue the same occupation throughout the year. For wage-labourers, the change in work is usually total, but for Travellers, most of whom have several types of work throughout the year, change is a gradual shift in emphasis over a long period of time eventually resulting in a new combination of occupations.

Thus the Travellers or Gypsies have found and retained a special niche within the wider economy, exploiting a multiplicity of occupations at one time and over time. Table 1 reveals the extraordinary variety of Traveller occupations. The vast majority are not generally those associated with Gypsies by the wider society. Gorgios have perceived employment for persons called Gypsies only where the Gypsy image is exoticised. They have overlooked the additional lucrative openings to be exploited by persons free of wage-labour and without a fixed abode.

In some occupations the Gypsies have to conceal their ethnic identity and any exotic Gypsy image. For example, as tarmaccers or antique dealers, the Travellers present themselves as respectable businessmen with a fixed address, and as scrap and rag collectors they present themselves as poor scavengers. Elsewhere (Okely 1979a) I have explored how in work relations the Gypsies' image may be exoticised (+), degraded (−), concealed (0), or neutralised (+−). Since only a minority

Table 1. *Occasional, seasonal and specialised goods, services and labour*

(a) Sale of goods	(b) Services	(c) Seasonal labour	(d) Specialised 'Gypsy' goods and services
Hawking of bulk purchased manufactured goods: blankets, linen, carpets, household wares, e.g. lace, brushes, combs, clothes-driers, plastic flowers.	*Clearance* of discarded goods and waste: scrap metal, rags, old cars, material from building demolition.	*Agricultural work* fruit and potato picking, beet hoeing, hop tying.	*Hawking* hand-made wooden clothes pegs and baskets, white heather, hand-made flowers, lucky charms, 'hand-made' lace.
Other sales: secondhand goods cars, caravans, household appliances, clothes, secondhand furniture and antiques.	*External building and gardening* laying tarmac driveways, crazy paving, kerbing, logging, tree pruning, gardening, slate repairs and roofing, painting.		*Fortune telling*

Knife-grinding

Waggon and cart construction |
| *Christmas decorations* Christmas trees, holly, wreaths, flower sprays. | *Casual entertainment* fairground booths, singing and guitar playing in pubs. | | |
| *Other goods* Fruit and vegetables on market stalls, horses, pedigree dogs. | | | |

of the Gypsies' occupations are those where their image is exoticised, much of their economy passes unrecognised. This has given credence to the assertions that the Gypsies' economic survival is threatened by industrialisation and urbanisation. In a study of Gypsies in Spain, for example, some development sociologists asserted that if Andalusia was to 'develop successfully, Gypsies would be left with no marketable skills' (Goulet and Walshok 1971:464).

Some rural occupations, such as fruit gathering and hop picking, have more recently been exoticised as those of the 'real' Gypsies, now vanished. Urban occupations are belittled or remain unseen. As Britain has become more industrialised, the Gypsies have adjusted accordingly. Whereas they once did such work as fencing, ditching and pest control (Wood 1973:46) for farmers, they have more recently worked at scrap clearance or tarmac laying. The type of goods hawked has also changed; manufactured goods have sometimes replaced hand-made ones. But it should be presumed neither that the 'traditional' Gypsy was exclusively rural, nor that Gypsies have abandoned all rural based occupations. Gypsies must be continually adjusting to technological and industrial development, albeit in ways unrecognised by their observers. One English Gypsy said, 'Work doesn't come to you, but the *muskra* [police] do.' So while external state control is regularly imposed upon Gypsies, they must simultaneously initiate economic contact with Gorgios. They are neither isolated from nor ignorant of the larger society and economy.

The theme of former isolation which appears in the literature (e.g. Croft-Cooke 1955:113) may have gained strength from the classification of Gypsies as nomads, who in turn tend to be presented as self-sufficient. Typologies of nomads have usually distinguished only two types: hunters and gatherers, and pastoralists. Gypsies are missing from this typology. The study of nomads has been distorted by the concept of 'pure nomadism' and, according to Dyson-Hudson, its presumed 'independence of settled populations and external markets' (1972:8), so that the inter-relation of nomadic and sedentary groups has been systematically under-investigated (Bates 1972:48). Gypsies are a special type of nomad whose economy can in no way be seen as independent.

It is presumed that both hunters and gatherers and pastoralists can subsist independently of an external economy, and although this presumption is often inaccurate, Gypsies have no such claim to potential self-sufficiency. The Gypsies have been able to hunt and gather only some of their food and fuel from 'natural' resources. This they have done always in territory owned and controlled by others. They must purchase or acquire the bulk of their food and fuel from others. Whereas other nomads may be more independent for subsistence, and move in territories under-populated by others, the Gypsies' subsistence and economy are directly dependent on a wider economy and on the presence of other groups from whom they gain their livelihood. Unlike many pastoral nomads, the Gypsies' main animals, horses, have been a means of transport only, and not a food resource. In contrast to the other main types of nomads, the Gypsies can survive and flourish as urban nomads, since they do not require vast tracts of land for hunting, gathering and pasture. Their prosperity is, even more than in the past, linked to that of the urban economy and population.

The Gypsy economy can be classified as part of the 'informal economy' within advanced capitalism, but not in so far as the term refers to economic activities which are either a temporary substitute for or mere supplement to wage-labour. For those Gypsies encountered during fieldwork, the opposite was the case. Wage-labour could only be a temporary substitute for self-employment, and a last resort for a tiny few. The informal economy has been identified and investigated in parts of the third world, for example among the shanty town dwellers of Latin America. There are important contrasts and comparisons to be made with Gypsies in Britain. The Gypsies differ in that they are a small minority, not the majority of the urban population. In contrast to the shanty town inhabitants, they are not recent peasant migrants. Moreover, the majority of the Travellers' ambitions are very different; not being directed towards wage-labour, fixed property and eventual passing into the wider society.

Self-employment

The Gypsies' history is also the history of their refusal to be proletarianised. In Britain's industrialised capitalist economy, the Travellers are one of the few groups who have remained independent of one of its fundamental features: wage-labour. Travellers only occasionally employ others and they have avoided being employees. For the majority, the closest experience to wage-labour is temporary farm work on a piece-rate basis. Self-employment is bound up with Gypsy identity. There is shame attached to a wage-labour job; one Traveller said: 'If we Travellers took regular jobs it would *spoil* us.' He did not mean work as such, but wage-labour, with its many limitations and restrictions. Contempt is expressed for Gorgio wage-labourers:

> 'There's not much to a Gorgio's life; working Monday to Friday from the same time in the morning to the same time in the evening. Then the man gets drunk on Saturday and he has sex with his wife once a week; that night, and a lay-in on Sunday. After all those years on the job, the man's given a gold watch at the end of it all.'

The same man was offered a regular job restoring the interiors of a block of flats in central London. The firm were paying him £100 a week in 1975. But, he told me, he would stay for 'six weeks and no longer':

> 'I couldn't work like that every day week after week. One day I might want to go [hare] coursing, then I'd want to go to Stowe Fair or Barnet.'

Some Travellers on local authority sites are confronted with jobs at the Labour Exchange:

> 'Wil had to call at a place about a job the employment people gave him. When he got there they said, "It's available." You should have seen Wil's face! It dropped. Ha! Ha! Ha! It was a shovelling job. Shovelling!'

Travellers proudly announce 'I've always worked for myself'. Self-employment not only gives a feeling of greater independence from the Gorgio, but also offers greater flexibility in choice of occupation at one time over a period of time. Set hours and the obligation to appear in a fixed work place limit the opportunities for alternative economic activities, both during the working day and throughout the year. Not understanding the nature of Traveller occupations, well-wishers have suggested that all Travellers need is some initial help in getting wage-labour jobs (see Okely 1975c:144). The presumptions that Travellers will spontaneously accept wage-labour and that no Travellers achieve affluence within their own society, on their *own* terms, are thoroughly ethnocentric. Moreover, by the 1980s, the earlier presumption that there existed a ready supply of wage-labour employment was clearly mistaken.

There are certain common characteristics in the mode of earning a living as a Traveller. Self-employment minimises the routine imposed from outside. Hours are not calculated in the same way as by an employer or employee. A 'job' is usually calculated in terms of days. Moreover, the number of hours amounting to a day's work vary considerably. There is no rigid demarcation between work and leisure. Some work can be done at home on the encampment and mixed in with other activities, surrounded by family and friends and interrupted for chats. Children and others assist. Information and advice are exchanged. Outside contacts are made during an evening in a pub.

The pace of work varies. Probably the pace is quicker when the Travellers are outside the camp on a job.

> 'People don't think we work. We don't work normal hours, but when we go out on a job, we work straight through, we work fast.'

Travellers are thus aware that Gorgios accuse them of being layabouts. Some Gorgio officials complained that the Gypsies never seemed to work; they were 'always on the site' or 'always passing the time of day'. In reality work is a continuing activity done in varying degrees of intensity. A Traveller may take days off, especially after earning a windfall.

Breaking up a dynamo to extract copper wiring. *Judith Okely*

There are times when work is less easy, depending on the weather and season. Slack periods may bring uneasiness, and sometimes hardship. For self-employed Travellers there is no concept of retirement. Ultimately the Travellers are also dependent on changes in the wider economy. Wage-labour unemployment will affect their trade.

In the exceptional cases where Travellers in trailers had taken up 'regular' employment, they were in poorly paid, unskilled jobs. Predictably, there were no examples of occupations where literacy was indispensable. Even in these exceptional cases, wage-labour employment was rarely seen as a permanent occupation. The job was treated as a temporary stop-gap by the less buoyant members of the society and by others in times of crisis (see Okely 1975c:139-40 for examples). After a temporary job a Traveller woman said:

> 'The wages weren't bad, but I hate factories; the same thing every day and you have to come in at the same times, otherwise they knock some money off your wages.'

She didn't complain about the money, only the monotony and conditions. The same woman resented even farm work:

> 'I like calling for scrap. It's much better than picking potatoes all day. I'd rather work for myself than a farmer or someone else.'

The majority of young people, even when they had attended school and lived on sites for several years, took up work similar to that of their parents. It cannot be assumed that a regular minimum income from wage-labour is a sufficient attraction. A Traveller is likely to demand a high compensation for the loss of self-employment.

Regular use of hired labour came only with sedentarisation, as for example when a Traveller family invested in land and property, established a scrapyard or demolition firm and sought further expansion by hiring outsiders. At the other end of the scale, sedentarisation occurred or was required when a Traveller undertook regular, wage-labour employment. The major structural differences between Traveller self-employment and wage-based employment are generalised in table 2.

The Travellers' craft

By avoiding permanent wage-labour employment in an organisation external to the family, Travellers have remained outside a work structure dominated by the division of labour with demarcated tasks, repetitive disciplines or long-term specialisation. The majority of Travellers encountered had not attended school. The majority were non-literate. Yet their lack of specialisation and training in terms of the dominant society's priorities is their very strength.

A Traveller's special ability lies in having a multiplicity of occupations, both at one time and over a period of time. Their use of the word 'Calling' exemplifies the multiple purpose of a work activity. It can include hawking, fortune telling, scrap and rag collection, the purchase of antiques or other re-saleable goods and the search for tarmac jobs. Most Travellers take pride in being able to turn their hand to anything, in any circumstances or environment. A frequent boast is 'You could put me down anywhere in this world and I could earn my living … you could even put me in a desert.' (Gypsies in Iran and Afghanistan have indeed attached themselves to nomadic pastoralists, supplying goods and services.) The greater the spread of occupations, the greater the advantages, rewards and chances of survival.

A multiplicity of occupations was both valued and practised by the vast majority of Travellers in this study. Moreover, the wealthiest, most successful families were those with a greater spread of occupations than the poorer ones. Literacy was also not the asset it is normally assumed to be in earning a living successfully as a Gypsy. Among the families of varying economic levels, literacy occurred *least* among the wealthiest families. Only a minority of individuals were literate, and they were most concentrated among the families of medium economic status.[2] Literacy occurred slightly more often among the poorer families than among the wealthiest.

Outsiders are inclined to assess the Gypsies' training and occupations in terms of the wider society's system of employment. Yet it is precisely

Table 2. *Wage-labour contrasted with self-employment*

Wage-labour employment		Traveller occupations	
(1)	Employee.	(1)	Self-employed.
(2)	Dependence on a single trade or industry.	(2)	Diversified occupations.
(3)	Capital-intensive technology.	(3)	Labour-intensive.
(4)	'Unskilled' labour or specific skills.	(4)	Less specific, more wide-ranging aptitudes or skills.
(5)	Work away from the family and home.	(5)	Family often involved in production. Some work in home setting.
(6)	Work/leisure division of hours, days and weeks. Set holidays.	(6)	No work/leisure division. Time off a personal choice. No set holidays.
(7)	Orders from above. Usually fixed routine.	(7)	Self-imposed orders and decisions. Routine is self-structured.
(8)	Training and education in institutions external to the family, e.g. school and college.	(8)	Family based training and education.
(9)	Wage payment.	(9)	Individually negotiable prices and profits.
(10)	Short-term security of a regular fixed wage.	(10)	Short-term insecurity with unpredictable losses, but the promise of a windfall.
(11)	Possibility of long-term insecurity: the sack or redundancy.	(11)	Some long-term security: independence from an employer and flexibility in occupation.
(12)	Sick benefit and unemployment money. Diminished support from kin and neighbours.	(12)	No sick benefit, no unemployment money. No Social Security benefits if no fixed address. Assistance from kin and neighbours.
(13)	Compulsory retirement in most cases. Pension or Social Security.	(13)	Some self-employment in old age. No pension. Social Security benefit available.
(14)	Fixed location.	(14)	Geographical mobility.
(15)	Work may be available but no housing.	(15)	Work may be available but no legal stopping place.

because the Gypsies' work categories are not found in the larger system that they are able to occupy them. It is said either that the Gypsies are 'unskilled' or that the 'real' Gypsies once possessed skills which are now outdated or defunct, namely rural 'crafts'. Yet it is doubtful whether Gypsies ever possessed these skills in a form which matched those of the sedentary population. Nonetheless, rural 'crafts' have been isolated and inflated by some writers to find a respectable niche for Gypsies in the past (see Croft-Cooke 1955:130-3 and Sandford 1973:206).

Travellers or Gypsies have their own criteria for what is a skill or craft and which are a source of prestige. They recognise that there are *two* types of skills, each related to a different work system and learnt in a different way. A Traveller who spent some of her childhood in a house and attended school before she returned to the road and married another Traveller aptly put it:

> 'I've got your [Gorgio] craft and the Travellers' craft ... I'm sending my kids to school to learn yours and I'm teaching them mine ... My children go out Calling with me. My son sits next to me when I tell fortunes, that's how they learn.'

As the woman is aware, 'Travellers' craft' is acquired not via a formal and external organisation like school or college, but through the institution of the family and inculcated from early childhood. The Traveller must apply him or herself to a variety of circumstances, using a set of general skills which can be formalised as follows:

(1) *Knowing the local economy and its potential where demand and supply are irregular.*

> 'New Towns is no good for scrap. There ain't much in their back yards. You've got to go to the old council estates where there might be stuff that's been hoarded for years.'

(2) *Knowing the local people, an alien population, and recognising their psychological needs and weaknesses.*

> 'When you're selling secondhand clothes, sometimes it's best to go to a house standing on its own. Then the woman won't worry about neighbours seeing. They don't like to show they're poor.'

> 'There was this woman on holiday at the seaside. She'd had a nervous breakdown. She'd been told to leave her house. I told her she should stop worrying, that when she got back she'd be offered a better house than the one she'd got now. Well she could enjoy her holiday then, couldn't she? It was no good her worrying. She paid me for it.'

(3) *Opportunism and ingenuity in choice of occupation in the local context.*

> 'One year was a bad'un for berries and the markets was looking for good holly. We got some dried peas, painted them red, then stuck a pin in each and pinned them on the twigs. We took the holly to the market and a man said he'd buy the lot.'

'Once I came back with three beasts and a nanny goat. The old man said "Whose are those?" I said "I've bought them." I sold them a few weeks later … we grazed them on the field where we were stopping.'

(4) *Flexibility in occupation at a given time and over a period of time.*

When I went out Calling with Aunt Moll we were asking at houses for 'any old scrap'. At one village we were given an old carpet and a heap of old clothing and rags. A few hours later in another village, Aunt Moll got talking with a housewife. The housewife had no scrap but Aunt Moll reassessed the situation and we were transformed into travelling salesman. She sold the woman the carpet and several items of clothing from the rag bag.

'I learn; I'm always learning, thinking of something better. You wear yourself out like a body wears itself out. So you go on to something new. I don't have time for people who pick 'tatoes.'

(5) *Salesmanship.* Establishing immediate face to face contact with customer, client or potential patron. This requires verbal skills of persuasion and boldness, to confront strangers on their doorsteps and risk rejection and abuse.

'Sometimes when you go Calling they swear at you. They could at least be polite.'

'It doesn't matter what you say. You tell them anything and you get them to buy.'

'I sometimes sell key rings and combs but you can't talk over them. You can talk over paper flowers and those wooden ones. Say they're hand-made by yourself. The person can see the key rings aren't hand-made. So you can't get much extra.'

(6) *Flexibility in role-playing.* Travellers adjust their clothing, mannerisms and general image to the demands of the particular occupation. Tarmaccers disguise their Gypsy origins. Fortune tellers play up to the exotic stereotype and scrap collectors dress like beggars (see Okely 1979a and above).

(7) *Manual dexterity and mechanical ingenuity,* especially where materials and equipment are limited. Running a motorised vehicle is now more or less indispensable. Some of the problems of loading vehicles' bodies onto their lorries without the use of cranes are overcome as follows:

> Tom attached one end of a chain to the front of the lorry, fling-
> ing the chain over a tree branch and attaching the other end to
> a car body behind. He then drove forward, thus lifting the car
> body up from the ground. Then he rapidly reversed so the car
> would fall onto the back of his lorry.

Some Travellers use a more sophisticated chain and pulley.
(8) *Bargaining skills* (both with other Travellers and outsiders).

> 'When you go to the yard with some good scrap, you've got to
> call on the man in the office and argue the best price.'

> 'Jim just sold some horses to Bryan. I wish I'd heard the old
> man get together with this old Bryan. It must be an education
> in itself to hear those two, They're both very tight. They won't
> let anyone else hear, go behind closed doors and no one can
> come until it's over.'

(9) *Highly developed memory*. Essential for a non-literate group for
instructions, messages, routes and places.
(10) *Physical strength and stamina*. Lifting of heavy materials, pushing
vehicles and trailers from the mud. Work outdoors in all weathers.

> 'When we first got married, we had no money, so I had to
> work very hard. We had to pick 'tatoes in gangs. Now they do
> it by the bag, but we had to do it by the acre and we moved in a
> long line while the trolley was in front. You had to put the
> 'tatoes on it as it moved. And you couldn't drop behind. I had
> to do it when I was "carrying" [pregnant]. Once I had heavy
> pains but I had to keep working.'

The family work unit[3]

The trailer unit, which usually coincides with the nuclear family (see
chapter 9), is a major unit of production and consumption. Each trailer
unit neither merges with others in a permanent work and budgeting
unit, nor offers itself as hired labour to other families. But each depends on the wider cooperation of kin, affines and camp neighbours
for mutual aid, temporary partnerships and protection. Within the
trailer unit there may be divisions; elder unmarried sons and sometimes daughters eventually work independently of their parents,
retaining their earnings.

Sharing of earnings varied between families. A Traveller wife who
worked at tarmaccing one summer with her husband retained her half
share and purchased a Land Rover. By contrast, one couple expressed
disapproval of a wife who did not hand over all the money to her
husband when they went Calling together for scrap and rags. Obviously when a woman went out on her own she retained greater control

over her earnings. As offspring reached the age of 15 or 16 they would no longer see themselves as 'apprentices' of their parents and would demand half the profits. The parents were usually reluctant, so their offspring chose to work independently. Upon marriage, the adult offspring formed an independent trailer unit and cooked, budgeted, and worked separately. The parents sometimes lent or donated money to the young couple. Older parents hoped for continuing assistance of some kind.

Work partnerships

In a relationship of equality, as neither employee nor employer, one member of a family may work in a partnership with someone from another family. This occurs frequently in tarmaccing. The Travellers themselves use the term 'partner' or 'pardner'. Profits are shared equally: 'We split the money down the middle', and work ideally should be shared. Where there is a great disparity in wealth, it is rare for a Traveller to work with another Traveller in partnerships unless they have a special bond, e.g. kinship, and where the wealthy man is deliberately offering assistance. Work partnerships usually occur between Travellers of roughly the same economic level and with a cognatic or affinal connection. Almost all the partnerships are limited in duration and changeable (for examples, see Okely 1975c:128).

Indeed, permanence is not sought: 'Sometimes Travellers might work together, then one lot might move off 'cos they want to see another part of the country.' Even when partnerships lasted for several months, the two trailer units remained economically separate. Amongst clusters of kin more frequent partnerships and greater mutual aid and cooperation occurred.

Sometimes the relations between individual families, especially when there were neither kin nor affinal ties, were marked by rivalry and out-manoeuvring rather than cooperation (for examples see Okely 1975c:129).

Occasional hired Gorgio labour

It is rare for an adult Traveller to work *for* rather than *with* another Traveller where profits are shared. Any Traveller seeking to employ cheap labour must resort to people outside the Gypsy community. There is a ready supply of Gorgio tramps and down-and-outs willing to work on a daily basis at a flat rate (e.g. £5 in 1972), and perhaps 'fags' and a meal:

> Ellen explained why her husband had recently ceased to work in partnership with her sister's husband: 'It's all right having a Gorgio dosser. You can pay them so much. But if you work with a fella [Traveller], then you've got to split it up.'

61

Some Travellers called at vagrants' hostels and offered a day's work to any inmate. These Gorgios are referred to as 'dossers', 'lurchers' (i.e. working-dogs), or even 'slaves'. One English Traveller claimed that the Irish 'buy and sell their slaves'. These Gorgios may sleep rough: 'John's got this ol' man working for 'im this week. John picks 'im up at the railway bridge where 'e sleeps at night.' Or they may be offered a night's shelter in the lorry cab; never in the family trailer. Dossers are only resorted to occasionally, usually for the heavy and monotonous work in tarmaccing. Without capital resources, transport and work contacts, they remain on the outside. Rarely permitted to marry in, they are comparable to the 'gaff boys' employed as cheap casual labour on the fairgrounds (Dallas 1971:84-96).

Now and again a married Gorgio couple, connected to Gypsies by neither descent nor marriage, may park their caravan alongside the Gypsies, for want of other land. They are not given equal work partnerships with a Traveller. A Gorgio wife described how her Gorgio husband was given a flat rate for heavy labour jobs for Travellers. When asked if he tried to bargain with them, she replied; 'No, they'd say, "You can go without." They stick together. They've always got work. They're out every day.'

In addition to the exclusiveness of Traveller society, the subservience of these outsiders can also be explained by the factors which made housedwellers, without Traveller connections, take to the road in the first place. The majority are drop-outs who have failed in housedwelling society for financial, legal or social reasons. Apart from the few 'tramps' their aspirations are still directed to housing and a sedentary life style. Meanwhile, they have neither the skills nor the contacts to compete with Travellers.

Key work contacts with Gorgios

The Travellers may have an equal or more subordinate relationship with Gorgio housedwellers who are in a position to give them tip-offs or do them services. Here they are not working together doing the same work, as in Gypsy partnerships, but in a relationship based on an exchange of different goods or services. One Traveller described a Gorgio with whom he had such a working relationship: 'I've known him a long time. He's like my own brother.'

It is in the interests of a Traveller to cultivate if not make friends with those Gorgios occupying key positions as patron to Traveller client, for example, the scrapyard owner, the caretaker of a rubbish dump, the builder with subcontracts, or the tarmac manufacturer. In these contacts the Gypsies' ethnic identity is known, accepted and neutralised (Okely 1979a:30). Here, on Gorgio territory, the Traveller is not in a position of dominance, although sometimes an equal. By contrast, in the work relationship between the Traveller and the Gorgio dosser

Economic niche

on Traveller territory, the Traveller is dominant, and the Gorgio never an equal.

Economic status and expenditure

There was enormous variation in the income and financial assets of different Traveller families in this study, but no systematic investigation of earnings or possessions could be attempted. Families hesitated to reveal financial details to other Travellers, let alone outsiders. Moreover, it is impossible to calculate earnings on a weekly or even monthly basis since self-employment entails irregular income.

Families were classified into three broad types based on observable wealth. The main indices for economic status were: the type of trailer – some were old and battered and bought for £30 in the early 1970s, others cost thousands of pounds; motor vehicles, their make, year and condition; domestic utensils, and other consumer goods; work tools; antique china, cut-glass and gold jewellery. The terms low, medium and high should be understood in the context of the Travellers' life style. It is likely that in relation to the sedentary society, families of both low and medium status would be classified as a low income group. Out of the 73 families, 26 were classified as low status, 21 as medium and 26 as high economic status.

Those of lowest economic status lived in very poor trailers, usual Gorgio 'tourers' designed only for summer holidays, so without thickly insulated walls. Some lived in 'bender' tents.[4] The families usually lacked reliable motor transport either for work rounds or for towing. Other possessions were minimal. Some cooked outside on an open fire and rarely used calor gas or coal.[5]

Families of medium economic status usually possessed secondhand trailers, weatherproof and solidly built compared to 'tourers'. The furnishings were modest but adequate. Heating was from a coal fire, cooking and lighting from calor gas. Cooking utensils were adequate and regularly replaced. Some had radios, and record players, most had televisions. They usually owned one serviceable lorry or pick-up for scrap work and towing. Such vehicles were rarely less than seven years old and had been lovingly patched and repaired.

The families of highest economic status sometimes owned two trailers, one specially commissioned with formica interior wall, decorated mirrors, lace blinds and cut-glass designs on the window. The exteriors sported chrome beading. The chimney, bumpers and steps were also of chrome. This trailer was the show-piece with new carpeting, velvet covers and cushions, antique 'Crown Derby' china and cut-glass vases. The second trailer, less lavish, was used for cooking and everyday use. Calor gas was used for cooking, lighting and sometimes heating. Some families owned small generators for lighting and the colour television. Whereas the lower and middle status families stored water in old milk churns, the wealthier families possessed chrome-plated 'Barnsley' cans. They owned at least one heavy lorry usually less than three years old. With a second trailer to tow, they relied also on a Land Rover or a Range Rover. Work tools included power saws for tree-lopping and mechanical vibrators for tarmaccing. Whatever the economic status, gold jewellery was apparent, among all families, but more plentiful and costly among the wealthier families, who were also more likely to own horses, pedigree dogs and plots of grazing land.[6]

Travellers have different financial commitments and priorities from most of the sedentary society. Rent, rates or mortgages are rare demands on the family income. Vehicles and their running costs have the greatest priority for a nomadic group. Many domestic goods can be obtained without payment, for example, firewood and 'game', even on the urban fringes, and clothing and furnishings given to the women out Calling. The ability to get by with minimum cash expenditure is highly valued and seen as part of a Travellers' identity. 'They're not Gorgios. They don't buy anything, not even curtains.' Goods are often obtained, cheap or free, from personal contacts either within or from outside the travelling community, for example, calor gas appliances, radios, work tools, spare parts, trailers and vehicles.

The major cash purchases from the larger economy for nearly all families are food, petrol and domestic fuel. Wealthy families made major outlays on new trailers, furnishings, clothes, domestic equipment and motor vehicles. Surplus cash is invested in gold jewellery, antique china, cut-glass, pedigree dogs and horses, all easily transportable. Some Travellers invested in land for their own occupation. Without planning permission, they usually found it only usable for grazing their horses.

Many of the Travellers' occupations make important contributions within the dominant sedentary economy. Travellers have traditions of flexibility and adaptation to changing economic circumstances, and they have been able to exploit new occupations when others have declined. Elsewhere (Okely 1975c:116-25) I have given detailed accounts of the major occupations of Travellers in the 1970s, including scrap metal re-cycling, tarmac laying and rag collection. The Travellers, whether rich or poor, had not specialised in one occupation. Diversity and a multiplicity of occupations have been the Travellers' strength; often overlooked by government studies.[7] Those families who have succeeded in the Gypsies' terms have often been the most mobile and able to travel widely. In this study, literacy was found least amongst the wealthiest families, thus throwing doubt on the popular assertion that Gypsies' lack of Gorgio schooling is a major handicap. The wealthy Travellers have acquired new lorries and Range Rovers, costly trailers and luxury domestic items. In this study, they only rarely indicated a desire to accumulate capital, invest in a fixed business and become sedentary, although more recently some families have made profitable ventures into buying and selling land. These wealthy families have been a model for other poorer Traveller families as a continuing disincentive to settle. This chapter has also explored the Travellers' ideology and practice of self-employment. The Travellers' resistance to plans either to force or to guide them into wage-labour emerges as entirely rational, given the massive increase in unemployment in the larger society by the 1980s.

5 Self-ascription[1]

Outsider's definitions

The sedentary society's attempts to identify Gypsies or Travellers have not coincided with the way Gypsies have identified themselves, and were often not intended to. Apparently 'objective' criteria such as country of origin, race, language, occupation or exotic culture have more often reflected the current interests of the Gorgio definer. For the central authorities, the problem seems to have been to find a sufficiently *inclusive* category which would cover all nomads or quasi-vagrants, whereas for folklorists and those charged with making local site provision for a select few, the concern has been with an *exclusive* category which would enable them, for different reasons, to discriminate between an acceptable minority and a mass of rejects. The different Gorgio definers' 'objective' criteria cannot survive the historical change to which country of origin, race, language, occupation and culture are all subject.

As an alternative Barth has suggested that 'The fact of continuing dichotomisation between members and outsiders allows us to specify the nature of continuity and investigate the changing cultural form and content' (1969:14). The dichotomisation between Gypsies and Gorgios is continuous. A broad definition of Gypsy and Traveller might be 'Not Gorgio'. Travellers mark themselves off from the Gorgio or, in the case of Scottish and Irish Travellers, the 'Flattie' (Rehfisch 1958), 'country person' or 'Buffer'. When Gorgios use the term 'Gypsy' or 'Tinker', however inaccurately, the Gypsies' consciousness as a separate group is also constantly reaffirmed from the outside. But it is crucial that the Gypsies continue to define *themselves* as Gypsies. Here self-ascription is decisive. Self-ascription should be taken to refer to group ascription rather than to that of the lone individual; i.e. if a group of Gypsies or Travellers recognises as a member a person calling him/herself a Gypsy, then his/her Gypsy identity is a social fact. The group would be by definition greater than a nuclear family. Acton, by contrast, tends to use self-ascription on a purely individual level (1974:59).

When self-ascription is the primary focus, then only those aspects of culture which the group itself emphasises as important have a bearing upon recruitment and identity. Concerning ethnic groups, Barth

Self-ascription

suggests: 'Socially relevant factors alone become diagnostic for membership, not the overt "objective" differences' (1969:15). Some cultural traits may be symbols of identity, others not. The important traits may also change over time and new ones take their place. Aspects of Gypsy culture may resemble aspects of the wider society. But cultural similarity with any non-Gypsy persons does not necessarily weaken the permanent feature in the Gypsies' identity; namely their conception of themselves as a distinct group. Some aspects of Traveller culture and values serve to reinforce the division, for example nomadism, self-employment, dress, language and rituals of cleanliness. But none of these is sufficient.

The principle of descent

The Gypsies use the principle of descent as a self-ascriptive mechanism for continuity. It restricts entry into the group and offers the means for its survival. Among Gypsies or Travellers it is the most socially relevant and the one necessary condition for being a Gypsy.[2] This main vehicle of separation between Gypsy and Gorgio has probably always been paramount. Among the Gypsies or Travellers, a person must have at least one Gypsy or Traveller parent (see also Rehfisch 1958). For this reason they differ from certain other persons with whom they have been mistakenly classed, for example, tramps, vagrants, and even criminals who may come to form a community of sorts with their own code and values, but their identity stems from an *assumed* or *achieved* status, rather than something *ascribed* at birth. A Gypsy's status is ascribed at birth.

The Gypsies' birthright is reinforced by their upbringing. A person claiming to be and recognised as a Gypsy by others has usually been aware of his/her identity from childhood and socialised into a community which caters for its members from the cradle to the grave. This is to be contrasted again with that of tramps whose identity is assumed after childhood and who form no community which can socialise each new generation. Whereas tramps have dropped out of one society, Gypsies on the road have remained in their own society, having failed to drop out.

Gypsy identity, as a birthright reinforced by upbringing within a distinct community, is made explicit and constantly validated by the additional features which the group itself considers to be indices of its identity. Here outsiders' assumptions have not often matched those of the Gypsies. 'Real' Gypsies are alleged to be a dark-skinned race; but among British Gypsies this is irrelevant for membership. Again, ideas of cleanliness, as important with Gypsies as with Gorgios, are focused differently (see chapter 6). The group's self-ascription as Gypsies therefore includes specific cultural choices as well as the principle of descent. Persons of Gypsy parentage are expected to live in a certain way and uphold certain values.

Self-ascription has also to operate at the level of the individual, if he or she is to retain active membership of the group. Although no person can call him or herself a Gypsy without fulfilling at least the condition of descent, an individual with Gypsy parentage can choose to adopt the life style and values of a Gorgio and 'pass' into the wider society. Individual assimilation and rejection of ethnic affinity can occur among persons from any ethnic group, however, it is technically less complicated for Travellers to cross the ethnic line. Living and working in a symbiotic relationship to Gorgios, Gypsies acquire an intimate knowledge of the Gorgio's alternative life styles and values. Moreover, the physiognomy of most British Travellers does not differ from most local housedwellers.

It is clear that a number of individuals and families have chosen assimilation into Gorgio society. Also a number of Gorgios have been co-opted into Gypsy society. Although individual Gorgios cannot, if they marry Gypsies, be allowed to forget their origins, they will participate in Gypsy life on a day to day level, and their children can be fully incorporated. The principle of descent provides a method both for incorporation and exclusion. Thus Gypsies, like any ethnic group, have procedures for releasing or absorbing a number of individuals without weakening their boundaries. Ascription by the individual is subsidiary to the groups's continuing self-ascription.

Descent is no less a self-ascriptive mechanism because of its association with biological inheritance. A purely biological model for Gypsy membership would be misleading both on an individual and a group level. Gypsies do not survive as a group simply because they are biological descendants of Gypsies. For, given the practice which allows offspring of a Gypsy–Gorgio marriage to call themselves Gypsy, many members or descendants are as biologically akin to Gorgios as to Gypsies. It happens that they choose to reject this biological affinity with Gorgios. Moreover, for centuries, numbers of Travellers have chosen to become assimilated into Gorgio society. The option of 'passing' is ever present. It is always possible that *all* the descendants of Gypsies could choose to assimilate. Biology is no determinant. The principle of descent is imposed upon a group with some flexibility in personnel. McCormick (1907:391-2) also refuted a biological 'blood' definition for Scottish 'Tinkler-Gypsies' but claimed it depended on Gypsies continuing to travel. This approach is nearer to self-ascription, but still rests on an 'objective' trait, i.e. travelling.

Ethnography of descent

Recognition among all the groups I encountered, including English, Irish, Welsh and Yugoslav born, appeared to require descent as a necessary condition. A Gypsy or Traveller may not have many of the other characteristics associated with Gypsies and particular groups, but if he or she can prove his or her kinship links with others accepted as Gypsies or Travellers, he or she will be received, though perhaps grudgingly.

> Bill had spent much of his time in Borstal and prison. He learnt to read and write and acquired the mannerisms and dress of a non-Gypsy. When he visited a site, the inhabitants called him a Gorgio, but an old man thought differently. 'I know his parents, he's a Gypsy.' A similar experience was recounted by a woman, 'When I came here, they saw my glasses and said "Here's the welfare." They didn't think I was a Traveller till I told them about my relations.'

Sometimes a group will denigrate another's claims. But this should be understood within the context of rivalry between groups. The principle of descent is not refuted where one group of Gypsies deny the birthright of others.

> An English-born Gypsy said of a group whose ancestors came from Yugoslavia at the turn of the century and who would have delighted a supporter of 'real Romanies' by their dark features: 'We don't call them Travellers ... they're not like us ... Those dark people are dirty.'

The Gypsies accept that all groups have Gorgio ancestors scattered in the family tree. In a dispute they may accuse the other party of being more Gorgio then they, but as a way of abuse. The accusation is only effective because both parties value Gypsy descent claims and distinguish themselves from Gorgios.

As already indicated, individuals with only one Gypsy parent and their children are not excluded by others with two Gypsy parents. It seems that a Gypsy must have at least one Gypsy parent in claiming identity. If he or she has one Gorgio parent, he or she is likely to be called 'half-and-half'. But if he or she marries a Gypsy, the offspring are usually called Gypsy without further modification, provided that they are brought up as Gypsies. The ideal is for both parents to be Gypsy. For those born of only one Gypsy parent, the emphasis on Gorgio or Gypsy background may be altered to suit the circumstances. One day I tried a new tactic to generate discussion and indulged in the sort of self-denigration normally adopted by Gypsies to housedwellers: 'I'm only a Gorgio', I said. Michael, whose mothers' mother was a Gorgio and father a Gypsy immediately pointed to his mother: 'She's a Gorgio.' Another Gypsy present said, 'I'm a Gorgio, my mother is.' Yet he had in another context called himself a 'proper Traveller'. His final observation was: 'If you took it seriously ... well I tell you there ain't a Traveller on the road.' Despite such flexible interpretations, a person who can offer no evidence of any Gypsy parentage is permanently vulnerable to the label Gorgio even after marriage with a Gypsy (for examples see Okely 1975a:40). Although marriage does not make a Gorgio a Gypsy, full participation may be finally achieved after unofficial endurance 'tests' of integrity, teasing and ostracism. The Gorgio must convincingly repudiate certain traits and values considered to be Gorgio. 'If you're born a Traveller, you stay one. If a person's not born one, he can fit in but he never becomes a real Traveller.'

Of the 73 families with whom I had closest contact, the majority of which consisted of nuclear families, four married couples were acknowledged as Gorgio. They were either temporarily or permanently attached to the Gypsies, but they were never fully accepted, were referred to as Gorgios, and they made no pretence to be Gypsy. These few Gorgio families had different aspirations from the Gypsies; they did not desire to travel, and would have preferred housing and regular employment. They had dropped out of the housedwelling society, usually after legal and financial problems. They were also incapable of success within the travelling society, partly because they had not been trained from early childhood in the necessary skills, and because they were linked to the group by neither descent nor marriage (for example, see Okely 1977:55).

In addition to the Gorgio couples there were single male Gorgio 'dossers'; vagrants or individuals on the run who were exploited as cheap labour and never fully incorporated. Gorgio women who drifted into the society without the formal status of a wife were exploited for casual sex and later abandoned. Of the 69 remaining families or domestic units, the vast majority of which contained a husband and wife, there were fifteen Gypsy–Gorgio couples, eleven where the wife was Gorgio and the husband had Gypsy parentage, and four where the husband was Gorgio and the wife had Gypsy parentage. It is possible that a female Traveller marrying a Gorgio is more likely to leave the Traveller community, while a male Traveller marrying a Gorgio is more likely to remain in the community. Examples of Gypsy–Gorgio marriages were found also among relations of the families. These marriages occurred among all groups, regardless of age, life style, wealth, or region. Every group of Gypsies whom I encountered had a few Gorgio ancestors mixed in with Gypsy ancestors. This evidence is inconsistent with any outsiders' classification of groups based on the presence or absence of marriages with Gorgios. Despite the regular occurrence of Gypsy–Gorgio marriages, it is significant that they formed a minority of the marriages, thus indicating a practice of endogamy. Four of the 69 Gypsy or Traveller families were originally from Ireland and four others originated from Yugoslavia one generation back. They had the same criteria of descent. Thus the majority of the families whom I encountered living as Gypsies fulfilled their own necessary condition for membership, despite the claim by many outsiders that the majority are 'drop-outs' and counterfeits.

Terminology and title

Contrary to another popular Gorgio assumption (e.g. Vesey-Fitzgerald in the Kent County Council 1952, Duff 1963:260), the term 'Traveller' does not have lower ethnic status than 'Gypsy'. If anything 'Traveller' is preferred, especially to outsiders because it is less stigmatised than Gypsy. It also emphasises the nomadic ideal. Whereas Gypsies are always prepared to acknowledge they are 'Travellers', they may deny being 'Gypsies'. Given the Gorgio meanings for these terms, it is preferable for the Gypsies to deny their ethnicity than risk suffering the negative responses to it.

> A local councillor visited a new council site for Gypsies and asked one of the teenage girls, 'Are you a Gypsy then?' She said, 'No of course not, I'm a Traveller.' He went away wondering if the warden had given a place to a 'drop-out'.

> A five year old girl told her mother that the teachers had called her a 'Gypsy'. The mother became very angry; 'You're not a Gypsy, you're a Traveller. There are no Gypsies on this site, only Travellers.'

In both examples the Gorgios had intended to be complimentary. Such questions have been met with similar answers in the past. A Gypsy told Hindes Groome: 'if any one asks ... plump out, "Are you a Gypsy?" we're bound to answer "No"' (1880:46-7). The term Traveller also had acceptable status in the nineteenth century. The same Gypsy said: 'To hear him talk, you'd fancy there wasn't a deeper traveller going' (Hindes Groome 1880:47). Among themselves or in the company of Gorgios whom they respect, Gypsies will use the word 'Gypsy' without embarrassment, although I heard it more frequently among the older generation. A woman who had only ever used 'Traveller' in front of me said after six months' intermittent acquaintance, 'So you've taken to the Gypsy way of life.'

The need to deny being a Gypsy to a Gorgio has also an immediately practical explanation, given the discriminatory clauses in the 1959 Highways Act and the 1968 Caravan Sites Act. Sometimes in conversations with Gorgios the word is used with pride. A grandmother said to a health visitor: 'I'm a Gypsy, and I've brought up my children my way.' The term 'Gypo' is also acceptable if used by a Gypsy, but obviously not when, as I heard it, used by a policeman to a Gypsy. The Gypsies also indulge in self-deprecatory jokes, permissible if told by a member of the stigmatised group. One such joke told between a group of teenage boys produced cathartic laughter, the punch line was repeated several times and explained.

> 'There's this dead body. How can you tell it's a Gypsy?'
> ''Cos 'e's got a peg in 'is arse!'
> 'You see the joke? Gypsies are s'posed to sell pegs!'

Didikois, Romanies and 'Gypsy blood'

The principle of descent, which gives a right to membership through a biased selection of ancestors, should be distinguished from that of 'racial purity', although both are manipulated. When the labels 'half-breed' and 'true-blooded' are used by Travellers among themselves, blood is mainly a metaphor for *social* categories made by the Travelling society. As among Gorgios, blood is incorrectly equated with race. Generally the terms would not refer literally to the genetic inheritance of an individual and certainly not to that of a whole group. In an internal dispute or when wishing to ingratiate themselves with Gorgio visitors, one group of Gypsies might denigrate their rivals by calling them 'Didikois', meaning half-breeds. In this way Travellers have exploited their own and their observers' theories of race (cf. the 'Romany' writer Wood (1973:96)). In other circumstances, and amongst themselves, 'Didikois' is often devoid of pejorative and genetic content, e.g. in the popular song,

> I'm a true Didikois
> I live in a tent,
> And don't pay no rent.

One Traveller indicated to me: 'Didikois sometimes means the tent dwellers or horse and trap people, but it's often used for any Traveller. It means the same thing as a Traveller' (cf. Acton 1974:70-3).

Whereas those with partial Gorgio ancestry are not consistently denigrated, those with no claims to any Gypsy ancestry are always vulnerable. One Gypsy told me a 'Gypsy story' in which the villain was a Gorgio 'foundling' adopted by a Gypsy family as a baby. This person turned out evil despite his good Gypsy upbringing. 'It was in his blood, that Gorgio blood. You can never change it.'[3]

Non-Gypsy theories of race have been expressed more in terms of physical appearance. Here the Gypsies' theories of race have not coincided. The *Oxford English Dictionary* for instance gives one definition of 'Gypsy' as 'member of wandering race … of Hindu origin … they have a dark tawny skin and black hair'. Whereas popular Gorgio ideas of a 'real' Gypsy may still be governed by such notions, these are rarely identifying facts for the Gypsies themselves. The majority have physical features hardly distinct from the sedentary population. One Traveller did say to me at our first meeting (which may have affected the content of her statement): 'My grandfather was a *rank* Gypsy, very dark. You don't see them like that nowadays.' But usually distinctively 'foreign' features had only a personal significance and were not exploitable for status as a 'full-blooded Romany'. For example, one Gypsy who had very dark hair and skin was given the nickname of a detergent brand. I was told 'He's so dark he needs it to make him clean.' A literate Traveller expressed to me the popular Gorgio ideal of the real Romany: 'They're supposed to be dark-skinned.' The idea of a Romany is still exploited when talking to outsiders: 'We're real Romanies. Not like some of those people round here', declared a Traveller to a Gorgio at first meeting. But sometimes the title is unfavourable; one woman who considered herself more a showground person said to some Travellers, 'My daughter married a real Romany – ignorant.' And another time: 'Those Romanies'll go on picking 'tatoes, that's all they can do.' Another Traveller said, 'There's no difference between a Gypsy and a Romany.' A literate Traveller affirmed the Egyptian and Indian mythical origins:

> 'The different Travellers, they're all from the same root. Years ago they came from Egypt and India. They're all the same at the bottom, all the same down the line.'

This contrasts with Gypsies talking to Hindes Groome in the nineteenth century: 'All these country Gorgios fancy we come from Egypt ... They'd swallow any mortal thing and ask for more' (1880:37).

Since the Gypsies use the term Didikois as pejorative or complimentary according to context, there is no clear fact–fiction distinction between Gypsies' and Gorgios' categories. The Gypsies will present to the Gorgio categories which both confirm Gorgio prejudices and protect the particular Gypsy speaker. The public categories which work best may actually be those with some connection with the Gypsies' internal categories. The Gypsies' ideology of 'blood purity' feeds also the Gorgio demand for the 'true-blooded' Romanies. This continuing relationship between Gorgio stereotypes and the Gypsies' internal criteria discredits any assumption that stereotypes of alien groups are created by popular ignorance and thrive for want of empirical information. Stereotypes are not images *in vacuo*. They may be inversions or projections of the ideal, or transformations of readily available information. Stereotypes are rooted in 'fact'.

Geographical and national affiliation

Self-ascription in Gypsy identity is relevant also to criteria other than descent, for example, national or regional affinity, membership of a subgroup and of a kin group, and language and general values (Barth 1969:34). There is an interconnection between Gorgio concepts of national and geographical origins and the Gypsies' use of them. 'Region' or 'state' are not very helpful when defining Gypsies since they neither possess nor govern their own national territory. Gorgios have sometimes tried to define 'real' Gypsies according to a group's present or former residence in a particular country (see Okely 1975a:37). For a sedentary society 'place of birth' is given crucial status in its ideology. A Gypsy woman was aware of this problem: 'We've all been born in different places – a family can't say it belongs to one spot when the children have all been born in different places.'

For a sedentary society, 'place of residence' may come close to replace 'place of birth'. Travelling Gypsies obviously have no permanent address, hence their definition in Gorgio law as persons of 'no fixed abode'. Some Travellers, especially those who have travelled beyond the British Isles, have a great variety of potential national identities (for example see Okely 1975a:38). In general non-Gypsies broadly define Travellers by the country their group prefers to frequent, e.g. as Spanish, American or British Gypsies. Within England, as elsewhere, one group is considered more authentic than another on the basis of its alleged national 'origin'. The name Lee is often associated with the favoured 'Welsh' Gypsies. Faced with the dominant society's hierarchy, the Gypsies will try to pass as the most favoured group in the current location. That is, they will not merely claim to be 'real Romany' but also by implication, English or Welsh as opposed to Irish or Scottish.

> In July 1975 I encountered a group of families on waste land in Islington. They had migrated from Ireland and had Irish accents. But they informed a local Gorgio sympathiser that although many were 'Irish' *each* family contained an English spouse called Lee or Loveridge. I found no such evidence. Their spokesman called himself Loveridge – a 'traditional Romany' surname. However implausible 'Mr Loveridge' seemed, talking in a broad Irish accent, any accusation of being a 'foreigner' or 'Tinker' had been pre-empted.

Attention has been directed to the flexibility of the Travellers' national affinities as presented to Gorgios (cf. Kaminski 1977). It should not be concluded that no such sub-categories are recognised among the Gypsies themselves. A recent discussion on sub-groups in the British Isles tends to give this impression. Acton rightly dismisses the varying dialects as a means of classifying Irish, Scottish, Welsh or English Gypsies (1974:58), but he gives no place for self-ascription in sub-group identity: 'individual families seem more or less Welsh' (1974:67). Sub-group categories here are presented as merely outsiders' labels without additional meaning for the Travellers. Sutherland, relying on Acton, appears to believe this (1975:307). Nonetheless, Acton acknowledges that the Travellers themselves appear to use national sub-group categories (1974:58) in self-definition. When confronted with Travellers who have regularly frequented Ireland, Travellers within England make a clear distinction between 'Irish' and 'English' Travellers. George and Sharon Gmelch (personal communication) have confirmed that the Irish regard themselves as separate from the English. This separation and self-ascription by national affiliation is accentuated when groups are competing for land and work. For those

Self-ascription

Travellers who frequent a single country the question of national identity is not significant except in opposition to rival 'immigrants' or until there is occasion to cross a national boundary. A Traveller born in England who travelled 'abroad' for the first time to Wales was surprised to find himself classified as 'English' in pubs (see Okely 1975a:38).

Given their geographical mobility, Travellers or Gypsies do not hold rights to a locality in the law of the sedentary society. They must resort to independent means of asserting territorial claims, or appropriate the sedentary society's categories for their own ends in order to protect themselves as Gypsies in opposition to Gorgios, or to defend a Gypsy sub-group in competition with another. Gypsies confronted by Gorgios complaining, for example, about 'rubbish' will say 'those foreigners' or 'strangers' dumped it, not themselves, the 'local' 'Romany' Gypsies. Simultaneously officials complain that the Gypsies causing offence are not the 'locals' but foreign 'invaders'.

Regional affiliations are predictably more flexible than national ones. There are recognisable differences between the accents of those Travellers regularly frequenting the north of England and those regularly frequenting the south. But the accents are rarely linked with one county. There is an amalgam of pronunciations and dialects in each individual, which housedwellers, ignorant of the speakers' Gypsy origin, find baffling. The national affiliations of individuals, if not groups, is made more flexible by marriage alliances and inter-generational assimilation. Here again self-ascription, however flexible, is the key to sub-group ethnic identity. Some Travellers speaking with an Irish accent have never been to Ireland, yet identify themselves as Irish. Others who do not speak with an Irish accent may emphasise Irish ancestry and on a personal and individual level call themselves Irish.

> Harry has never been to Ireland and speaks with an accent associated with southern England. In confidence he calls himself 'Irish' and 'Catholic'. His surname is mentioned by Sampson in referring to the 'tinker clans, who still infest Wales', and who 'commonly speak both Shelta and Romani' (1930:345). Harry is prepared to denigrate Irish Travellers in discussion with officials. He has married into a family with no claims to being Irish, who frequent the south-east. If, as I suspect, his parents, along with other kin, escaped to Ireland during the war, their Irish connections would have been made more explicit in that context.

Other Travellers with 'Irish' surnames may also acknowledge some Irish ancestry but call themselves 'English'. They have no Irish accent and have married into groups using names traditionally associated with English Gypsies. Thus national and regional affiliations are flexible in time and place, while remaining significant categories.

To conclude, persons calling themselves Gypsies or Travellers have survived in the shadow of external categories, and distorted them accordingly. Some categories have enhanced the Gypsies' self-definition. Fieldwork reveals the people's internal perception and experience. Travellers or Gypsies are members of an ethnic group based primarily on the principle of descent. A minority of persons have married in or out, but this has not affected the group's social and ethnic distinctness. Descent is reinforced by upbringing and a commitment to the values and life style emphasised by the group. 'Cultural' or 'objective' factors are subject to change and adaptation, and have been variously selected by both Gypsies and non-Gypsies for definitions which may not coincide. In relating to outsiders, Gypsies may manipulate their image, but their independent self-ascription and ethnic identity are no less permanent.

6 Symbolic boundaries

Explanations

It is often assumed that 'culture contact' brings change by a kind of contagion; the most technologically advanced economy and the dominant political group 'infecting' or rubbing off its culture onto the least technologically advanced and perhaps subordinate group. The Travellers are a case study for such relations. They have changed and adapted to some extent on their own terms. Their ritual beliefs show similar marks of independence within the system of the larger society. The Gypsies may indeed incorporate symbols, rites and myths from the larger society, but there is a systematic, not random, selection and rejection. Some aspects may be transformed or given an inverted meaning. The Gypsies, and possibly other oppressed groups, can be seen as *bricoleurs* (Lévi-Strauss 1966:17-21), picking up some things, rejecting others. The ideology of the dominant society is de-totalised, and the ultimate re-synthesised cosmology takes on a new coherence with perhaps an opposing meaning, and one which accommodates the Gypsies as an independent group. The Gypsies are not passively 'copying' the beliefs of the dominant society.

The Gypsies are under constant pressure from the dominant society to become assimilated. The problem is how to remain separate and different, while maintaining daily contact with Gorgios, to whom Gypsies must present many disguises. All roles, whether trickster, exotic or victim, carry the risk of self-degradation and a dangerous sense of un-reality, unless the 'inner self' is protected intact, and unless the actor can distinguish between the self and the part. Group integrity must be maintained and expressed in some independent way.

One way of remaining different is by pollution beliefs which both express and reinforce an ethnic boundary.[1] The Gypsies' beliefs not only classify the Gorgio as polluting, but also offer the means to retain an inner purity. If certain observances are maintained, the Gypsies can enter Gorgio territory unscathed. Here I part company with liberals and educationalists who, by nature of their position as mediators, deny the continuity of these boundaries. Sometimes lip service is paid to the Gypsies' pollution taboos which are vaguely justified by edu-cationalists as part of 'Gypsy culture' which must be respected, as if 'culture' is politically neutral and can be merely tacked on to a programme of liberal integration, or preserved, out of historical context, after ethnic assimilation. Since these taboos express a fundamental division between Gypsy and Gorgio, they cannot be viewed with such neutrality, nor explained as merely quaint survivals of a previous set of beliefs, e.g. from India, nor as the left-over 'superstitions' of a lost rural, non-literate culture.

The Gypsies' beliefs cannot be seen independently of those of the larger society, mainly because they create and express symbolic boundaries between the minority and majority. The beliefs are allied to daily, often commonplace practices concerned, for example, with eating, washing, the use of space and the placing of objects in that space. Conformity with these practices affirms the Gypsies' separation from Gorgios. However, the extent to which these beliefs express symbolic boundaries may not necessarily be made explicit nor articulated by members of the group. The Gypsy writer, Fred Wood, has asserted: '–a list of taboos of things that must never be done in a wagon, and items that must not be brought into the wagon – could fill a book; but it would merely be a list of customs for which there is no explanation' (1973:78).

One task of the social anthropologist is to examine these taboos and to expose their hidden logic and underlying meaning. The discussion that follows is not simply a descriptive record of Gypsy beliefs acquired by straight question and answer. It should not be misread as 'only ethnography'. Instead, apparently meaningless and inexplicable statements, incidents and taboos encountered both in fieldwork and from the literature have been assembled, pondered over and systematically explained. When I introduce the hidden notions of an 'inner' and 'outer' body, the former representing the inner ethnic self, then seemingly bizarre practices such as the Gypsies' rejection of sinks in their trailers and their abhorrence of cats make sense as part of a coherent cosmology.

Public health or inner purity

The Gypsies' idea of purity and cleanliness, even in their most explicit manifestation, are often concealed from non-Gypsies. There may be a clash of views. Here it is important to examine also the specific ideas of cleanliness held by representatives of the dominant society, especially where there are contrasts. A common Gorgio attitude is that, in terms of the housedwelling ideals of cleanliness and hygiene, Gypsies are dirty. Two examples, one of an illegal encampment, the second of an official site, reveal the Gorgio notion of public health in conflict with the Gypsies' notion of inner purity.

The heath 1961
Local Gorgio residents complained that the caravan dwellers

used the heath for their personal needs without digging pits or using screens. 'This we think causes a very serious hazard to health and may give rise to an epidemic when the warmer weather comes' (local *Advertiser*, 28 April 1961). Residents also complained about litter, scrap-iron and rags. After his visit, the county health inspector reported: 'While the bonfires and piles of scrap material make the Heath unsightly the main objection is that owing to their being no lavatory accommodation on the site, excreta is to be found everywhere – on paths, between bushes, under the bushes themselves and on the edges of surrounding fields' (council records, 1961). However, in answer to the local vicar who feared an epidemic, the medical officer wrote: 'Don't worry too much about the menace to the health of the village and your family ... Please do not quote it ... the possibility of danger to health must obviously be an important lever in trying to remove the nuisance' (council records, 1961).

An official site 1974

From the first example it might be concluded that Gypsies would conform to housedwellers' concepts of health and hygiene once officially provided with washing and toilet facilities. However, a front page headline of the *Oxford Journal* reads:

> SQUALOR
> Disillusioned warden quits council caravan park to run Isle of Skye youth hostel. The wife of the warden said of the Travellers: 'They are filthy, I just cannot understand how they can live like that ... They seem to want to live in squalor ... We set out with such high ideals and now we are completely disillusioned. They don't want to be helped.'

The *Journal* continued:

> The outhouses which have lavatories, washing facilities and a room for sleeping were filthy ... old clothing, human excreta and dirt were everywhere. Every window in the outhouses had been smashed. The park was littered with wrecked cars and old rags. The scene was one of utter desolation apart from the three caravans parked on the site.   (8 March 1974)

The last reference to the caravans, apparently devoid of squalor, unwittingly indicates the main focus for the Travellers' sense of order and cleanliness. The installation of modern plumbing and other facilities on official sites for Gypsies did not always appear to be reducing the conflict over hygiene. The council provision was adjusted to the value system of Gorgio housedwellers. The underlying intention was to change and convert the Gypsy tenants, for ultimate assimilation. But so long as the Gypsies retain their ethnic and economic independence, their differing ideas of cleanliness will survive. It is pointless to expect change by operating only at the level of the symbolic.

Inner/outer body symbolism

The problem of the Gypsies' relations with Gorgios is expressed and resolved in their symbolism of the body, and pollution taboos. These are found by extension in the Gypsies' treatment of domestic space, classification of animals and attitude to death. The complex pollution taboos indicate that the Gypsies can be said to make a fundamental distinction between the inside of the body and the outside. The outer body symbolises the public self or role as presented to the Gorgio. The outer body or public self is a protective covering for the inside which must be kept pure and inviolate. The inner body symbolises the secret ethnic self, sustained individually and reaffirmed by the solidarity of the Gypsy group.

Usually taboos among English Gypsies are presented merely as evidence of 'Eastern origins' (Seymour 1970:187). Undue emphasis on a theory of origins or 'survivals' risks the loss of the current coherence and meaning of the system. The observance of these taboos among English Gypsies has been explained more meaningfully but vaguely by Acton as a 'commitment to a culture which will remain Gypsy' (1971:109), but, he does not escape mentioning a 'hygienic function' (1971:120) in addition to a symbolic interpretation. The anthropologists Miller (1975:46) and Sutherland (1975:8) in their studies of American Rom have recognised the role of pollution taboos in maintaining an ethnic boundary, and have found greater emphasis on the Gypsies' distinction between the upper and lower parts of the body (Sutherland 1975:264), with the waistline emphasised as the symbolic boundary.

The inner/outer dichotomy operates among English Gypsies as follows: the outer body (or skin) with its discarded scales, accumulated dirt, by-products of hair and waste such as faeces are all potentially polluting if recycled through the inner body. By contrast, anything taken into the inner body via the mouth must be ritually clean. Attention is directed not only towards food, but also vessels and cutlery which are placed between the lips; the entry to the inner body. Chipped and cracked crockery must be jettisoned. The outer body must be kept separate from the inner – a person's shadow can pollute food.

> A Traveller attending a Town Hall luncheon with Lady Plowden and Council officials explained why he did not finish his lunch: 'I could not finish my cheese. A shadow has fallen on it. It is one of our customs. You do not know our customs. We cannot expect you to understand.' Lady Plowden's comments reveal the familiar explanation in terms of origins: 'We learn that this custom is also current today in districts of India, from where the Gypsies came in the tenth century.'
>
> (1972:7)

Gypsies distinguish between something being dirty and something ritually unclean. The word *chikli* (from *chik* for dust or soil) means 'dirty' in a harmless way (see Acton 1971:110). But the word *mochadi* means 'ritually polluted'. Another meaning offered only by Borrow is 'unclean to eat' (1874:46). In most circumstances the Gypsies' outer appearance, for example, when returning from scrap metal work, has no significance for ritual cleanliness. A person's face and clothes can be black with grime but not *mochadi*, so long as the inner body is clean. The Travellers are very conscious of Gorgio accusations that they seem dirty, but for them the *context* of washing, not washing in itself is crucial for defining pollution.

The primary distinction is between washing objects for the inner body and the washing of the outer body. Food, eating utensils and the tea towels for drying them must never be washed in a bowl used for washing the hands, the rest of the body or clothing. Ideally the Gypsy should have a whole collection of bowls: one for washing food, another for washing crockery and cooking utensils, one for the main laundry, one for washing the body, one for a woman's body, one for washing the floor and trailer, and one for washing a newborn infant. In practice, the number is often reduced. The Gypsies speak more readily of 'two bowls', distinguishing the crockery from the personal washing bowl. The focus of purity is the washing-up bowl which should be reserved exclusively for associated activities. The tea towel must be washed in this bowl and never with the laundry (cf. Acton 1971). The tea towel hanging out to dry on its own becomes a flag of ethnic purity.

A washing-up bowl used for any other activity becomes permanently contaminated and can never be made clean. A Gypsy woman explained to me that previously both her washing-up bowl and the personal washing bowl were made of expensive stainless steel. She never confused them but sensed that others accused her of doing so. She therefore threw away the personal washing bowl and replaced it with an old plastic bucket. The personal washing and laundry bowls are potentially polluting and often placed outside the trailer whereas the washing-up bowl takes pride of place *inside* the trailer.

The conflict between the Gypsy concept of cleanliness and Gorgio concepts of hygiene are brought out as follows:

> A Gorgio *health* visitor discovered that a Traveller had a deep cut in his foot. Well versed in Gorgio germ theory, she grabbed the first bowl she saw inside the trailer – the washing-up bowl – poured in disinfectant and water and bathed the man's foot in it. Afterwards the Travellers threw away the bowl and recounted the incident with disgust. The bowl was permanently *mochadi*.

The Gypsy writer, Gordon Boswell, recalls the dirty habits of some Gorgios encountered as a young man: 'They'd perhaps be boiling a sheep's head in a bucket, to eat, and then be boiling their shirt in the same bucket later on, and that wasn't my way of life' (1970:63-4).

The Gorgio is condemned as *mochadi* by definition since he or she is not Gypsy. This is confirmed by the Gorgio's failure to distinguish between the inner and outer body. Gorgios design and use kitchen sinks for multiple purposes. This is proven by the Gorgios' habit of placing hand soap or even tooth brushes near the kitchen sink. Hand soap must be kept away from the sink and crockery. One day the Gypsy children offered to clean up my trailer. Among other things I noticed was that they had hidden my hand soap in a cupboard and wrapped it up in several layers of paper tissue.

Another example indicates how for Gypsies soap is seen as potential dirt, not cleanliness. The ideas cannot be explained by a Gorgio medical theory of germs nor 'medical materialism' (Douglas 1966:29-32):

> Nelson told me about Jack, his Gorgio dosser, who was working for him after leaving prison. 'One morning Jack put a fork on the table near a bar of soap. My wife Sheila said "Oh dear, there's another fork gone!" and threw it out the window.'

It was frequently asserted that Gorgios urinated in their sinks. Travellers buying Gorgio-designed caravans board up their sinks. Wealthier Gypsies commission trailers without them – instead they have a continuous formica ledge on which they place crockery bowls. Personal washing is either done at the far end of the trailer or in the

Trailer interior, with no sink. *Homer Sykes*

second trailer, not used for cooking. All waste water, especially that used for body washing, must be thrown away, a distance from the trailer. I soon learnt to use several bowls, but continued to pour the different types of water down the sink until the children voiced their disapproval. Waste water must also be scattered when emptied from the bowl. There is one exception – on Good Friday dirty water must be tipped and not scattered, as that is the day, I was told, when the Devil threw dirty water in the face of Christ (an example of the Gypsies' reinterpretation of Gorgio Christian theology to fit their own).

The Gorgios' failure to make the same distinction between inner and outer body is not seen by the Gypsies as merely accidental, but a means of drawing positive ethnic boundaries. A Gypsy is partly defined or defines him or herself by an adherence to these rituals of cleanliness. A Gypsy woman said: 'He's a *real* Gypsy. You wouldn't find him washing his hands in the same bowl as he washes his cup.' A Gypsy man said: 'If you look at a Gypsy's trailer, you won't find a sink, that's what Gorgios use.' These ritual beliefs have historical continuity. The *Journal of the Gypsy Lore Society* (1910:156) recorded how a Gorgio charity invited Gypsies to a local hall for a 'high tea'. Before the giant meatpie was brought in, the local baker wrapped it in a blanket to keep it 'piping hot'. The blanket, associated with the outer body, would thus have contaminated the food. One Gypsy informed the others. Consequently no Gypsies would eat the pie, except for an old man who took one taste to spare the Gorgios' feelings. From then on he was nick-named 'Blanket Pie'.

These general taboos associated with the body among *both* male and female have not been formalised by the English Gypsiologists, but confused with the pollution associated specifically with women, animals and death. It is important to clarify the primary pollution taboos associated with the symbolic separation of the inside of the body. The other taboos follow from this.

Food and health

Food, the sustenance for the inner body, presents an additional problem for the Gypsies in their ambivalent relationship with Gorgios. They must obtain the bulk of their food from the dominant society. Only a certain amount is obtained from the wild, and Gypsies are neither pastoralists nor cultivators. Sustenance for the inner body comes paradoxically from the dirty Gorgio. Most food must be purchased, begged or stolen from the enemy. Great care has to be taken over the type of food acquired. Food in tins, packets or bottles, not perceivably contaminated by the Gorgio's body or shadow, is usually most acceptable. Obviously factory food can be hideously manhandled, but first, the event is more distant, not visible, and secondly this confirms the symbolic rather than the empirical character of the system.

> A Gorgio wife of a Gypsy described how members of her camp found a cache of tinned food thrown out from an American airbase. The tins were bent and slightly rusty. The Gypsies avidly consumed their clean contents and suffered chronic diarrhoea. The food had seemed acceptable because not exposed. They had not considered the possibility of food poisoning inside the tins.

Unwrapped food is treated with extra caution.

> One old man recalled proudly how his father would travel a great distance to a 'clean' baker, but even then he stripped off the outer crust, recently hand touched, and ate only the interior.[2]

Any left-overs from meals are instantly jettisoned – stews, sandwiches and vegetables. Nothing once cooked or prepared is saved. When out Calling, the Gypsy woman prefers to accept only wrapped food from the Gorgio housewife. A fear often voiced among English Travellers is that Gorgios might deliberately or inadvertently poison the Gypsies' food.[3]

> Dolly was talking to her neighbours about a mass murderer in the States who poisoned his victims. Her immediate comment was – 'It makes you think, they could put poison in your tea in cafés.'

> Louise found some black specks in a lettuce after washing it. She shouted angrily, 'They're out to poison us!' then wrapped the offending article in newspaper and put it in her dustbin.

Thus the Travellers feel ever vulnerable to Gorgios. The most dangerous places for the consumption of food are on Gorgio territory where the Gorgio has control over its preparation – not simply its production. In a Lévi-Strauss sense (1970) food cooked by Gorgios (as opposed to food cooked by Gypsy women) is Gorgio 'culture', which must therefore not be consumed. Since commensality is a sign of and an affirmation of intimacy, the sharing of eating places with the Gorgio risks not only direct pollution via 'poisoned' food, but also secondary contamination by a weakening of the social boundary betwen the two groups. The precautions and limitations in these circumstances serve as continuing reminders of the need for differentiation. Travellers will eat only in cafés where they are sure the crockery is washed correctly, where no hair can fall in the food and where there are no cats and dogs. If worried they will drink only factory beverages from glass bottles and eat with their hands rather than with utensils. Some Travellers frequenting select pubs may reserve a tankard or take one with them. Gypsies will only rarely accept a cup of tea when visiting Gorgio homes. If a Gorgio is offered tea in a Gypsy trailer, a special compliment, he may be served with a special cup, reserved for outsiders and considered unusable by the Gypsy family.

The eating places where Gypsies risk contamination by Gorgios include prisons and hospitals, as well as private homes, cafés and pubs. Hospitals are the most dangerous, partly because of their suspect ways of cleaning and cooking. Some Gypsies there temporarily have been known to refuse all food except the fish and chips brought in by visiting relatives (see Okely 1975d:66-7 and chapter 11). Such food is more acceptable, because although cooked by Gorgois, it is not perceivably touched by hand after cooking, and is placed in clean paper or new plastic containers rather than on dubious crockery.

The Gypsies' conception of hospitals as concentrations of Gorgio disease is wholly consistent with a medical theory of germs and Gorgio practice. However, for the Gorgio, hospitals are also optimistic centres for curing and overcoming disease with full faith in modern science and medical technology. The Gypsies, in contrast to many Gorgios, will resort to these places only at certain times. Babies are more often entrusted to Gorgio medical care, especially when suffering respiratory problems. Adults may use hospitals for curing venereal diseases and tuberculosis, both perhaps visible signs of contamination of the inner body and sources of shame.[4] The Gypsy writer Boswell recalls 'our people had always been against vaccination'. In the army he protested 'I will not be poisoned' (1970:71). Internal operations are usually avoided, even when the symptoms become increasingly apparent. At other times the Gypsies prefer to pay private fees to doctors in their surgery and then only in emergencies. Since hospitals are polluted, places of death and disease, they are the best place for handling the Gypsies' most polluting *rites de passage* - childbirth and death (Okely 1975d and chapters 11 and 12).

Spatial organisation

These examples of polluting acts (birth and death), taking place outside (in hospitals), or formerly on the edge of the camp, reveal that the inner/outer dichotomy in body symbolism is expressed in the Gypsies' organisation of domestic and public space. Whereas the washing/eating separation is maintained by all groups there are slight variations in spatial separations according to variables like mode of shelter, emphasis in occupation and level of wealth.

The distinction between inner and outer in spatial terms is now more pronounced among those who live in trailers, as opposed to tents or waggons. Horse-drawn waggons were a focus of cleanliness except that cooking (as opposed to tea-making) was done outside, just as with tent dwellers. Now with calor gas cookers the Gypsies have retreated inside. The cooking pots are scoured inside and out. For those cooking outdoors the black outer coating on pots and kettles is an acceptable protection of the inside. The fire for cooking must never be confused with that for burning or cleaning metal.

Many objects and activities are banned inside the trailers (including most animals). The trailer must not risk being a storehouse of pollution; childbirth and death must occur outside. Clothes-washing, defecating and urinating must be done outside and some distance away.

Gorgios design lavatories for their caravans: proof of their dirty habits. Gypsies use these cupboards for storage. Frequently public health inspectors prosecute them for not having elsans in their trailers. Whereas Gorgio hygiene consists to some extent in containing, covering or hiding dirt, for the Gypsies, polluting dirt can be visible, but it must be a clear distance from the clean. The sight of faeces is neither polluting nor shocking, as seemed to be the case for the local house-dwellers and visiting health inspectors described above, but its proximity to food and domestic quarters is. It is not surprising that the tenants of the official site had no respect for the council designed huts which combined all the polluting activities of washing, laundering and defecating with cooking facilities. I noticed on encampments that so long as faeces were distanced from the trailers, and by implication contact with the inner body, there was no problem.

The same focus on the inside of the trailer applies to domestic rubbish. No waste bins are kept inside. The practice was observed among Gypsies who had moved into houses. By contrast Gorgios accumulate and store their rubbish in bins in every room in their houses. Attitudes towards the disposal of rubbish outside the trailer varies according to the Gypsy group. Those families who may cultivate a 'respectable' outer image and do not concentrate much on car breaking tend to keep dustbins. The space outside the trailer is not so vital a work space. The area or order is extended by laying pieces of carpet or new linoleum immediately outside the trailer. Territory is also claimed by laying down left-over tarmac. But even this group may sometimes act in a way similar to those doing scrap breaking, where a large amount of rubbish is simply thrown 'out the window'. A man slung his dinner of half a chicken and roast potatoes straight out of the window, because he said he'd lost his appetite. His wife didn't take this as an insult. Cakes, tins, clothes, faulty T.V.s, shoes, all have the same fate. A frequent comment is 'chuck it out', as opposed to 'put it up', meaning put it inside the trailer. 'Break it up' is reserved for anything metal for the scrapyard and 'burn it' is the appropriate treatment for polluted articles, including the possessions of the dead (see chapter 12).

Obviously nomadic Gypsies cannot expect rubbish disposal services, and also some of the material is valuable scrap iron. But there is an element of defiance in the way Travellers indiscriminately scatter the stuff they themselves classify as rubbish. Their liberal supporters urge them to be tidy, but the Travellers know from experience that the police will move them on anyway. The Travellers don't see external tidiness as important in these contexts. They are perfectly aware of Gorgio priorities, the health inspectors and local residents see to that.

Here there is a one way exchange of information. Whereas Gypsies know about Gorgio ideals of cleanliness, the Gorgios are not informed of the Gypsies' alternative ideas. This is standard between dominant and subordinate groups. The Gypsy is not, as is commonly believed, hampered by ignorance, he or she merely refuses to imitate Gorgio values.

It is commonplace for officials to judge the success of a council site, as opposed to a roadway camp, in terms of the area surrounding the trailer. The 'before' and 'after' pictures do not show the interiors of the trailers which are often dazzling displays of mirrors, antique china, formica walls and ceilings. Instead the Gorgio officials look for cultivated gardens, in what for the Gypsy is a shifting no-man's land and work space. One Traveller woman said:

> 'People say we're dirty. They don't see that we think *they're* dirty. Sometimes you go to houses and maybe the *outside* and the garden look all right. But you should see what's *inside*. And people in houses have got electricity and water. We haven't got those things but we keep clean.'

An inside view. *Farmers Weekly*

Site layout

Since the Travellers' encampments were condemned for their public health hazard, 'permanent' council sites have been installed with elaborate and costly facilities. The 1968 Caravan Sites Act specified 'adequate' accommodation. This has been interpreted in terms of the ideology of a housedwelling society. Facilities are not geared to transitory, temporary use but to permanent settlement. The Gypsies are given unnecessary duplicates of the facilities they must continue to possess when travelling. The planners and architects resort to a spider's web of regulations all purporting to represent a rational universal concept of public health and order when their priorities are equally ethnocentric: 'The Chairman of the Housing Committee ultimately responsible for the official site said, "The Council produced the facilities they thought were reasonable"' (*Oxford Journal*, 8 March 1974).

Temporary sites with simple cheap facilities have not been acceptable in the long run to local authorities, although many Gypsies generally prefer them. On some new 'permanent' sites, each family was given a bathroom in their small hut. On other sites where cooking, washing and lavatory facilities were combined in a single area, the Gypsies referred to such 'pre-fabs' as 'flea-flabs', thereby indicating their contempt and fear of pollution. But ignorant educationalists explained this different pronunciation as the Gypsies' illiteracy.

The sites have also reflected the Gorgio's rigid distinction between industrial and residential zones. Scrap breaking, an industry which the Gypsy pursues on home territory, has been banned on sites by some authorities. The camp layout as designed by Gorgio architects and officials also reveals a contradiction between the ideology of the dominant society and that of the travelling Gypsies. Ideas of public order combined with personal privacy are reflected in many official sites, by the placing of caravans in rows of straight lines. To the architect the aerial plan looks 'tidy' and to the passing motorist rows of caravans appear to be 'under control', self-consciously placed. The result is that no occupant can see all or be seen by all the other occupants of the site at one view. The assumption is that each caravan or nuclear family is a private unit, wishing minimum contact with neighbours. Sites are not designed for a group of self-selected families united by cognatic and affinal ties.

When Gypsies choose the layout, they often place the trailers in a circle, with a single entrance. The main windows, usually the towing bar end, face inwards. Every trailer and its occupants can be seen by everyone else. When the camp members are self-selected, usually in a political cluster (see chapter 10), there is no need for privacy and protection from Gypsy neighbours. Few draw curtains, even at night. Within this circle of group solidarity there can be no secrets – domestic quarrels are for all to see, the centre is a place for chatting, and a safe enclave for children to play. Every driver pulling out or coming in can see if children are in the way. The single entry to the circle is a deterrent to Gorgio visitors. Outsiders are enclosed as if in a trap. One authority, having noted the Gypsies' use of space on the temporary sites, recognised their preference for a circle and built two new sites accordingly. But the concept of individual privacy was maintained by the erection of twelve feet beech fences between each family plot. This made excellent firewood. A Department of the Environment plan for some Gypsy sites placed the toilets in the centre (D.O.E. 1977a:13 and 15).

Elsewhere in the world, e.g. in Latin America, the colonisers have required a similar spatial reorganisation into straight lines in order to control subordinate groups:

> The circular arrangement of the huts around the men's house is so important a factor in their social and religious life that the Salesian missionaries ... were quick to realise that the surest way to convert the Bororo was to make them abandon their village in favour of one with the houses set out in parallel rows
> (Lévi-Strauss 1973:220-1)

Once the Travellers feel security of tenure or access, rubbish is cleared, and the spatial boundary extended to the edge of their plots or the camp itself. Rubbish may be pushed over the hedge or fence on the outer rim of the circle. The toilet places will also be sought outside. The inner/outer boundary of dirt and cleanliness is thus completed in territorial space. Hedges are symbolic as well as physical boundaries. A Gypsy accused of illicit sex is said to have 'gone behind the hedge'.

Since caravans are considered offensive to the ideals of a house-dwelling society they must be well screened by fences, walls and trees, and placed in back lanes and hollows, if planning permission is to be awarded. Many permanent sites have been so selected and designed. A local councillor explained to me why a site on unwanted land near a dual carriageway would have to be closed: 'It gives a bad first impression to motorists approaching the city.' The site was bulldozed, unevenly surfaced and planted with trees at enormous cost. But the Travellers do not like to be concealed from Gorgio public view: 'We like to see what's going on ... watch the traffic.' Advance warning is thus received of visiting Travellers or Gorgio officials. Where possible the Gypsies have pruned the trees around the sites. They do not feel vulnerable when exposed to the disapproval of Gorgios, on the contrary they feel safer – in their circle.

Animal categories

In analysing the Gypsies' classification of animals,[5] I found pollution to be an important underlying principle. Animals are graded on a scale of pollution ranging from the completely clean to the extremely *mochadi*. The extent of an animal's pollution can be a factor in its edibility. Those characteristics of the animals which Gypsies select for significance reveal boundary maintenance in several ways. The classification of animals appears intelligible if seen in terms of their outer bodily appearance and their eating and washing habits, which are consistent with the Gypsies' priorities of the inner and outer body. The general body symbolism, as discussed earlier, is related to Gypsy–Gorgio political and economic relations. Similarly, the classification of animals uses not only body symbolism, but also depends on the animal's position or use in both Gorgio and Gypsy space. Since Gorgios are the agriculturalists and landowners, as well as housedwellers, their spatial categories (e.g. Leach's categories: house, farm, field and far, 1972:48) impose themselves on the Gypsies' own often conflicting spatial categories. Gorgios control, if not own, many of the animals on their land. For Gypsies, all farm animals are Gorgio bred and owned, and all wild animals are on land controlled by Gorgios. The Gypsies' relations with each animal are affected by the Gorgios' relations with that animal. The acquisition of an animal will be affected by the extent of Gorgio control.

What is 'wild' or 'far' for Gorgios may be more like 'home' for Gypsies, and what is 'home' and house for Gorgios may be 'wild' or 'far' for Gypsies. The placing of some animals may be roughly equivalent for both Gorgio and Gypsy, but the placing of others among Gypsy and Gorgio may be diametrically opposed. Some animals will also have a special place for the Gypsies in economic and political exchanges with Gorgios. Given these differences in the two groups' relationship with and use of animals, their ideas about animals will also differ. In understanding the Gypsies' classification of animals, it is also essential to appreciate the Gorgio classification, more specifically, how the Gypsy *perceives* the Gorgio classification, i.e. how Gypsies see Gorgios see animals. The Gypsies' idea of Gorgio animal classification may be a distortion, but with an element of truth. It is no coincidence that the cat, the animal which the Gorgio is considered to find the cleanest, the Gypsy finds most polluting. Here aspects of the Gorgio belief system are transformed and inverted.

Sharon Gmelch (1974) refers to certain attitudes of Irish Tinkers towards specific birds and animals, including their association with good or bad luck, as 'superstitions'. The Tinkers' unorthodox relation to Catholicism has been explained as a technical result of illiteracy. Aspects similar to the dominant society's religion are explained by an inarticulated contagion theory, as if the Tinkers' beliefs are merely a case of culture lag. The Tinkers' beliefs have not been interpreted as a coherent system. It is my contention that Gypsies in England, and just as likely Irish Tinkers, may incorporate aspects of Gorgio culture, but not arbitrarily. The Travellers themselves, however, may not fully articulate the underlying system (see also Wood 1973:78 quoted above).

As in the general pollution taboos, there is a one way transmission of information. The Gypsy takes note of Gorgio values and may adopt inverse ones. An asymmetrical power relation, where the Gorgio sets the constraints within which the Gypsy must operate, is balanced by an asymmetrical system of information. Both groups may classify themselves as 'culture' and the other as uncivilised, if not of 'nature'. But whereas the Gypsy knows he or she is classified by the Gorgio as of the wild, if not always an animal, the Gorgio does not see how the Gypsy sees the Gorgio – a dirty beast. Whereas the Gorgio animal symbolism for the Gypsy is often mere fantasy (Cocteau compared the Gypsy to a 'jungle tiger'), the Gypsies' animal symbolism, however selective, is based on a more detailed acquaintance.

The analysis of classification here goes beyond the internal ethnography of one group and is also very different from that proposed by Lévi-Strauss in his discussion of symmetrical oppositions among different groups of Australian Aborigines. Lévi-Strauss's ideal was to computerise all the transformations if and where known all over Australia (1966:89). He made contextual comparisons between Australian Aborigines and peasant villages in France. In both cases the groups accepted a 'general conformity' (1966:90). There is then no direct comparison with the oppositions between Gypsy and Gorgio where the same overall rules are not accepted by both parties. A more satisfactory comparison might be the relations between Australian Aborigines and the immigrant whites. Contemporary studies of Aboriginal animal classification still treat them in isolation from the invading white man's systems (e.g. McKnight 1975).

Animal body symbolism: washing and eating

The Gypsies' classification of animals in terms of their outer body and their washing and eating habits is comprehensible – in the light of the Gypsies' symbolic separation between the inside and outside of the human body. The animals upon which the Gypsies choose to focus attention are the horse, cat, dog and hedgehog. The cat (*matchka*) is possibly the most polluting and associated with death and the Gorgio. Dogs are also polluting, but respected as hunters and protectors. The horse (*grai*) is absolutely clean and an important mediator between Gypsies and Gorgios, as well as between Gypsies. The hedgehog (*hotchi-witchi*) is edible, sacred medicine and associated with the Gypsies' better self, i.e. the self which is not involved in deception of the Gorgio.

Cats, rats, mice, dogs and foxes (called red or dirty dog, e.g. *mokada-jook* (Wood 1973:71) are all *mochadi* partly because they lick their fur, taking their hairs and outer bodily dirt into their mouths and inner body. Thompson has also recorded the Gypsies' discrimination between animals based on washing habits: 'Lias objected especially to the way dogs and cats lick themselves all over: this he said, was the chief reason why Gypsies regarded them as *moxadi*. He did not consider a horse to be *moxadi* because it does not lick itself and he would if necessary drink after it' (1922:230). The polluting powers of dogs were documented even earlier by Thompson (1910) and Dutt (1910), but not explained in this way. My own fieldwork confirms the Gypsies' condemnation of cats' and dogs' self-grooming. The cat's regular washing is seen by Gorgios as a sign of laudible cleanliness, but the same practice is seen by the Gypsies as shamefully dirty. Cats and dogs are also possibly condemned for being carnivorous; eating the outer and inner bodies of other animals. Cats eat rodents, also extremely polluting. Dogs eat the faeces on the camp site. If these animals or their hairs, also polluting, come into contact with cooked food it must be immediately jettisoned. Dogs' bowls must never be washed in the same bowl as crockery for humans. Dishes are smashed and containers destroyed if touched by dogs and cats (see also Wood 1973:70). Thompson and Dutt recorded a similar practice at the beginning of the century.[6] My fieldwork confirmed this:

> On the camp where I was living, a Gorgio's dog, not trained to keep outside, rushed into a Gypsy's trailer and stole some meat from a valuable Crown Derby china plate. The Gypsy woman smashed the set.

Johnny described to me a visit to a Gorgio household, which incidentally somewhat discredits the obsessional explanation of Gypsy customs in terms of mythical Indian origins:

> 'I called on Peggy's husband; you know he's an Indian. He made me some tea and his little dog kept growling at me. When I spoke about it, Peggy's husband said "That's because you're drinking out of his cup!" (Johnny imitated a retch.) I put that cup down quick! There's a *mochadi* thing.'

Cats are generally considered untouchable and their hairs polluting. It is recognised that dogs may have to be handled sometimes, but a person must wash afterwards (see Wood 1973:70).[7] The Travellers expressed disgust to me that Gorgios not only stroked cats and dogs freely but allowed dogs to lick them on the mouth, very *mochadi*. It is said that a dog licking the human face can cause blindness. Additional evidence of the polluting powers of dogs is provided in a handout of the National Gypsy Education Council: '*Mochadi* regulations should be respected ... In Romani *mochadi* can mean in different ways "dirty, immoral, unhygienic" ... dogs or other animals should not be let into the school. Do not let dogs lick your hands or face, or stroke them' (1973).

Gorgios are condemned for keeping cats and large dogs in their beds. One Gypsy man accused Gorgio women of bestiality with their 'lap' dogs. Cats and dogs are banned from the trailer (see also Wood 1973:70).[8] The Gypsies permit one category of dog inside their trailer, small ones like Yorkshire terriers or chihuahuas, acceptable because they cannot jump onto tables and touch or leave hairs near crockery. Their movements outside the trailer and around the camp are controlled. They are kept on leashes. They are permitted in the lorry cab, another arena of cleanliness. The following incident reveals these dogs' expendability and the extreme untouchability and *mochadi* quality of rodents:

> One evening on my camp, some rats seized a favourite Yorkshire terrier (also considered valuable for breeding), and dragged it down the bank. The Gypsy owners slammed their trailer door and left the animal to its fate. A Gorgio neighbour rushed to save the dog and in the process got bitten. She complained to me that the Gypsies showed her no gratitude for having rescued their dog. The Gypsies thought her *mochadi* for approaching the rats.

Rodents are condemned partly for their carnivorous or indiscriminate diet. It is considered 'bad luck' to utter the word 'rat' or 'mouse' inside a trailer, thus threatening the trailer's ritual cleanliness by a *mochadi* category. The term 'long tail' is preferred.

Rabbits and hares are ambiguous, being somewhat *mochadi* since they conspicuously lick their fur. However, they are edible partly because they are not carnivorous and their edibility rests on the special precautions required in their preparation before cooking; every trace of fur must be removed. A Gypsy boy was horrified to see a tiny number of hairs remaining on the rabbit I was cooking. Dead rabbits are stored outside the trailer before preparation for cooking. Birds of prey are *mochadi* and inedible because carnivorous. Wood, the Gypsy writer, states: 'As to food, there are some animals that you could never eat because it is *mokada*. A fox ... you could never eat him; nor a cat; nor a rat; in fact not any beast of prey or bird of prey, vulture, raven or crow' (1973:71). The owl is polluting and associated with ghosts and death, and perhaps because it 'lives inside old rotten trees'. Gypsy bred chickens or bantams and eggs are *mochadi* and inedible partly because of the chickens' observed diet of Gypsy waste, including faeces. Since chickens live in the vicinity of the Gypsy domestic space, eating prohibitions may symbolise tabooed incestuous relationships (see Leach 1972, Tambiah 1973). They are bred not for sustenance, but for cock-fighting (see Boswell 1970:49).

The frog has been associated with the devil (*beng*), and with cripples (Sampson 1926:IV, 32). Smart and Crofton recorded the following statement by a Gypsy about the frog: 'A four-legged devilish thing which goes into water for drinking' (1875:174). For the Gypsies, the presence of this creature in water has been seen as an indication of the water's suitability for human consumption, i.e. its cleanliness (Smart and Crofton 1875:243), but at the same time the frog walks in its own drink: by analogy it drinks its own bath water. Fish of course do the same, but they are not anomalous legged land creatures (see Douglas 1966: ch. 3). During my fieldwork the Gypsy children revealed a violent attitude to this creature:

> The children noticed a frog under my trailer: 'Miss you've got company!' they said. Despite my vigorous protests, they frightened it out by throwing stones, then stoned it to death. Still not content, they sliced and squashed it into the ground by riding over it repeatedly with a bicycle.

Snakes and lizards are associated with or inhabited by the devil and extremely *mochadi*. Both are constantly shedding their outer skin or body, so revealing no clear distinction between the inner and outer body. As with rodents, it is bad luck to utter the word snake or *sap* inside the trailer. Hindes Groome noted the Gypsies' exclamation at a Gorgio comparing a Gypsy woman to a serpent (1880:329). Sampson later recorded that an older Gypsy woman carried a cast-off snakeskin for luck (1926: IV, 325). The post-menopausal woman thus displays her ability to control pollution.

Creatures considered edible and not *mochadi* include most non-carnivorous birds, i.e. not 'birds of prey', for example, birds in the Gorgio 'wild' now usually regarded as inedible by Gorgios: finches, blackbirds, sparrows and thrushes (see also Boswell 1970:38). Also edible are Gorgio bred pheasants.

Wood states that 'traditionally' (a word which is usually synonymous with contemporary ideals) Gypsies were supposed to kill and eat only those animals with bristles or antlers (1973:71). I conclude that such animals are favoured because they have either a tough outer bodily covering or a substitute protection for the inner body. Animals such as deer are additionally acceptable because they are not carnivorous. The wild boar and pig are unfavourably carnivorous, or omnivorous, but graded above dogs, for example, because of their protective bristles. Animals with bristles are less able to resort to extensive licking of their outer body. Gorgio farm cattle including bullocks and sheep are favourably non-carnivorous and edible.

The horse and hedgehog are viewed most favourably. Both are attributed special qualities in connection with the inner and outer body. The horse is absolutely clean. It is not carnivorous and does not lick its coat. For the Travellers, the horse's special fastidiousness is proven in the saying: 'You can take a horse to the water, but you can't make it drink', that is, it will never drink dirty water. This is another example of the Gypsies giving their own meaning to Gorgio utterances. I was told also that a horse is especially clean because it drinks through closed teeth, thus filtering the water. The horse is considered so clean that a man can eat off a plate a horse has licked (see also Seymour 1970:183). In contrast to cats and dogs, a horse can be touched without ill effect. On my camp a Shetland pony was brought every night into a luxury carpeted trailer for a bowl of milk while the alsation dog was kept permanently outside.

The Gypsies are renowned for their predilection for hedgehogs. This animal obviously fulfils the preferred category of animals with bristles. Its prickly outer casing offers a rigid separation between the outer and inner body and a protection for the inner body, so that it requires special preparation by baking or singeing in the fire; the ultimate cleanser. In Romany it is referred to as *hotchi-witchi*, a thing which requires burning.[9] Its fleas are also burnt; their presence merely emphasise the separation between the inedible exterior and edible interior. The hedgehog is considered neither carnivorous nor herbivorous, but an insectivore, so unlike other animals is seen to do a positive service, and in several spatial categories. Wood writes: 'The hedgehog will eat every kind of garden-, farm- and forest-pest' (1973:71). The hedgehog's spines prevent self-grooming. In fact, hedgehogs deposit saliva on the tips of their spines, the function of which is not clear. The Travellers did not remark on this practice.

The hedgehog is attributed by Gypsies with a special ability to counteract poison or pollution; it 'has an antidote in its system against most animal and plant poisons; it is supposed to be immune to the deadly nightshade; and it will go for an adder or a viper and kill it with a bite on the spine and then eat it – poison sacks and all' (Wood 1973:71). For the Gypsy, the hedgehog is the antidote to any poisonous and *mochadi* substance within. It is good not only as food but as a medicinal cure.

Ideological and spatial relations: the cat

In acquiring animals considered edible, the Gypsies confront their political and economic relations with Gorgios who are the breeders of animals, and who own and control the land. The ideological place or meaning which different animals, edible or inedible, hold for Gypsy and Gorgio rarely coincides.

The cat, *matchka*, is seen by Gypsies as one of the most loved among Gorgio animals.[10] It is usually a pet within the Gorgio household. Moreover, it is considered one of the cleanest precisely because it licks itself and because it buries its faeces. 'It licks its paws after burying its dirt', a Gypsy told me. The cat in Gorgio houses jumps onto tables and shelves, so it scatters its hairs near food and crockery. Gorgios feed it from their own saucers. The cat is associated with a sedentarised people, not nomads. It cannot, like a dog, follow the horses and waggons. Living inside the Gorgio home and house, it lives with the

95

Gorgios' uncleanliness and has their *mochadi* habits. Houses are generally described by travelling Gypsies as unhealthy: 'All those bricks and mortar are bad for your health.' Houses are suffocating; Gypsies say they feel 'stived in'. The cat is the house's inhabitant – fondled, tamed and loved by the Gorgio. The Gypsy does not want to be housed and domesticated by the Gorgio. Wood writes: 'The cat is the most unclean animal there is, even more so than a rat; it used to be considered unspeakably dirty and a harbinger of death, if a cat got into your tent or wagon you had to go through a purification ceremony' (1973:70). The cat, assimilated by the Gorgio, represents death to the Gypsy.

The Travellers volunteered stories reflecting their hatred and aggression towards cats.

> 'You know what we think of cats, well young Tom [aged 6] and I were visiting this Gorgio lady and she asked Tom what he'd like to do with her dear little cat. Tom said, "Give it a kick when you're not looking!"'

> 'When we were working at Mrs Martin's place I got my old dosser to hold her cat and put mustard on its back-side. You should have seen it. It *shot* up the tree!'

> 'Billy was in lodgings [on parole]. He used to shit out the window for a laugh. He did it on a man's hat when the man was walking underneath. He was fined £5 for that. Then he was fined £10 for doing it on a cat.'[11]

Black cats especially are considered 'things of the devil' – the inverse of Gorgio beliefs.[12] One Gypsy woman encountered in fieldwork regularly sells 'lucky black cats' to Gorgio housewives. Consistent with children's relative immunity to pollution, I found that young children were permitted to handle kittens (mysteriously 'lost' when fully grown). A few older women owned cats: one living alone with her children while her husband served a long prison sentence, two elderly sisters living with the husband of one, and one elderly widow all owned cats. When I asked about the two sisters, the Travellers explained: 'They grew fond of the cat, 'cos it was a stray. But whenever their relations come, they throw it out the window.' I was also told that stray animals were 'lucky' and should not be turned away. Of the widow it was explained: 'She only has a cat so people think she's a *chovihanni*, a witch. They leave her alone then.' This woman lived on an official site among families with whom she had no affiliations and felt somewhat vulnerable. The post-menopausal woman can no longer threaten the purity of her race by conceiving a Gorgio child. With her sexually polluting powers diminished (see chapter 11 and Okely 1975d) she acquires or can demonstrate magical abilities to control general pollution by owning cats. The presence of her cat gives credibility to the devious powers she may exercise.

Dogs, game and contest

In contrast to the cat, dogs are present in large numbers on Gypsy camps but, with few exceptions, banned from the trailer. Dogs perform valuable services as watchdogs against Gypsy thieves and Gorgio intruders and are trained as hunters. Rabbits may be caught with the aid of terriers. Whippets are also favoured. Hare coursing with the aid of dogs is a regular pursuit by some Travellers, and like other hunting is done secretly and separately from Gorgios. Hunting with dogs is a male preserve. I was unable to observe it directly. Only after some trust in me did the Travellers admit to these pursuits. The ideal hunting dog is a lurcher of mixed breed with a rough coat, the intelligence of a collie and the speed of a greyhound. Seymour writes: 'A pure bred greyhound will very seldom catch a hare by himself; a good lurcher will, because he uses his head as well as his legs' (1970:189). This breed respond to command by gesture and 'hold their tongue'; important for the Gypsy owner. Seymour mentions a Gypsy dog trained to go straight back to the camp, i.e. away from its owner, on the command 'come here!' (1970:189). Boswell describes the special training for these dogs: 'A man needn't walk about a field with a dog; he could put the dog over a gate and it'd go on the field and kill something and bring it back and the man would never trespass' (1970:47). Leland recorded similar preferences in the nineteenth century: 'Gypsies almost invariably prefer, as canine manifesters of devotion, lurchers a kind of dog which of all others can be most easily taught to steal' (1893:164). Gypsies have described how they 'used to' train their lurchers to steal joints of meat from butchers and bring them to their masters. Although the dog is *mochadi*, it does not apparently contaminate the meat in a raw state, only after cooking.

The Gypsies' alternative form of game hunting would be described in the dominant Gorgio ideology as poaching, given that the *Oxford English Dictionary* defines it as 'to take game or fish illegally, or by unsportsmanlike methods'. Leach describes pheasant and hare as 'game' because 'they are killed only at set seasons of the year in accordance with set hunting rituals' (1972:54). The Gypsies choose their own season, their game is always for their own consumption, and they have their own methods of hunting. Pheasants can be hunted by catapults so that detection is reduced. A Traveller prides himself on being able to 'shoot' a pheasant from several hundred yards. Boswell describes how 'pheasants was very tame and you could sit on your cart and cut the head off with a whip' (1970:48). He recalls how the older Gypsy people 'was hot on pheasants' eggs and partridges' eggs in the restricted areas ... The old womenfolk ... kept pockets in their petticoats', and would take and hide the eggs, unsuspected by a keeper (1970:47).

Something of the antagonism between the travelling people and the Gorgio landowners is revealed by Boswell:

> We travel about, we can't keep pheasants, we can't keep chickens: what was wrong if we went to a farm? ... They didn't want anybody: they wired you in and they wired you out; there were locks on gates; there were keepers to keep you out; there was 'trespassers will be prosecuted' on common land that was self-claimed by these people. (1970:48)

The Travellers' interests in acquiring Gorgio bred bird and beast cannot be explained entirely in terms of the practical difficulties for nomads in breeding their own. The Travellers do in fact breed bantams, but which together with the eggs they regard as inedible. These birds are used for cock-fighting (for comparisons see Geertz 1975). I noticed that Travellers gave their bantam eggs to grateful Gorgio wardens and social workers. In the struggle to acquire bird and beast from Gorgios, the Travellers are enacting a wider political struggle with the dominant society which controls the land to which the Travellers must have access. With each bird and beast acquired by devious skills from the Gorgio owner, a wider victory is scored.

Ideologically, it seems that for Gypsies, Gorgio bred chickens and their eggs are edible *precisely* because they are located on Gorgio territory, the farm yard as opposed to the Gypsy camp. Eggs from supermarkets are edible, but ideally this kind of food is stolen from the Gorgio farm yard. I was asked:

> 'Do you know how to make a Gypsy omelette?'
> *Answer* 'Well, first you steal your eggs ...'

I was given detailed descriptions of how to steal a *kanni* or hen at night, and told that chickens and pheasants must always be plucked by a fast moving stream, 'so the feathers get carried away, then no one can prove anything'. Boswell denies that Gypsies enter farm yards for chickens, but instead describes how one on the roadside might be chopped with a whip, then its head put under a cartwheel. 'If it was found it had been run over' (1970:49).

Other Gorgio farm animals are regarded as edible and have in the past been acquired in unexpected ways. Formerly pigs and cattle were killed by a special Gypsy poison (*drab*), or mysteriously suffocated. According to Borrow the *drab* 'affects the brain, but does not corrupt the blood' (1874:174). After the poisoning, the Gypsies then acquired the seemingly worthless animal, dead from 'natural causes', from the farmer to whom the Gypsies professed a liking for carrion. Hoyland (1816:153) was misled by a Gypsy woman into thinking this was a genuine Gypsy custom. When I asked the Travellers if they ate carrion they were horrified. Yet it has suited Gypsies that throughout Europe the literature has recorded their preference for this (e.g. Grellmann 1787:11).

Thus, Travellers have their own procedures for obtaining animals from Gorgio territory, whether Gorgio wild animals such as rabbits, or Gorgio game such as pheasants, or Gorgio animals from farm or butcher. In all cases the contest or the game is played not merely with the animals, but also with human beings from the dominant Gorgio society.

Gorgio sports such as fox hunting are ignored. To the Gypsy, the fox is *mochadi* and called a 'red dog', but clearly not despised for its reputation as thief. The Travellers have also their own sports between themselves. They race and place bets on their whippets and lurchers. Rivals sometimes race their horses. The *Guardian* reported a horse race where it was alleged that the Gypsies closed off a section of the A1 early one Sunday morning (22 August 1977). Whether true or not, some Gypsies have enjoyed telling the tale. Cock-fighting, banned in England since 1840, continues (see also Boswell 1970:49). It may occur between individuals and groups with other rivalries, but it is conducted in the knowledge that the activity is banned in Gorgio law.[13]

The horse

The horse has a special place in relationships between Gorgios and Gypsies. It is both a mediator between the Gypsy and Gorgio, and between groups of Gypsies. Remaining ritually pure, the horse is continually crossing boundaries, passing through the enemy lines. It cannot bring dirt from the other side. When it is exchanged between Gypsy and Gorgio, any 'dirty game' goes, any horse makes its passage from Gypsy to Gorgio; the broken winded and lame are 'faked up' and passed as good and sprightly. The Gypsy's horse is not always as its appearance promises. Horses can be deviously acquired and as cunningly disposed of. Some are 'whistled' out of Gorgio fields. One image painted or engraved on Gypsy waggons is of a horse standing by an open gate. Although no longer used by the majority for transport, the horse remains a prestige possession and a conspicuous investment.

Horses have also had a political role with Gorgios, who would not forcibly move a Gypsy family with horse-drawn waggon too many miles if the animal needed a rest. Now Gypsies with lorries and trailers cannot obtain the same delays. Formerly Gypsy horses were impounded by Gorgio authorities for 'straying' in grassy fields. Today with no horses to 'do time' for them, Gypsy men are imprisoned for 'straying' on the highway.

The identification of the Gypsy with the horse is ambiguous. Horses can be equated with humans, but it is not clear whether these humans are Gorgio or Gypsy; male or female. It is said that a menstruating woman must keep a great distance from a stallion who would jump over a hedge to get at her. Male/female segregation is rigid in Gypsy horse-dealing; only men own and deal in horses. At the Fairs, occasional post-menopausal women stand near the horse-dealing clusters. These women 'have privileges', I was told. 'It's all right for them to listen so long as they don't interfere.' Horses are compared to women. Gypsy men play at exchanging their wives. 'The men sit round the fire and one might say, "Who'd like a chop for my wife? She trots well and she's only had one owner."' Horses may be exchanged as if women:

> I have a woman
> Legs like bars of iron.
> Built to last a life time.
> Eyes like diamonds
> A mouth like jelly.
> Short in the flank
> And lean in the belly.
> Steps as high as the ducks can fly
> Comes right out of Wales
> Where you can touch the tip of the sky
> And the girls wear no bloomers.

So men exchange horses as women – faked for the Gorgio, genuine among themselves. Women must have no share, because subordinate to men: they are not permitted to organise their own exchange. Horse-dealing between Gypsy men especially at the fairs affirms their manliness as well as ethnic identity (see chapter 10 and Okely 1979a)

While a mediator between Gypsy and Gorgio, in the Gypsies' history the horse simultaneously ensured their independence as nomads from Gorgios. While the requirements of the larger populations have been perforce a fixed abode, land tenure and wage-labour, the Travellers have exploited the very absence of these, thanks to the horse as their mode of transport and an item of exchange. Franz Liszt observed the Gypsies' liking for the horses: 'they feel its superiority over other domestic animals and know that it alone can afford them any real help, in that it aids their flight' (1863 in Sampson 1930:255-6). To every Gypsy family a horse was an indispensable part of the travelling unit, a friend and equal, never a pet. For the Gypsy to eat horse flesh is the most heinous crime. Here the Gypsy taboo against eating horse flesh coincides with that of the English Gorgio.

In the last 25 years, since motorisation the horse is no longer the transporter of the Gypsy nomad but it retains its historical significance as the Travellers' ally and mediator. The horse remains a symbol of travelling identity. Horse emblems abound in Gypsy interiors. One family newly moved into a house commissioned a special fireplace decorated with brass horse heads. The horse's special purity is affirmed in the Gypsies' frequent selection of crockery with the horse motif. Horses are prestige possessions and their exchange between Gypsies is a major feature of the Appleby Fair. Certain types, e.g. the 'coloured' or piebald, are favoured, and recognisable as 'Gypsy horses'. Such a horse is visually refracted, ambiguous; neither brown nor white, neither black nor white, half shadow, half light. Ambivalent, as the Gypsy is to the Gorgio, it is a broken image.

The hedgehog

In contrast to all other animals and birds, the hedgehog is both supremely edible and given high status. This is for reasons additional to its eating habits and tough outer skin, and to do with its ideological and spatial position. It lives on the fringes of the wild, or to be more exact in shrubs and hedges, neither in open fields nor in the thick of woods. Like the Gypsy, it lives in *liminal* areas, the very boundaries which demarcate a Gorgio's property. Another term for the *hotchi-witchi* is *pal* of the *bor*: brother of the hedge. Gypsies select those traits with

A horse deal at Appleby. *The Times*

101

which they can most identify. Sampson recorded the statement: 'He lives in one place and another like a hedgehog' (1926:IV, 387).

The hedgehog is unique in Gypsy–Gorgio relations. Unlike farm animals or pheasants it is not Gorgio bred. In contrast to hares and rabbits, it is unwanted, laughed at or generally ignored by Gorgios and regarded by the majority as inedible. When Gypsies talk to Gorgios about hedgehogs they are conscious of the Gorgios' humorous image, and they invariably adopt a joking manner, but not among themselves. Even though Gorgio folklore is that hedgehogs steal eggs, suck milk from reclining cows and impale apples on their spikes to carry back to their lair (Harrison Matthews 1968:63-4), these attributes rarely inspire Gorgios systematically to destroy these animals. The Gypsies never mentioned such beliefs to me, but even if they had incorporated them, the accusations of stealing Gorgio produce would make the hedgehog more endearing. Sometimes Gorgios befriend hedgehogs by leaving saucers of milk in their gardens. But domestication is limited, the hedgehog remains outside the house.

Unlike other edible animals, the constraints on acquiring and killing the hedgehog are self-imposed. Wood records: 'A hedgehog you were never supposed to kill at all in the old Romany way unless there were plenty in the area. This had to do with the hedgehog being thought of as one of the creatures of *Moshto,* the god of life' (1973:71). I was told that hedgehogs were not to be eaten with young in the spring, that boars tasted bad in the mating season. The Gypsies have established rules as to when hedgehogs are to be eaten. 'We don't eat them every day, you know.' It was also emphasised that a hedgehog is 'too rich to be eaten just by one person'. A hedgehog is ideally eaten in a communal meal. With its antidote which cleanses poisons in the blood and inner body, the hedgehog is a symbolic antidote to any *mochadi* substance and to pollution from the Gorgio; freeing the Gypsy from the problem of deceit and falsehood which could threaten the inner self. Sampson recorded the tag of a folk tale: 'A nice hedgehog's liver for the great falsehood I have told thee' (1926:IV, 388). The liver, a coveted delicacy and the ultimate cleanser, is introduced in circumstances where deceit is to be overcome.

In a Gypsy folk tale (Leland 1893:203-4) a hedgehog is warned not to go to the right, lest it be trampled by hunters' hooves, and not to go to the left, because the Gypsies would eat it. The hedgehog replies that it would prefer to be eaten by the Gypsies who liked him than be trampled by people who despised him. The tale concludes: 'It is better for a real Gypsy to be killed by a Gypsy brother than be hung by Gorgios' (1893:204). Here the identification between the hedgehog and Gypsy is explicit, although possibly this identification is usually unconscious. The hedgehog is the Gypsy's ideal and inner self. Eating this sacred food is a totemic act.

The hedgehog need be neither purchased nor poached, neither begged nor stolen. Gypsies informed Hindes Groome that hedgehogs are '*Romané's baulé* [Romany pigs], 'cause they are pigs the Gorgios can't deny us Gipsies' (1880:163). The hedgehog is free food, undomesticated and outside the Gorgio's control, unlike any other animal considered edible. While consuming the hedgehog, the Gypsies liberate themselves from all relations with the Gorgio.

Elsewhere, Gypsies have placed special emphasis on hedgehogs. Otter wrote of Viennese Gypsies: 'The favourite food of the Gypsies is hedgehog' (1931:110). Leland notes of Liebich: 'the only indication of a belief in a future state which he ever detected in an old Gipsy woman, was that she once dreamed she was in heaven. It appeared to her as a large garden, full of fine fat hedgehogs' (1893:13). Gypsies I met in the Toulouse area of France in 1980 spoke enthusiastically of hedgehogs. When they ate several in a shared meal the most succulent pieces were equally apportioned.

To conclude, I have concentrated on an analysis of animal categories which reflect the Gypsy–Gorgio boundary as opposed to those various transformations used to distinguish Gypsy sub-groups both in England and elsewhere. My analysis has prompted Marek Kaminski to examine his data on Gypsies in Poland and Czechoslovakia. He has noted a similar aversion to cats, dogs and snakes as polluting, and a predilection for hedgehogs. Moreover one group of Polish Gypsies condemns another group for not distinguishing between two types of hedgehog. They say there is the hedgehog with 'a dog face' and the hedgehog with 'a pig face'. One group will eat only the pig-faced while the other Gypsy group are accused of eating also the dog-faced hedgehog.[14] As among English Gypsies, the pig is edible, the dog is not. My investigations have revealed that there are indeed two species of hedgehog in Europe, the 'western' species found in the British Isles, Sweden, northern Spain, France and Germany; and the 'southern and eastern' species found in Italy, Bulgaria, southern and eastern Europe. In the west of Poland alone both species are to be found. The most marked difference between the two is in their heads; the shape and colouring (Van den Brink 1974).

Anne Sutherland has confirmed that Gypsy sub-groups in California identify themselves by the animal eaten at ritual feasts and accuse each other of selecting one with relatively polluting attributes, measured sometimes by its washing and eating habits.[15] If, as it seems in the examples from Poland and California, animal categories are used also to distinguish Gypsy sub-groups, the underlying principles are still in terms of the primary ethnic boundary, i.e. one group of Gypsies is accusing another of being more polluting than itself, and so less Gypsy and more Gorgio.

In this chapter, I have outlined and explained the ways in which Travellers or Gypsies use notions of the body, cleanliness, space and animals to draw boundaries between themselves and Gorgios. The

Travellers' beliefs cannot be viewed independently of the dominant Gorgios, their power and beliefs. Ideas of cleanliness and spatial layout often conflict with those entertained and imposed by Gorgios. Some Gorgio notions are seized upon and turned inside out. The Gypsies' classification system is allied with specific daily practices concerning eating, washing and spatial proximity, all of which can be described and comprehended as religious observances. The Gypsies have used the differences between animals to stress occasionally the differences between themselves, but more often to differentiate Gypsies from Gorgios. Some animals, viewed negatively, are associated with the Gorgio, others are seen as more independent, or in one case, as entirely free of any degrading relationship with the Gorgio, and therefore the ideal. The ideas and practices are an attempt by Gypsies to comprehend the vulnerability and power of their minority state.

7 Gorgio planning

1960: Gypsy sites closed. 1970: council sites required

Major political and legal constraints are set by the larger society on the Travellers' use of land for residence, work and travel. Evidence of the influence of the state and its representatives need not be confined to the national level, it can be found also at the local and micro level. For this chapter, information has been drawn from both national and local government reports, documents and newspapers, and discussions and interviews with national and local officials. The majority of examples of local authorities are from the south-east of England, but generalisations are corroborated by evidence from elsewhere in England. Documentary evidence has been taken both beyond and from the main areas of my fieldwork. Exact references to sources have been excluded in order to preserve the anonymity both of the local authorities and of the Travellers. A composite picture emerges. Details of some of the negotiations and activities leading to legislation in 1968, and case studies of several local authorities in the 1970s, are to be found elsewhere (Okely 1972, Adams *et al.* 1975: chs. 1 and 8 and Sibley 1981:93-100 and ch. 10). This account points only to some aspects, and more specifically to those which appear to have had the most immediate implications for the Gypsies' travelling patterns, especially during the period of fieldwork for this study from 1970 to 1979.

The 1968 Caravan Sites Act marked a change in government policy towards Gypsies or Travellers in England and Wales. Previous legislation was notable for its wholly negative character, where the practices of dispersal, harassment or *laissez-faire* were seen as the only means of dealing with Gypsies. Now, for the first time, local authorities were required by the state to provide official sites specifically for Gypsies This new welfare intervention also bore some of the traces of previous policies of dispersal. After having made provision for a certain number of families, the local authorities could apply for 'designation' or 'control powers' which could be used to remove *all* remaining Gypsies on any unauthorised camping sites from the locality. The control powers were applicable only to 'any person being a gypsy' and were severe; for example, the police could make arrests without warrant. Some local authorities could be exempted from making any provision and simultaneously acquire designation. The then county boroughs and those of London needed to provide for only 15 caravans, regardless of census returns (Adams *et al.* 1975: 297-303). The Act was therefore double edged, although it was presented as humanitarian at the time (but see Sibley 1981: 93-100).

The 1968 Act was also intended 'to put an end to the unauthorised, scrap-littered roadside Gypsy camps' (Adams *et al.* 1975:1). What was not so apparent was that the increasing conflict between the sedentary society and the Travellers over encampments during the 1960s was exacerbated by, if not partly a result of, earlier legislation which entailed the widespread closure of the Travellers' independently established sites and stopping places. Clearly, there were other factors contributing to the conflict, for instance the Travellers' shift from horse-drawn to motorised transport during the 1950s; the development and compulsory purchase of patches of land once frequented by the Gypsies, and possibly their increased activities in scrap metal work. However, legislation gives an indication of the authorities' response to these circumstances. That response helped to create rather than alleviate what the non-Gypsies described as 'the Gypsy problem'.

The Gypsies were victims of the 1960 Caravan Sites and Development Act, which was not specifically addressed to Gypsies but apparently aimed mainly at the increasing number of non-Gypsy house-dwellers resorting to caravans during a housing shortage. The Gypsies, for whom caravans are the preferred abode, were subject to the universalistic and inflexible law of the dominant housedwelling society. Other disfavoured minorities may also find themselves unaccounted for in laws apparently for the majority, but they are at least potential voters. The Gypsies, however, with no fixed address, have neither vote nor representation, so that elected officials and others have even less incentive to consider their special needs. Moreover, given that hostile response which the sight of a Gypsy camp has seemed to generate among local residents, albeit a strident minority, councillors have sometimes found positive advantages in supporting policies of dispersal and repression (see Adams *et al.* 1975:ch. 8).

The new Gypsy 'problem' was created both by intervention and by omission. Some local authorities were fully aware that the residents of sites to be closed under the 1960 Act were Gypsies, but there seemed little thought for the consequences. New measures for the complete dispersal of Gypsies were hardly likely to succeed, when centuries of similar previous policies had failed, so by the end of the decade the same authorities were to find themselves obliged to build official sites at massive public expense; the price for some of their earlier actions. Alternatives to the twin policies of closure of Gypsy stopping places or private sites, and the later public provision of council sites for Gypsies, were not seriously explored.

The 1960 Act required all owners of land with residential caravans to obtain planning permission and a site licence. The planning authorities did not grant these easily. Gypsies who had lived on or regularly frequented land which they owned or rented, and even where they had installed their own facilities and paid rates, were faced with new forms of prosecutions and fines. If, as it appears in the majority of cases, they or their landlords failed to obtain licences, they were forced on to the road, on to the grass verges, and common and waste land where the landowners, often central government, were unlikely to be prosecuted. Evictions from one roadside verge to another was obviously pointless. Instead, other measures were taken to disperse the Travellers. The 1959 Highways Act which made it an offence for a Gypsy and no one else in a caravan to camp on the highway was used. As of old, the Travellers often clustered at county and other boundaries, after being driven from one set of authorities to another. Repeated visits by the police, public health inspectors, and the hostility of certain local residents and the melodrama in the press could not drive the Gypsies away, since they had nowhere to go free of prosecution and further harassment. The numbers of Gypsy families in specific encampments then became more concentrated and increasingly conspicuous.

The following examples from the south-east of England reveal the kind of actions taken by the authorities to deal with different kinds of encampments, the first a private Gypsy site, the second a favourite stopping place where greater numbers had begun to congregate. Similar incidents occurred throughout England.

(1) A private Gypsy site was described by a county planning committee in early 1961 as an example of 'the growing tendency of Gypsies to settle in permanent camps' (planning committee report 1961). It had its own water supply and elsans. A rural district council was collecting rates from the occupants. Health authorities sent there in the hope of finding grounds for prosecution could find none. The health visitor reported: 'In spite of their various ways of living, the children seemed to thrive on it.' Eventually, the same district council, which had previously collected rates from the occupants, prosecuted the site owner under the 1960 Act and the Gypsies, after a fine of £50 with £10 costs, took to the roads.

Nearby was a roadside camp. The rural district council prosecuted the Gypsies under a by-law. The £20 fine failed to close the encampment. So the Gypsies were prosecuted under a 1935 County Council Act. By the winter of 1961 both sites were closed. The roadside camp was not closed under the 1961 Act, but it had become more vulnerable as the authorities began to scrutinise all the sites in their area. A council sub-committee indicated its policy as follows: 'There are many other caravans in the Rural District singly and in groups of varying sizes ... In some cases the caravans will be allowed to remain and in others, steps are being taken to "run down" the sites' (council report). A few private sites remained, but often after their residents had paid fines and resisted many attempts to remove them. Generally, the initiative among a number of Gypsies to provide their own sites was brought to a halt. The Gypsy Council in 1971 considered that more places had been closed to Gypsies under the 1960 Act than had been made available under the 1968 Act (Adams *et al.* 1975:9-10). Private Gypsy sites continued to be closed in this way throughout the 1970s.

(2) The most dramatic event at that time for Gypsies in the same area was the closure of a local heath in 1961. It was recalled by the Travellers over a decade later: 'If we'd had people like the Gypsy Council in those days, it would never have happened.' There had been an increase of numbers on this 'traditional' stopping place partly because Gypsy families were forced onto land where prosecution was less effective. Residents in the parish protested at the rural district council's 'lack of action' against the Gypsies (local *Advertiser* 1961).

The council neither directly assisted in an eviction nor offered any immediate alternative. Ownership of the heath was vested in the Lord of the Manor who did not want any responsibilities for seeking a proper licence. As in other areas at this period, the local authority took steps to acquire ownership of the heath or common. Meanwhile, the power of the public health authorities could only be used to improve conditions, and some temporary provision was made. The Gypsies were charged minimal fines in court and regarded them as 'rent'. In one court appearance nineteen Gypsy men were named, ten of whom were in the area a decade later. One Gypsy said 'My family have been coming to this heath for generations. We all regard it as home' (local *Advertiser* May 1961).

By mid-August ownership of the heath had been procured by the parish council who were then able to take action against the Gypsies as trespassers. *The Times* reported that the Gypsies believed they had 'a statutory right to be there' (August 1961). But when the council's tractors and van loads of police arrived, the 40-50 families left without a struggle. Their few supporters, who included a Conservative woman councillor, discouraged resistance. Later it was reported, 'All week residents of the district have caught glimpses of parties of caravanners making their way in search of new parking places' (local *Herald* August 1961). The authorities had in no way solved their problems since the Gypsies eventually moved to a neighbouring common and inevitably to the roadside verges and laybys where it was less easy for the authorities to block access or to prosecute. This general shift in location was noticed later by non-Gypsy residents: for example in 1963, a local branch of the National Farmers' Union, in complaining of Gypsies in their area whom they said 'live outside the normal code of human conduct', reported that 'caravans have been moved off land in other parts of the county and have virtually taken over the roadside verges' (local *Mercury* September 1963). This was to be the pattern for the next decade and beyond. The farmers agreed that permanent sites should be found but said that 'no one would welcome these sites on their doorstep' (*ibid.*).

Gorgio planning

The following example reveals the kind of difficulties encountered in establishing private Gypsy sites, even when instigated by the local Gorgio gentry and aristocracy. After the closure of the heath described above, the Conservative woman councillor who had been one of the few outspoken supporters of the Gypsies appealed for, and collected, funds to set up a private Gypsy site. She was assisted by a local earl. Planning permission was refused on land offered by a marquis. It took two years and an appeal to the Ministry after 'bitter' opposition from one of the local authorities to open a private site for just five families. Years later, the county council were bold enough to include this site in their figures of families for whom official provision had been made.

Another example shows the kind of tactics used by the local authorities when a Gorgio leaseholder permitted Gypsies on to his land. In December 1970, Travellers were on a small triangle of land hidden from the main road. The leaseholder, a London solicitor, had no objection to their presence. On receipt of a letter from a solicitor demanding their removal, he telephoned the urban council public health inspector whom he said was 'quite offensive ... He told me I hadn't got planning permission for Gypsies to be there and if I applied I wouldn't get it. He suggested I moved them or the council would sue me' (local *Echo* Dec. 1970). He was obliged to appoint an agent to remove the caravans.

The 1960 Act had in fact given the local authorities the power not only to close sites, but also to provide their own. A tiny minority of authorities did begin to consider one or two special council sites for Gypsies before the 1968 Act made it a requirement (e.g. Kent, Buckinghamshire and Hertfordshire). All local authorities had received some encouragement to do so from a Ministry circular in 1962. Negotiations were marked by delaying tactics by district councils when, for example, a county council considering site provision had to obtain planning permission from them. Since there was little political advantage for any councillor appearing to support Gypsy sites in the locality, not surprisingly closures of unofficial sites and sudden evictions often coincided with imminent local elections, or a new stage in plans for a permanent site. For instance, one county council obtained planning permission for a site from a district council in return for a guarantee that other Gypsy encampments would be cleared. The county council then proceeded to arrange evictions and the banking and fencing of land on which the Travellers had once appeared to be tolerated. The costs of these exercises were sometimes as much as facilities for sites. The Travellers' experiences of these unpredictable events merely confirmed their views of Gorgios as untrustworthy and capricious.

The 1962 circular had generally failed in its attempt to exhort local authorities to provide sites. At the same time there was increasing pressure from local authorities upon central government to give direct powers to them to remove Gypsies from private land, rather than rely on prosecuting the landowner. In response to persistent questions from the Kent M.P. Norman Dodds on the Gypsies' behalf, the Minister of Housing and Local Government, Richard Crossman, ordered the national census of Gypsies in England and Wales. This took place in March 1965 and was carried out by members of the police force and by public health inspectors (M.H.L.G. 1967:4), and was therefore unlikely to encourage cooperation from Gypsy families. During the weeks and days preceding the census, local newspapers reveal a sudden increase in efforts to disperse or evict Gypsies from their current encampments. The local authorities appeared to be competing to drive Traveller families beyond their own boundaries. The smaller the count for each authority, the less would be their future responsibility. Even if families were not driven out of a specific area, their new location would have been hard to determine. It was accepted later that the numbers were a serious under-estimate, but the 1965 figures for each authority remained for many years as the yardstick for future site provision, exemptions and designation.

The 1965 census recorded about 15,000 individuals or 3,356 families in England and Wales. By the late 1970s, the Department of the Environment was organising counts twice a year of Gypsy caravans and recorded 8,528 caravans in England (excluding Wales) in January 1980. The number of families would be slightly less than this, given that some families have two caravans. Already by 1977, it was generally accepted that the total number of families in England and Wales amounted to between 8,000 and 9,000 (Cripps 1976:8); many more than the number recorded in 1965.

The preliminary findings of the census were released in another Ministry circular to the local authorities in 1966. It again exhorted them to provide sites, but was still 'reluctant to make the provision ... mandatory' (Adams *et al.* 1975:13). In December of that year, the newly formed Gypsy Council asserted the Gypsy people's right to 'self determination and the recognition of their special needs by national governments ... and a legitimate need for camp sites' (Gypsy Council 1967). Concerning sites, it called for a measure of independence, e.g. consultation with Travellers by authorities setting up sites, and it called for work areas, transit pitches and Traveller wardens. The Council's most immediate interests in its first deputation to the Ministry in 1967 were the evictions and harassment, and the necessity for 200 temporary sites throughout the country (Adams *et al.* 1975:13-14).

The Ministry's report, based on the census, reiterated the need for camp sites 'to enable the travellers to avoid the use of unlawful sites' (M.H.L.G. 1967:66). It was not suggested that some existing 'unlawful sites' could be made lawful by special consideration in licence applications. Both the 1966 circular and the 1967 report appeared to presume that many, if not the majority of families, wanted to settle. Even if this were not the case, the circular stated that the Travellers 'must be helped to improve their living conditions and encouraged to settle down and send their children to school' (M.H.L.G. 1966).

The 1968 Act which followed did not spell out any policy of sedentarisation. Indeed the sponsor, Eric Lubbock, had insisted that provision should be made 'not only for the Gypsies belonging to an area but also for those who travel through it' (Adams *et al.* 1975:17). The authorities had the duty 'to provide adequate accommodation for gipsies residing in or resorting to their area' (1968:part II,6.i). Thus, there was in principle allowance for families who continued to travel, although in the long run it was perhaps presumed that settlement and assimilation would occur (see Sibley 1981:95-101). It was the term 'adequate' which was open to flexibility in interpretation with regard not only to type of accommodation but also to the numbers of families. It was clearly in the interests of the local authorities to minimise the numbers of families for whom they should take responsibility in order to obtain either exemption or designation.

The new national policy may partly explain a changing emphasis in the non-Gypsy's classification of the acceptable or 'real Gypsy'. Those authorities who resisted making any provision whatsoever would still be most inclined to assert that they had no 'real Romanies' in their area, only housedwelling drop-outs, e.g. in 1970 a Walsall councillor, defending his council's refusal to provide a Gypsy site, said that they would agree to one for 'Romany Gypsies' but not for 'Tinkers'. All the Travellers in his area he claimed were 'Tinkers' (B.B.C. 'Man Alive'). Irish Travellers in any area were already seen as an anomaly. But a different sub-division began to emerge: that between 'local' Gypsies and those allegedly belonging to another district or county. Although the Act specified that the authorities were to be responsible also for those 'resorting' to an area, greater emphasis was now placed on those presumed to reside all the time in a single locality. A new type of 'foreigner' was thus created; one not from another land but one who had crossed a Gorgio administrative boundary. The Travellers soon became aware of this and described themselves or others as 'Bedfordshire', 'Kent', 'Hertfordshire' or 'Essex' Gypsies, depending where they were at the time. Some evictions in the early 1970s were justified by the authorities because it was said that the families were 'not local'. They had 'invaded' the area.

Authorities who had begun to provide sites both before and after 1970 when the 1968 Act was to take effect protested that their sites had acted as a 'magnet' to 'foreigners'. There was no evidence to support this claim. First, as chapter 8 indicates, caravan dwelling Gypsies can rarely if ever be said to 'belong' to a single county since they frequent several. Secondly, it would have been communicated among Gypsies that site provision was for a minority and that vacancies were immediately filled. Thirdly, economic opportunities rather than sites

An eviction. *Evening Post-Echo Ltd*

were more likely to attract Travellers, and even then, few families would suddenly risk an unknown region. In the short run, the numbers in an area with an official site may have increased for quite different reasons; some families, especially those taking up welfare benefits and needing a fixed address, were encouraged to settle on sites and were less likely to move to adjacent areas for short-term travelling. Thus the numbers of families in an area with an official site may at a given time have been inflated without the addition of newcomers.

Given that the authorities were using the 1965 returns as the basis for their obligations, it was inevitable that the actual numbers of Travellers in their locality appeared to have increased as they began to be more acquainted with Travellers. In one county in 1971, a local voluntary group conducted its own census of two-thirds of the county and recorded nearly double the number of families recorded in the 1965 census. The figure was so alarming to the county, hoping to apply for designation in the near future, that one official tried to persuade the group not to circulate its findings. But a few years later, the county's own returns to the D.O.E. were very similar and acknowledged as accurate.

Sites and settlement

I record here some Travellers' comments between 1970 and 1973:

> 'They think they've got us pinned down on these sites.'

> 'We had a grand time till this talk of sites. Now we can't go anywhere. They've closed our old stopping place.'

> 'When's the next reservation opening?'

> 'I don't believe in sites. They ought to let Travellers go on as they were; stopping different places ... These sites aren't good for Travellers.'

The 1968 Act was not to come into effect until 1970. After that there was still no time limit set for the mandatory building of sites. By the summer of 1972 there were only 50 such sites, and about a quarter of these had been established before they became obligatory (Adams *et al.* 1975:246). By January 1977 there were 142 sites (109 permanent, 33 temporary) with 2,254 pitches (1,759 permanent, 495 temporary; D.O.E. 1977b:8). By the same date, designation had been granted to fifteen London boroughs and to ten former county boroughs, all of whom had in accordance with the 1968 Act to provide no more than fifteen pitches, regardless of any census returns. Two of the London boroughs, including Westminster, were exempted from provision. Designation had also been given to 26 former county boroughs after exemption from any provision, 'on the grounds that the number of gypsies resorting to their areas was not sufficient' (D.O.E. 1977b:11).

Up to the mid 1970s at least, while no clear policy was acknowledged, the underlying assumption among influential officials both in central and local government was that Gypsies would eventually be assimilated into the dominant sedentary society. Site provision was equated with settlement, and in turn equated with assimilation. The 1966 Ministry circular had suggested not only that families should be encouraged to settle but that as many as possible should eventually be housed. 'Families who show a capacity for a settled way of life should be given every encouragement to move into permanent dwellings' (M.H.L.G. 1966:para. 11).

Despite the Gypsy Council's demands for temporary sites, both as an emergency measure but also as an indication that in many cases legal access to land, without necessarily elaborate, fixed facilities, was the major demand, the general preference by the non-Gypsy authorities was for 'permanent' sites. Although in the dominant society's law the words 'temporary' and 'permanent' ostensibly refer only to the length of planning permission (ten years for a permanent site), rather than to their *use*, the Travellers correctly interpreted 'permanent' as

113

'settled'. The authorities feared that temporary sites with minimum provision would be used as 'transit' sites. The notion of the 'transit' site is generally misplaced, since it presumes that there are two 'types' of Travellers: those who rarely travel, i.e. who are 'local', and those who 'move all the time'. Chapter 8 reveals that Traveller-Gypsies cannot be so easily classified. Indeed the fictitious dichotomy is inappropriate for a whole range of nomads. The 1967 Ministry report supported this kind of classification:

> A variety of provision is probably the answer: housing for those who wish to be housed; permanent pitches for those waiting to be housed or who prefer site life and do little or no travelling; and short stay pitches for those who *travel continually from place to place* and have no wish to settle.
>
> (M.H.L.G, 1967:55, my emphasis)

The report gave little place for Travellers who fit neither of the last two extremes.

Both the Cripps Report (1976) and the Department of the Environment booklet (1977a), written under the supervision of Don Byrne, showed greater flexibility in the kind of sites which would fit more with the various Travellers' needs. A more subtle distinction was made by the D.O.E. between 'residential sites with minimum facilities' and 'permanent sites for long term residential use' (1977a:13-14). But by 1979, in a guide to Gypsy sites design from the same office in the D.O.E., that distinction had again disappeared. 'Transit sites' were contrasted with 'permanent residential sites', and local authorities were informed that there were just two types of Gypsies: 'settled families' and 'itinerant travellers', who were to be kept quite separate; the former in 'permanent residential sites', the latter in 'transit sites' (D.O.E. 1979:1).

Site provision has therefore often been based on the assumption that many Travellers fitted the 'permanent resident' category. In practice, many Travellers travel regularly and wish to continue to do so. As chapter 8 indicates, residence for some months in one place was often part of the yearly cycle. Very few Travellers move 'continually from place to place'. The proposed 'temporary' sites, with greater flexibility over tenancies, were most suited to the many Travellers who did not wish to become permanently sedentarised. This was perhaps why the temporary sites were unacceptable to the authorities who wished to and indeed were encouraged to facilitate settlement, not travelling.

Transit or temporary sites with minimum facilities were not in accord with the 'model standards' outlined in the 1960 Act. But the sections of the 1968 Act concerned with Gypsies did not require the 'model standards' which were originally designed for sedentary, non-Gypsy caravan dwellers. However, earlier, the 1966 Ministry circular had seen added advantages in advising model standards: 'The sites established for gypsies should not be inferior in this respect to others;

good site conditions may indeed be instrumental in raising their standards of living and behaviour' (M.H.L.G. 1966:para. 9). According to Cripps, local authorities argued that model standards were necessary, otherwise non-Gypsies would demand similar relaxations (1976:20). Again here we find the belief that the rules and provision should be in accord with the requirements of the dominant order, rather than with those of an ethnic minority.

The same attitude was reflected in an argument put forward by a D.O.E. representative in 1980 (personal communication), namely that local authorities were increasingly against sites with 'low level' provision because local residents (i.e. the dominant population of housewellers and potential voters) objected. But a reading of local newspapers from several regions indicates that local housedwellers also objected to the high costs of the permanent sites, as well as to the existence of *any* type of sites.

The costs of 'permanent residential' sites with model standards were considerable and could be used to provoke further hostilities towards Gypsies and to delay provision of any kind. It was rarely reported that many Gypsies were not demanding the model standards devised for Gorgio ex-housedwellers. For example, one local authority had in the early 1970s a variety of sites: (a) one opened in the late 1960s with basic facilities suitable for short- and long-term stays, (b) 'temporary' sites with the absolute minimum of facilities and opened in the 1970s, with the understanding they would be closed when the district councils gave planning permission for type (c), which were those with the fullest provision. Type (a) had individual flush toilets, taps and rubbish disposal, and communal laundry facilities, and was subsidised in the early seventies at £1.50–£2.00 a week. Its initial cost was relatively small compared to type (c) where each pitch cost up to 70% of that of a council house and was subsidised in 1971 at £7 a week. One opened in 1972 for 15 families cost £34 000, excluding the price of the land. By 1975 the estimate for a similar site had risen to £90 000. The facilities for type (c) included a brick chalet for each pitch, with living room, bathroom, w.c. and store room. Electricity, immersion heater and coal-fired courtier stove were provided. There was also a 'community hut'. The temporary sites of type (b) had hardcore, elsans, a rubbish skip and sometimes a tap. Tenants of type (b) paid half the rent of those on type (c), and the subsidy was small. Many Travellers expressed dismay when they were obliged to move onto the new expensive sites after the temporary ones were closed. Obliged to decorate and furnish their chalets themselves, some complained this wasn't worth doing if they were only staying a while, and when the buildings did not belong to them. They would have preferred their own portable huts:

> 'They ought to let us buy these plots and huts because you haven't got the heart to make it nice and put money in it when it isn't your own.'

115

Another Traveller sensed the unhappy compromise in the council chalets:

> 'Having one of these huts you'd be better off in a house, but I'd rather travel.'

Given the considerable increase in public expenditure, these newer sites were subjected to greater scrutiny. Full-time resident non-Gypsy wardens were required to oversee the public property and, by a circular process, their salaries multiplied the costs. The wardens took upon themselves additional social work functions. Some families, relatively independent on the road, were now seen as 'problem families'. Moreover, the Travellers expected and demanded the wardens to make telephone calls, fetch doctors and do endless repairs in exchange for loss of privacy and independence.

The justification for wardens was not only as rent collectors and caretakers of council property but also as social workers. In 1975, one local authority referred to the wardens' 'task of trying to control and help families'. One warden gave his opinion:

> 'There is harassment on the roads, but there's a new kind of harassment on sites. They create more problems than they solve, and I know I'm just as responsible for this because I want things my way and I try to make it so. I want to make the site pleasant to look at. The sites discriminate against the car-breakers who are forced to move on to the roadside, also the sites disrupt the cultural set-up; visiting relatives or newly married couples can't stay with their relatives. This site is really made up of three distinct groups and I try to respect that by grouping them that way.'

From the early 1970s, there was a dramatic increase in salaried staff concerned with Gypsies for one authority studied here. They included wardens, cleaners, social workers, part-time assistants and play-group organisers, as well as extra office staff. A site warden said: 'The Social Services are mushrooming. Soon two thirds of the world will be looking after the other third.' Future estimates for sites had to cover the mounting costs of non-Gypsy salaries. In 1973 a liaison officer confided: 'given the cost of the wardens, their travelling expenses and the office processing, it would pay us not to collect rent'.

The costs of repairs to council property became an increasing liability. Some vandalism is inevitable when tenants on sites with a regular turnover do not themselves own the property. In 1971 one site warden was claiming £10 a week for materials and tools. In 1976, four years after the opening of a permanent site for seven families, £10 000 was allotted for repairs. By that time, another site for 15, opened five years previously, had lost fencing, piping, water tanks, doors and courtier stoves. Then two years later, only two pitches were habitable, the rest of the amenities having been demolished. Such destruction is inconsistent with the local authority claim to Cripps that 'the more informal the provided site, the greater the degree of cost of supervision' (1976:20). In 1979 and 1980, several local and central government officials revealed that considerable amounts of money had to be allocated for repairs (personal communication). These outlays reduced the financing of initiatives for new sites.

Plans to build sufficient sites of the most elaborate kind become even more unrealistic as the counts carried out by individual authorities revealed the extent of their Gypsy population. In 1975, one county council reassessed its policy to build pitches of site type (a) for its target figure before obtaining designation. It would take at least ten years and by that time, with a population increase, the minimum responsibility would be for 300 families. The capital expenditure alone, and excluding the cost of land, would amount to £1 200 000. The estimated annual revenue cost would be nearly £525 000 (county council report 1975). They decided to adopt a policy of sites of mixed facilities as a matter of financial expediency and as a means of gaining designation within a shorter time.

Thus there were a number of arguments on both sides against high cost provision. The Cripps Report also showed scepticism as to the usefulness of costly sites for the majority: 'Apart from the cost, these sites suit the needs of only a proportion of gypsy families. Others, and especially those who still travel frequently and over long distances, regard them as too elaborate' (1976:11). There appeared to be some disagreement among representatives of Gypsy organisations. Some continued to argue that the immediate priority was the provision of legal stopping places as soon as possible and for the vast majority. Others argued that Gypsies should not be treated as second class citizens with low grade facilities. Their interest in a network of high quality sites, whatever the likely delays and future rents, was consistent with a feeling that designation was inevitable. Whereas the first group rejected designation in principle, the second group sought the maximum financial outlay from the authorities in return for designation. They justified their actions in terms of political realism. At local level negotiations they were often more popular with officials advocating 'respectable' sites for minimum numbers.

Clearly the idea of 'minimum facilities' could be open to abuse. Moreover, even the sites originally supplied with costly installations were often allowed to deteriorate completely over time, and in no circumstances could be said to satisfy the requirements of their residents. Here the choice of location is as important as the type of facilities installed. For instance, a site for 20 families, supplied by two London boroughs in exchange for them both acquiring designation, was built on land that was unlikely to be used for residential building because of the noise level and dangers of lead poisoning. It was under two raised motorway access roads and bordered a railway. Reputed to have cost over £100 000 in 1975, it was installed with individual wash houses and electricity. The facilities deteriorated, and rubbish was infrequently collected. In 1981, its general conditions were such that a law centre, on behalf of one of its residents, sued the councils under the 1936 Public Health Act (*The Times* 5 Aug. 1981).

In addition to differences of opinion over the type of facilities, there was also the question of size. The size of each site favoured by the non-Gypsy decision makers tended to reflect the interests of the dominant society rather than those of the Travellers. The 1966 circular helped to influence the local authorities and was quoted by some of them: 'Experience suggests that sites for between 12 and 20 families ... are the easiest to manage satisfactorily.' I was informed by one local liaison officer for Gypsies that 15 was the most economic in terms of plumbing installations and rent collection. The criteria were those of the engineer, architect and bureaucrat. He also mentioned welfare visits. Certainly this seemed an important factor for one county council which, in the late 1960s, rejected a parish council's suggestion for small sites to be spread throughout the area. A senior official stated:

> 'In addition to such individual "private" sites, there is however a need for larger sites where positive work can be carried out by the various public services with the ultimate aim of integrating the families into the community.'

Thus there were assimilationist as well as merely technical priorities in the decisions to encourage sites for 15 or more families.

The decision bore little relation to the Travellers' preferences, because the usual political and kin-based groupings of Travellers staying in one place at a given time are rarely as large (see chapter 10). The result was that sites of 15 or more invariably contained several feuding factions. In 1975 a local authority, reviewing its experience of managing a number of sites, recognised that 'most gypsy families would probably prefer small sites occupied by their close relatives and friends, the extended family, which is their main social support and consistent with their established pattern of living' (council report). But they continued to ignore this in their future plans.

That particular local authority had also recognised the Travellers' use of what was referred to as the 'extended family'. But again this was hardly taken into consideration by the policy makers at local and national level. Responsibility for site provision was measured in terms of the nuclear family. Obviously, census counts and pitches could not be considered in terms of other units, partly because the Travellers' domestic unit tends to be the nuclear family (see Okely 1975b:3 and chapter 9). However, in site provision there was little or no awareness that individual families prefer to be surrounded by allies in the competition for work and camping places. Clusters of kin and allies, for example, assist the aged and others in times of crisis. The Travellers have depended more on their own forms of mutual aid than the welfare state. Neighbours are self-selected.

By contrast, the selection of tenants by the non-Gypsy officials for council sites is based on very different criteria: e.g. whether a family has children whom the official thinks should be in school, or whether a couple are likely to keep up with rent payments. Kinship links, fundamental to the Gypsies' political and social organisation, risk being rejected by Gorgio wardens as mere nepotism. I observed Travellers seeking pitches for their kin, describing them in terms which would most appeal to the Gorgio gatekeepers. Rival factions sought to manipulate the Gorgio warden. The selection of families from rival groups as tenants was sometimes the cause of major confrontations, resulting in damage to the council property, as well as to that of the Travellers. The costly and somewhat naive erection of a 'community' hut on several sites did not, as had been hoped, create site solidarity and neighbourliness to override those of the Travellers' own clusters (see also chapter 10).

During the late 1960s and early 1970s a major point of friction between the Travellers and housedwellers and their representatives had been the sight of scrap metal and gutted cars on the roadside encampments. Official sites only rarely solved the problem, since car breaking was generally banned. It was also hoped that 'settlement' on sites would change the Travellers' way of life. In fact it was only with the collapse of the steel industry by 1980 that Travellers persuaded themselves that such employment was unprofitable. Meanwhile, in 1972 a senior official in one local authority like many others considered that: 'We have to take the hardhearted view that the families must be weaned away from this activity or alternatively make their own arrangements ...' Some Travellers did 'make their own arrangements', by driving in the daytime from the council sites to the roadside verges where they carried out their most spectacular car breaking and tyre burning. Eventually, in the mid 1970s, some officials found it preferable to permit car breaking in a controlled way on sites.

As the earliest central government circulars indicate, the long-term policy was the sedentarisation and housing of the majority of Gypsies. By 1974, there was some indication of realism in the Department of the Environment found in a revised development control policy note quoted later in the Cripps Report: 'Their need, unlike that of the settled population, is for caravan sites, not houses' (Cripps 1976:7). As Cripps points out: 'there is nothing in the [1968] Act to indicate that the creation of sites ... was to be a stage in enforced settlement or assimilation ... Many local authorities, however, seem to have acted on the assumption that eventual assimilation is desirable' (1976:7). In one local authority I found such evidence in a 1975 report on future strategy: 'It is to be hoped that a transfer of a number of families from authorised sites into permanent housing may be possible and hence reduce the need for additional pitches' (council report 1975). Without any evidence to support their claims, some local officials would assert publicly that the vast majority if not all the occupants of their sites had 'settled down'. The officials possibly felt the pressure to reassure their employers and the local electorate that Gypsies would 'disappear' in the long run. The alleged settlement is based on several mistaken assumptions:

  (i) that there was no movement on and off the 'permanent' sites,
 (ii) that non-nomadic Gypsies inevitably cease to be Gypsies,
(iii) that, in the absence of official Gorgio managed sites, no Gypies would choose to settle on private sites, on their own terms.

I was able to record and examine site tenancies over a number of years (1968-75), both on 'temporary' and 'permanent' well-equipped sites in a number of localities. My broad findings were that only a small number of families came to regard the sites as a permanent base. Tenancies indicated that less than half, in some cases only a tiny minority, of the original tenants of the 'permanent' sites were still tenants between two and six years after their opening. In effect, the majority of families used the 'permanent' sites as temporary stopping places, or as regular bases from which to travel; which was not what the authorities intended. Those more likely to settle on sites were the aged, the widowed and sick, some of their close kin, wealthier families with local

A Traveller woman argues with a council official. *Evening Post-Echo Ltd*

contracts, and those least dependent on car breaking, which was then banned on 'permanent sites'. It is possible that families who became long-term tenants would have settled independently, if planning laws had not restricted caravans on private land. While the authorities hoped that an end to travelling would lead to housing for many families, this occurred only in exceptional cases and there was no evidence that site residence had induced this. Despite formal Gorgio control and management of the sites, the Gypsies remained relatively independent, able to manipulate the authorities and resisting assimilation. Even in the few cases where children received several years' schooling as site residents, their aspirations, job interests and choice of spouse were all consistent with the traditions of their Gypsy parents.

Independent sites and stopping places

Both before and after official site provision, some Gypsies tried to settle in their own ways; this was either overlooked or impeded by the authorities. Several of the wealthy families described their attempts to buy land with planning permission for a caravan:

> 'Once my husband and I bought some land. They told us we had planning permission but you know how it is … We found out it wasn't so, and we sold the land again and bought a new trailer.'

> 'My husband's sister tried to get permission to move onto our relations' land where they've already got a trailer. It's near A— . They only offered her temporary permission until a site's built. But we don't want it temporary, and have to move again after we've made the place nice, like putting down tarmac.'

A few Travellers had succeeded, and they were not necessarily the wealthiest families.

> Harry, a Gypsy, and Jane, a Gorgio, had been living on a plot for 20 years. It's right near a farm where Jane has always worked, while Harry does scrap collection from factories. When Harry first bought the land he had continual trouble from the council who refused planning permission. After several fines, they stuck it out until they gained permission. The plot is about the length of two and a half trailers and completely tarmacced. They have a tap and a w.c. There are hedges all round and a large corrugated iron gate. Electricity is connected and they pay rates. There was no trace of scrap or rubbish.

Throughout the 1970s, controls over any existing private sites remained strict and in this way merely increased the authorities' own responsibilities; for example, planning permission for a second trailer was refused by a district council to the Gypsy owner of a market garden. Instead, the newly married daughter was offered a tenancy on the nearby permanent site, thus depriving another family of a place.

Another form of independent settlement has been on farm land. Whereas a farmer does not require planning permission for those camping on his land for a few weeks' seasonal fruit picking, it is required when the caravan is stationed throughout the year. In one case planning permission was refused by the district council, then the local 'Gypsy Support Group' encouraged the farmer to appeal to the D.O.E. and he won the case. Several families alternated in using the camping place and working for the farmer. Another example comes from my fieldwork:

> By chance I was asked to drive Cilla to visit her widowed mother Rose, in her late seventies. After eight months' fieldwork this was the first I had known of her existence. Rose is the grandmother of three young married brothers all included in the 73 families known in detail. She has lived for over 15 years on a piece of farm land. She pointed to the screen of trees planted when she first came. Her youngest son aged 30 has never married and works part-time for the farmer. 'He won't marry till she's gone', said Cilla.

Policy developments in the 1970s

By the mid 1970s, there were a few innovations in central government policy towards Travellers. A local authority Gypsy Liaison Officer was appointed to a new post as Advisory Officer on Gypsy Encampments at the D.O.E. His practical experience and first hand acquaintance of Gypsies at grass root level promised a more informed approach. Previously, Gypsies had been the concern of rotating civil servants whose experience of them was often limited to some encounters with Gypsy 'leaders' and perhaps a few visits to sites, escorted by other officials. As late as 1975 a senior civil servant telephoned a researcher for the Centre for Environmental Studies project on Gypsies (published some months previously and specifically addressed to such policy makers) and asked, 'Are you sure you were studying the *real* Gypsies?' He was informed that an entire chapter had dealt thoroughly with the very question. Gradually, however, within the D.O.E. a new Advisory Unit was built up with a small number of staff, and one or two Gypsy organisations were given regular grants.

The C.E.S. research had, among other things, recommended 'that a duty be laid on every ... district authority to specify at least one area where Gypsies will be authorised to stop' (Adams *et al*. 1975:279), that official sites should 'be only one of several alternatives', and that local authorities 'should make plots of land available for family sites' (*ibid*.:283).A copy of the concluding chapter was sent to every local authority, representatives of who were also invited to a conference at Caxton Hall. The platform included a representative of every national Gypsy organisation, alongside speakers from the C.E.S. and the D.O.E. Copies of the publication, aimed mainly at such policy makers, were liberally displayed in a hall containing hundreds of local authority officials concerned with Gypsy sites. Despite these efforts, at the end of the day, only two copies were sold, one, by good fortune, to a Gypsy.

By 1976, both representatives at the D.O.E. unit and some Gypsy organisations were informally suggesting that government land, of which there was no shortage, should be made immediately available for Gypsy stopping places. There was no requirement for planning permission on central government land. The matter could be treated as an emergency (see also Okely 1976). Few such measures were implemented.

In 1976, the then Minister for Planning and Local Government, John Silkin , asked John Cripps to carry out a study of the effectiveness of arrangements for Gypsies. The report's recommendations corrected some of the earlier faults of the 1968 Acts. Cripps not only called for central government funding for the capital costs of sites, but also suggested that local authorities should help Gypsies to buy or lease land for their own use. Central government land could be sold for such purposes (1976:36). The report challenged the assumption that site provision was to be 'a stage in a process of enforced settlement or assimilation with a house-based society' and put on record that 'The Secretaries of States now have no wish to deny gypsies the right to a nomadic existence' (1976:7). Cripps also rejected designation for parts of counties. But there were ambivalences in the report, especially Cripps' discussion of so-called 'gypsy habits' (see Sibley 1981:109-113).

Later that year, a D.O.E. circular recommended (i) that the local authorities 'concentrate first on the provision of a number of sites with minimum facilities', (ii) the 'curtailment of indiscriminate evictions', and (iii) 'more help ... to gypsies who are prepared to develop their own sites' (1977a). The latter suggestion, influenced by the Cripps Report, was an important reversal of the implicit policy of discouraging independent Gypsy sites, so disastrously enforced by the 1960 Act. In 1978 the government agreed to give full capital grant costs for site provision. This money was to come out of the local authorities' housing budget. Plans to legislate for other changes recommended by Cripps were eventually dropped after the 1979 general election. Central funding for the sites was temporarily suspended. The Advisory Officer died suddenly in 1979 and his post remained vacant. Future policies were unclear under the new Conservative government. One D.O.E. official described the time as a 'watershed'.

In 1980 central funding for local authority sites for Gypsies was made law, along with the possibility for district designation, i.e. before a whole county had been considered to have made 'adequate' provision. Most of the other proposals by Cripps were dropped. These additions to the 1968 Act were brought in under a wide ranging planning Act. In the first year of its 100% funding, central government paid out £2.6 million for approximately 260 pitches, given that each pitch was not to cost more than £10 000. By December 1981, it was nonetheless discovered that the numbers of Gypsy families on unauthorised sites had remained constant (personal communication, D.O.E.). Such findings appear to be wholly consistent with my earlier findings that sites geared more for settlement were likely to attract those Gypsies who wished to cease travelling, and possibly those who would prefer to move from housing into caravans or merely chose not to become housed. By April 1982, the D.O.E. had committed itself to the further expenditure of £3.8 milllion for approximately 380 pitches. The large number of applications from the local authorities for funding was something of an embarrassment, given the Conservative government's policy of cuts. By the same date, designation had been given to forty-two authorities, including approximately nine districts. There were no government initiatives for Gypsy-run sites either on rented or Gypsy-owned land.

This chapter has outlined the changes over two decades, during which any attempts by Travellers towards self-determination have been increasingly outlawed. Travellers have been barred access to land which they have regularly frequented, rented or purchased. They are beginning to experience the consequences of an alternative policy of official site provision which can only partially suit their needs. This policy entails considerable public expenditure and increasing surveillance. As more designation orders are granted, travelling Gypsies may find large areas of the country legally impassable.

8 Travelling

The Gypsies' need for intermittent access to land, over which they also have minimum control, has been a major source of conflict with the dominant society. Their requirements are more often for flexibility and mobility, rather than for permanent residence. The Gypsies' movements, like those of so many other nomads, are misconstrued and seen either as irrational and unpredictable or as a response to some compelling urge or 'tradition'. In the study of nomads, detailed case studies and specificities are still hard to come by (Dyson-Hudson 1972:8-9). With regard to Gypsies, the Cripps Report recommended that government departments 'undertake or initiate research or experiments on such subjects as travelling patterns' (1976:36). This chapter aims to provide a detailed account of aspects of the Travellers' movements and struggle for the use of land during my fieldwork.

The Gypsies do not travel about aimlessly, as either the romantics or the anti-Gypsy suggest. Neither do their movements follow fixed and invariable routes. The Travellers' movements are governed by a complex inter-relation of political, economic and ideological factors. There are some broad seasonal patterns, some historical regularities in these, and other influences like work opportunities and relations with both local Gorgios and Gypsies.

Seasonal and historical regularities

Seasonal regularities in movement are influenced partly by the Gorgio economy, especially the demands of agriculture. Many Travellers in this study moved to rural areas at certain times for casual farm work. For a large part of the year from autumn to spring, these families tended to restrict their movements within a radius of a few counties near or within urban areas. Then they made direct journeys from spring onwards to specific rural areas beyond these counties, and where they had often established regular contacts with farmers. If unable to move to other farms when one type of work was over, they returned to their more urban bases.

For many Travellers, seasonal regularities were influenced also by the climate. Spring and summer months facilitate the exploration of lesser known areas, when budgeting for domestic heating is eased and when in warmer weather going out Calling in strange places is less exacting:

'It's lovely in the summer: a fortnight here and a fortnight there.'

'They say when the grass is green and the birds are singing, that's the time to be going.'

The area travelled mainly by those families which I classified as 'travelling regionally' does not appear to have radically altered over the past 150 years, if I compare my evidence with that of Hoyland. He listed a number of counties including my later fieldwork area, and noted that 'The Gypsies ... are continually making revolutions within the range of those counties' (1816:165). In addition, Hoyland recorded numbers of Gypsies who clustered in London either all the year or for the winter (1816:168, 182). Some moved out of the urban area for farm work and other occupations:

> A few of the gypsies continue all the year in London, expecting their attendance of fairs in the vicinity. Others, when work is scarce, go out twenty or thirty miles round the metropolis, carrying their implements with them on asses; and support themselves by the employment they obtain in the towns and villages through which they pass; and assist sometimes in haymaking, and plucking hops in the counties of Kent, Surrey and Sussex. (1816:187)

In the 1970s, increasing mechanisation and the gradual decline in casual work on farms affected the travelling patterns of the poorer families. Whereas in the past they could afford the expense and risk of travelling longer distances away from habitual work contacts to guaranteed and lucrative work in the fruit and potato picking areas, later they were prepared to travel only shorter distances for this. Alternatively, the migration of families for seasonal agricultural work was reduced in time span rather than eliminated altogether.

The availability of casual farm work did not affect the travelling patterns of those who travelled widely or interregionally, especially the wealthy, whose male members rarely did such work. In the warmer months they ventured longer journeys, to familiar or unfamiliar places to seek or re-establish work contacts, but usually in urban areas. If and when farm work was available in their current locality, the wives of these families availed themselves of this. Broadly, these families' long distance movements were more likely governed by the search for non-agricultural work like tarmac laying, tree lopping, carpet and linen sales. Greater mobility also enhanced opportunities in hawking and fortune telling. Even in the days before motorisation some Gypsy families travelled widely. According to Hoyland: 'Among those who have winter-quarters in London, there are a few that take circuits of great extent. Some of them mentioned going through Herts into

Travelling

Suffolk, then crossing Bedfordshire and Buckinghamshire to Herefordshire, Monmouthshire, Bristol, etc., others spoke of being at Yarmouth, Portsmouth, South Wales, Wiltshire etc.' (1816:187).

Long distance travelling is also influenced by the various fairs which are seasonal landmarks in the Gypsy calendar. In the summer months regional groupings of the rest of the year are dispersed over a wider area. Then on specific days or for a week or more, brief, alternative concentrations are formed with Travellers from regions all over the country. Epsom during Derby week in June continues to be a national gathering: 'You're not a proper Gypsy if you don't go to Epsom' I was told. A Traveller explained that there's just enough time to pull off from Epsom and reach Appleby in the north for that great annual fair a week later. In mid summer, Wisbech in Cambridgeshire also attracts families from several regions. This is not a fair but a centre for strawberry growing. The Gypsies come together at picking time, even when such work is no longer profitable: 'They don't just go for the money. It's also to meet the other people – your relations, or maybe people you haven't seen in years.' There are other smaller regional gatherings and fairs – for example at Stow-on-the-Wold several times a year, and the September Barnet Fair. The latter marks the seasonal return to the surrounding region for the harsher conditions of oncoming winter.

The spring and summer migrations away from the urban areas were confirmed by independent data. Between 1970 and 1972 one county council near London with the aid of the police made rough monthly counts of Travellers. These figures showed an influx in the winter months and a partial exodus in the summer, reaching a peak in June and July (council records). Some families, especially groups of Irish Travellers, did not follow the same season migrations but travelled all year nationwide. They did not depend on farm work and showed less association with one county and one region.

Non-seasonal factors in movement

Within the broad seasonal patterns and for those who did not maintain a regular 'winter base', movements were more random, depending on a variety of factors including the availability of work, access to camping places, harassment by police and other authorities, competition or solidarity with other Travellers, occasional crises, weddings and funerals, or a desire for change. Travelling was also used to escape ill health or the ghosts of dead Gypsies (see chapter 12).

The availability of camping land is unpredictable. Travellers might return to a pocket of land frequented for years, only to find it barricaded. They might occupy land where previously they had camped without complaint, and then face sudden opposition from local Gorgios whose petitions to the council would herald a dramatic eviction. Such policies rarely succeeded in driving the families from the locality if they had found lucrative work. The families would seek out some-where else in the vicinity and the authorities eventually lose interest. When harassment, summonses, arrests and evictions were followed by exorbitant fines or prison sentences, the Travellers had no option but to abandon their work and the area. The authorities did not pursue them for fines. Their main object was banishment, if only for a while.

Gorgio supporters are inclined to lament the lack of political 'sophis-tication' among Gypsies who only intermittently organise sustained re-sistance to those who would deny them certain 'rights'. It is not under-stood that the Travellers' strategies of evasion and dispersal or even 'disappearance' were often the most effective when faced with a direct confrontation. Travellers also faced competition between themselves for land. Some might find a favourite stopping place monopolised by a more powerful rival. A dispute between existing camp neighbours might be resolved by the departure of one of the parties. Travelling was a rational response to conflict, whether it occurred between Gypsies or with Gorgio authorities.

The ideology of travelling

Consistent with the various priorities in movement from one place to another is the belief that travelling is the ideal way of life and part of what it means to be a Gypsy. It is significant that Gypsies often prefer to be called Travellers, especially when talking to Gorgios. Travelling marks them off most dramatically from housedwellers. In discussing the possibility of a house, one Traveller said: 'I wouldn't mind a house as long as it had wheels on it.' Official sites pose new questions because of the idea of permanence attached to them and the pressures to 'settle'.

> Jack who, with his wife and two children, had stayed on a site for several months was talking with some other Gypsies. He pointed to the tyres of his lorry: 'My tyres aint worn. You know why? Cos I ain't been travelling ... I gotta.' He looked at the wheels of his trailer; 'I've got 50 000 miles left in this trailer. You know what those wheels are for? To keep turning.'

It is repeatedly asserted by Travellers in conversation with outsiders:

> 'They'll never stop us travelling. There'll always be Travellers on the road, that's for sure, no matter how many sites they build'. 'Once you've travelled you always will.'

The desire to travel is considered to be an inherited quality.

> 'We have to travel. It's in our blood ... Children of Gypsies who've lived in houses all their lives take to the roads. It's in them to travel, maybe way back.'

Travelling

One woman said to me after I had been living with the Gypsies for many months: 'You must have a Traveller in your family way back. It had to be in you, for you to travel.' Travelling is used as a criterion for group membership. I was often told: 'I'm a Traveller, I was born in a waggon [or tent], on the side of the road.' Another time I was told:

> 'A Gypsy has to keep travelling. Otherwise he isn't a Gypsy. That's why I had to pull off the site for a few weeks.'

Each group will try to outdo their rivals in terms of the travelling ideology: 'They aren't proper Travellers, they never leave Essex.'

Travelling and movement demand the qualities of versatility and flexibility, especially in hostile territory. The need to make quick decisions without melodrama is consistent with a way of life where long-term planning would be irrelevant and irrational. The majority of Gypsies on the roadside or on sites, even after a stay of several months, were able to pick up their belongings and leave within the hour if necessary. Planning was unequivocally condemned:

> Bill, a young married man, was complaining that the temporary site was soon to be closed. 'I'll be back here at Christmas, you see, even though it's going to be closed.' John, an older and respected man, replied: 'You're here today and gone tomorrow.' (This was not a criticism.) His wife Laura said: 'Bill, don't cross your bridges ... Wait till it comes ... I never plan ... You know Anne and Willie, well Anne's uncle had ordered a Vickers trailer. He kept ringing up asking when it was ready. They said he'd get it in a week. The man came down to tell him the trailer was ready, but he met the wife – now a widow. Her husband had died, so she said, "You can count me out". *You must never plan, you don't know what'll happen.'*

The moral of this tale is applicable to every aspect of the Gypsies' way of life, and demonstrates basic incompatibilities between the Travellers and a bureaucratised, literate, society where planning is ideal.

Housing

Travelling as the ideal is upheld in practice by large numbers of Gypsies in England. But the change from caravan or trailer to housing does not necessarily end Gypsy identity. Gypsies in Czechoslovakia with a long history of settlement, and whose current travelling has been more appropriately described as urban/rural migration (Guy 1975:215-18), still identify themselves and are identified as Gypsies. Some Travellers in Scotland (Rehfisch 1958, Lineton 1976), Ireland and Sweden, as well as some in England, regularly spend the winter in housing while travelling in trailers in the summer, and this has not affected their ethnic distinctness, so long as they have maintained a group solidarity. In fact, permanent housedwelling for Gypsies may not inevitably bring sedentarisation; for example in the American case (Sutherland 1975:44), the Rom move frequently from house to house and travel a large part of the year.

Although housing does not prevent a Traveller retaining ethnic identity, if he or she and parents were always housed, he or she must be able to point to ancestors who have travelled (cf. Barth 1955:288). The birthright is retained by children of Gypsies who have moved into houses as long as they associate with other Gypsies. A young woman explained to me: 'They are still called Travellers *if they keep in touch* with Travellers.' A Gypsy family may move into a house without Gypsy neighbours and, if socially isolated either through choice or misfortune, might cease to be recognised as a Gypsy by any others. One woman referred to relatives in a house: 'They're more Gorgio than Gypsy. Their ways is Gorgio.' The family might choose to drop its Gypsy identity. Then birth claim would become irrelevant; the individual or family would be of Gypsy origin but not Gypsy. Continuing self-ascription by the individual or family is essential. Experience of housing or lack of it remains a significant divider among Gypsy families in England. A *kennick* is the Romany word for a Gypsy in a house and is pejorative.

I was able to obtain fairly reliable information on the housing experience of 54 of the Gypsy female spouses and 60 of the Gypsy male spouses in the 73 families (The eleven female and four male Gorgio spouses of 'mixed' marriages and both spouses of the four Gorgio couples were excluded). Table 3 reveals that only 26% of the women and 23% of the men had experienced housedwelling life. I have excluded army, prison and borstal experience, and the very rare overnight stays with relatives in houses. The two Gypsy women and eight Gypsy men who had experienced their main upbringing in a house had taken to travelling after marriage to another Gypsy on the road.

Table 3. *Housing experience*

	Women	%	Men	%
Main upbringing in a house	2 ⎫	26	8 ⎫	23
Some experience of housing	12 ⎭		6 ⎭	
Never lived in a house	40	74	46	77
Total	54	(100%)	60	(100%)

Housedwelling was usually denigrated, and rarely seen as the ideal, despite a popular Gorgio view that the majority of Gypsies would opt for housing if given the opportunity. 'I don't like bricks and mortar – bad for your health. You need the open air.' To some of the younger Gypsies at least, housedwelling seemed baffling. I was often asked: 'What's it like living in a house?' Moving into a house may be stigmatised: 'None of the Travellers will speak to Cliff and Linda since they moved into a house.'

> A Gypsy husband and wife paid a visit to a Gorgio voluntary worker in her home. There they met Charlie, another Traveller, whom they had not seen for years. Charlie's father had known the wife's father years ago. Charlie seemed obliged to apologise for his present life: 'Here I am living in a *kenna* [house], I don't know what's become of me. I have to pay me rent regular and keep my motor taxed and insured. Who would have thought it?'

Travelling in time and space

Detailed information was recorded of the travelling patterns of the 73 families or trailer units known in detail. Additional observations on 30 more families confirmed the broad findings. Each trailer unit had considerable independence in travelling while cooperating in access to land. Since the exact groupings of families was so changeable, the most detailed information on travelling patterns relates to the movements of individual trailer units, usually nuclear families. The majority had motorised transport. Except for some Irish Travellers, they did not travel in large groups while *en route*, but more often as single trailer units, or accompanied by one another. Each converged with a greater number from several directions onto specific camping places, then later dispersing.

For each of the 73 trailer units I noted the location where I had known them best during the total period of fieldwork (see table 4).

Table 4. *Main location of trailer units during period of closest acquaintance*

Permanent official site	7	
Temporary official site	34	(including 3 Gorgio units)
Private site	2	
Illegal encampment	30	(including 1 Gorgio unit)
Total	73	

Given that in the area of fieldwork there were places on permanent sites for about 40 families, my acquaintance with only seven families in that location appears to indicate a bias towards the less 'settled' families. But many of the families on temporary sites or on the roadside were former tenants of the permanent sites which were marked by a regular turnover. There was often no clear distinction between tenants of a permanent or temporary site. Only 15 of the 73 had never stayed on any official site, whether temporary or permanent.

Tables 5 and 6[1] give details of the movements of the trailer units over a period of time. Thus 57 of the 73 stayed less than six months in the one location.[2] Those whom I got to know best in a location of only a few weeks or less were visited in other locations during fieldwork.

Table 5. *Length of stay at main location for my acquaintance*

Less than 1 week	2	
1-3 weeks	14	
1-5 months	41	(including 1 Gorgio unit)
6-10 months	2	(including 1 Gorgio unit)
1-2 years	5	
2-4 years	6	(including 2 Gorgio units)
5-9 years	1	
10-19 years	1	
20+ years	1	
Total	73	

Others whom I had known for several months in one place also experienced shorter stays at other times. The 14 families who had not

Table 6. *Travelling patterns through 12 months*

Did not travel	14	(including 3 Gorgio units)
Travelled part of year (i.e. up to 10 months)	34	(including 1 Gorgio unit)
Travelled all year (less than 2 months in one location)	25	
Total	73	

travelled for 12 months all lived in trailers and could not all be presumed to have become permanently settled. As table 5 indicates, five of these fourteen had been in the single location for only up to two years. Only three of the fourteen had been in the one place for five years or more. Even these could not be presumed to have become permanently sedentarised, as travelling can be suddenly resumed after an apparent process of settlement. The four Gorgio trailer units are not easily classified with the Gypsies, since they had neither an ideology nor a life style of travelling. The one non-sedentary Gorgio couple were former housedwellers from Scotland, on the run from the police, and who, after a few months, moved into a flat.

In addition to travelling patterns over time, information on distance was also recorded. Table 7 classifies families broadly into three types: first, those who did not travel, and secondly those who travelled 'regionally', that is within a single region consisting of several counties

Travelling

including Buckinghamshire, Essex, Bedfordshire, Hertfordshire, Cambridgeshire, Berkshire, Greater London and the fringes of Oxfordshire, with summer sorties into East Anglia and Worcestershire. Each family or trailer unit had different orientations within this region. Finally, there were those families who travelled inter-regionally, often countrywide and sometimes beyond England.

Table 7. *Travelling distances (12 month period)*

Did not travel	14	(including 3 Gorgio units)
Travelled regionally	26	
Travelled inter-regionally	33	(including 1 Gorgio unit)
Total	73	

A comparison between tables 6 and 7 indicates that the families who travelled all year were not necessarily the same as those who travelled widely and inter-regionally. For instance, some families moved within a relatively small radius, whereas other families stayed several months in the research area, especially during the winter, and at other times travelled the length and breadth of England and some to Scotland, Ireland and Wales. Table 8 gives a more detailed breakdown of the three categories in table 7.

Table 8. *Travelling distances (12 month period)*

Did not travel	14		(including 3 Gorgio units)
One county only	4	} 26	
Adjacent counties	22		
Further afield, but not countrywide	17		
Countrywide (England)	11	} 33	
Beyond England, e.g. to Scotland, Wales and Ireland	5		(including 1 Gorgio unit)
Total	73		

Specific movements

The 1965 government census attempted to assess the Gypsies' reasons for travelling by means of a questionnaire. Traveller families were asked whether they had travelled in 1964, and if so why (M.H.L.G. 1967:75). They were asked to give a single reason for *all* movements during the previous year. I rarely asked such a general question about travelling; it would have distanced me further from my companions.

133

Direct questions about a specific move usually met with little response. Instead, I observed the total context of specific movements and noted any reasons volunteered by the Travellers in conversation. In the minority of cases where the contextual information was confirmed by a direct question, this cross-checking enhanced observations of other cases.

The inappropriateness of direct questions about specific moves on most occasions is confirmed by the general secrecy surrounding the decision making. Discussions about when and where a family would move were usually held privately among the members. Information on a family's imminent departure was conveyed among camp neighbours in the form of rumours, substantiated by little clues, for example, if the china was no longer displayed in the cabinets, but packed away. An exact time of day was never volunteered. Close associates were more likely to know details of a specific departure and the next location of the family. Such information was closely guarded. Among Irish Travellers, travelling decisions were more a group concern since many tended to move nationwide as clusters of families.

Among the 73 families, I recorded 138 moves which I was able to observe usually at first hand, including the events and deliberations leading up to each, or which, in a minority of cases, were recounted to me in detail. A few of these moves were recorded during follow-up fieldwork and among some of the 14 families who, having not moved during a previous twelve month span, then resumed travelling. My fieldwork conditions were such that attempts to travel with one family were unsuccessful and would have had mixed advantages, since continuity in observing other families with whom I had established relations would have been lost. Thus, I was rarely able to analyse the factors in any arrival *at* a specific location as opposed to a departure *from* it. However, some of the factors which I have isolated, such as 'leaving for agricultural work', or 'inter-regional migration', include implicit reasons for choice of direction *to* a broad locality. There were some instances where the reasons for arrival were explicit and observable, as when a family travelled to a camp to join kin and associates in a crisis. Generally, the whereabouts of kin and associates is a crucial factor in choosing to stop at a specific location.

Whereas it would be misleading to suggest that each separate movement had a single explanation, excluding all others, nonetheless it was possible to isolate a *major* factor, one more obvious than others. Statistical generalisations based on percentages of each factor should be viewed with caution. Economic and other factors appear to outnumber internal political reasons, in that a Traveller probably moves more often to seek work than to escape conflict with camp neighbours. But the latter variable is often implicit, because a family or a group of Travellers is watchful of the location of rivals and may deliberately avoid camps where conflict and enforced departure would be inevitable. The purpose of this numerical exercise is to indicate the variety of factors in travelling and the differences between moves directly inflicted by Gorgios and those made more independently by Gypsies.

Major factors are isolated and enumerated in table 9, followed by a description and some case studies indicating the type of evidence used in classifying each type of move. The very different methods used in the 1965 census (see above) recorded that 'travelling was mainly motivated by economic considerations', although it was stated that many families had what the Ministry described as a 'deep-rooted habit of nomadism' (M.H.L.G. 1967:17). Straight answers to outsiders would have been less likely to reveal the variety of factors in each move, indeed the extent of intervention by the Gorgio authorities.

Table 9. *Major factor in a movement from a specific location*

Gorgio harassment	23	
Gorgio fine	16	
Gorgio eviction	8	57 moves induced by
Theft or other offences against Gorgios	6	Gorgio authorities
Imprisonment (of husband)	4	
Agricultural work	19	
General 'migration' (long distance)	21	
Regular 'circuit' (short distance)	20	81 moves initiated by Gypsies
Conflict with other Travellers	14	
Death	7	
Total	138	

Gorgio harassment

It is often more effective for the police to encourage the Travellers to move off before court procedures, and after a build-up of threats, dawn raids, examination of motoring documents, requests for dog licences etc., and constant observation from parked 'panda cars'. Other officials have been used for these purposes; health inspectors asking if the Travellers have elsans, or education officers threatening prosecution because the children are not in school. The Travellers recognise a certain 'game' between themselves and the authorities:

> 'We use every excuse and play for time. Once I said we had no petrol money. We were sent to the social security. That gave us a few more days and a bit of extra cash.'

Harassment was most effective after a family had made a court appearance, perhaps been fined and then either stayed put, or moved only a short distance. The reappearance of the police would eventually break further attempts at resistance.

Case study a

A family was parked in a small woodland area, off the road. This place periodically aroused complaints from the few local residents in large houses a quarter mile away. Then the police would try to move the Travellers off. On this occasion, police parked nearby and watched the family. The husband drove in an old car which he planned to break up. The police moved in, after finding he had neither tax nor insurance for this vehicle; only for his lorry. They examined the car and listed every item for which he could be prosecuted. A couple of days later he was presented with sheets of paper listing over twenty offences for which he would be prosecuted. These included: faulty headlights, faulty indicators, worn down tyres, poor brakes, poor steering, failure not only to have the car taxed, but also to display a tax disc, failure to produce a log book, in fact every possible offence. The family moved off. The charges were not followed up.

Case study b

Two families returned to a disused loop of road adjoining a roundabout. Frequently used by Travellers, it had been blocked by earth mounds dumped by the rural district council. The Travellers cleared the earth. An official from the rural district council told them to move. The local support groups encouraged the Gypsies to stay, as it was not council land. Efforts to remove them on health grounds failed. 'He made a remark about sleeping space in my caravan' one of the mothers said to a reporter, and 'We have been told that the Council will keep coming back until we go' (*Evening Echo*, 27 November 1970). In early December a county council official told the women (the men being absent) that *he* didn't mind them being there, but the R.D.C. were hostile. Moreover there were plans to widen the road. Plans for storing materials were instigated. The women were told that the contractors wanted to put their hut near where the trailers were parked. In my notes I wrote of the women: 'Why this placid approach? No hostility, extreme politeness when there was a threat of having to move altogether.' Later I recognised this as a standard approach. Friends of these families recounted the officials' suggestions with anger. They intended to stay.

The next day the council officer, accompanied by two site wardens, 'to show them we're serious', met the contractor who said to the women, 'I'm sorry. I've lived in a caravan myself on jobs.' The families were given a week to move. They resisted, but, after private discussions with the contractor, agreed to move after Christmas. This they did.

Travelling

The disused loop was only temporarily used for gravel and then closed off by fencing where it remains today. As has been verified elsewhere, it is likely that the contractors were introduced for the specific purposes of justifying moving the Travellers.

Gorgio fine

Where harassment alone proves ineffective, the authorities take the Gypsies to court. There are a number of by-laws or Acts which can be resorted to, for example the 1959 Highways Act and several Public Health Acts. Some Travellers have been fined for possessing milk churns, which, even if purchased from farmers, remain technically the property of the Milk Marketing Board. Alternatively, the Gypsies may be fined for motoring offences. Again the authorities are interested only in ensuring speedy departure after the first instalment of a fine. Sometimes Gorgio supporters encourage the Travellers to stay put, once the fine or first instalment is paid but, faced with continuing harassment and the threat of further harassment or fines, the Travellers recognise that departure is best.

> Two families pulled onto a long deserted army camp owned by the Ministry of Defence. There were protests from the local health inspector and local residents. The Ministry were loath to evict, and instead put barbed wire at the entrance, leaving space for a vehicle, but preventing the entry of more trailers. A Gorgio supporter wrote to the Ministry pleading the Gypsies' case. Meanwhile local pressure increased. A rural district councillor complained (*Gazette*, 4 February 1972) that the Ministry 'has put itself above the law'.
>
> A representative of the Ministry visited the site and claimed he found one of the Travellers, Smith, chopping up an old door frame of one of the huts and burning it. Smith was charged under the Criminal Damages Act. In fact the army camp was derelict and due for demolition. The hut roofs had been stripped long ago, few windows remained and there weren't many door frames, let alone doors. In court, legal aid was rejected 'because the offence was too small'. A voluntary solicitor advised the Gypsy to plead guilty so a Gorgio supporter could appear in mitigation. Smith had also to get this Gorgio to stand bail.
>
> Next week Smith was given a conditional discharge, but had to pay compensation, witness expenses and costs of prosecution. In fact there had been no need for a prosecution witness from the Ministry as Smith pleaded guilty. But the witness said that as Smith didn't have a solicitor he didn't know in advance what Smith's plea would be, although he could have telephoned the court. Smith paid the full amount and returned to

the airfield. The police visited constantly and threatened summonses for motoring offences. So the families moved off. Earlier, the Ministry had threatened an eviction. Alternative measures had saved them the embarrassment.

Gorgio eviction

Such direct confrontation occurs when Gypsies have failed to respond to harassment, fines or threats, but when the authorities can obtain the collaboration of the landowner and are prepared to face adverse publicity. Evictions are resorted to when the Gypsies are occupying plots of land rather than roadside grass verges where the Gypsies can merely move a few yards further on. Legal evictions may take up to three months to prepare through the courts, and were undertaken by one county council when the Gypsies' presence threatened the credibility of the council's guarantees to district councils that site provision would rid the locality of any remaining Gypsies. Some authorities have employed full time 'clearance' officers to evict Gypsies.

In no place did harassment, fines or evictions guarantee the Gypsies' permanent departure from a location. The same stopping places, after a temporary absence, were 'opened up' again – to use the Travellers expression. Imprisonment remained the ultimate deterrent. Since caravan dwelling Gypsies own and transport their home, an eviction is less consequential than for a householder. However, the direct and often violent confrontation which occurs at an eviction expresses and reinforces a boundary of hatred between Gypsy and Gorgio.

In the 1970s, seven Gypsy families moved onto a grass verge near a temporary site. After police pressure to go, one night the Travellers broke down the fencing of a field adjoining the site. The council immediately contacted the Department of the Environment and the private citizen who part owned the land. They agreed to a request that the council 'act as agents to clear the land'. The continued occupation was considered undesirable partly because 'their presence ... was likely to attract other families', said one official.

The council mobilised tractors, twenty policemen and three members of the Social Services Department. 'We wanted to avoid any possible breach of the peace. It is a situation of conflict', said the council officer (local newspaper). The council believed prompt action was necessary because 'Legal process through the Courts would take too long.' After one trailer was towed off, the other families left voluntarily and were 'escorted' to the council border by the police. 'It's not possible to suggest anywhere else for them to go ... their removal to any other land would constitute various offences' said an official, i.e. the council would itself be liable to prosecution if they had simply towed the caravans onto the highway.

Many of the Travellers on the temporary site expressed anger at the eviction and one woman, already in a dispute with a neighbour, blamed it on him: 'It was him who rang up the police and told them about the people who'd pulled onto the bottom field. He had them pulled off. Someone told the *gavvers*. No one would've known 'cos they pulled on at night.' She could find no other explanation for the Gorgio's prompt action. She was unaware of the council's need to guarantee clearance of the area in exchange for a district council's consent to a local site.

Theft

If prosecution for theft (or other offences against Gorgios) seemed imminent, a Gypsy family would move on. Sometimes this coincided with the family's intention to leave for work in another area.

Imprisonment

Men rather than women usually risked prison sentences. The wives, left with their children, would usually move to kin who would also assist in towing the trailer.

Agriculture

This was listed as the main reason for a move when the family arranged to travel to specific farms for seasonal work. The following example shows the various factors leading up to a specific move where opportunities in fruit picking offered the final incentive.

A short time before Millie's baby was due, her parents and unmarried sibling pulled their trailer onto her plot at the temporary site. They reassured the Council they would only stay while Millie was recovering. At first they expressed interest in a plot on the permanent site to be opened shortly. During their stay of two months I noticed some conflict between Millie's father and husband. The older man, in a drunken mood, threatened Millie's husband to a fight and was ignored. One Traveller told me that Millie and her husband wanted them to leave in the long run. One day, another Traveller woman on the site told me: 'Those people are leaving today or tomorrow ... going to Wisbech for fruit-picking.' (It was June and the height of strawberry picking.) 'Millie's father doesn't want a trailer site. He wants to be his own guv'ner. Doesn't want other people telling him what to do. His wife doesn't mind ... The old man drinks a lot. When the others are fruit-picking, he doesn't do any. He asks for money for drink and they give him some so as he'll keep away.'

The next morning I watched Millie's parents and sibling leave. As the trailer was towed onto the centre, Millie's husband's brother and another male Traveller, both camping on the temporary site, walked over and exchanged a few words. The family left with their ex-army lorry (sides cut out) towing the trailer, followed by a small grey van driven by Millie's young brother.

General migration

A movement was explained in these terms when the family made preparations for long distance travelling, beyond the local counties, usually in the warmer months and not specifically for farm work, but for a variety of work opportunities more randomly located.

Elisa and Noah had lived for several years on a permanent site, then pulled off in January, possibly after a dispute. After summonses for encampment, they pulled on to an abandoned road with some of Elisa's kin and affines. Even when on the site they had travelled for some months in the summer. In the first week in May after seven months within an area near Greater London and four months in the one place, they pulled off. A few days later, Elisa's sister said they had gone to Leeds. A Gorgio warden said they were in Leicester. Shortly after, Elisa's brother's wife visited me. She'd just received a phone call at a set time at a warden's office. Elisa and Noah were on a 'pull-in' at 'Nogginum' (i.e. Nottingham), 'near Loughborough', and asked her and her husband to join them. They were going further north.

Regular small circuit

Very often a family might move for no apparent reason than a stated desire for change, or, as was once said to me, 'because he's restless, he doesn't like to stay too long in one place'. The distance between locations would not be great; the current and previous locations being in the radius covered during the daily work drive by those efficiently motorised. Obviously the nearest hawking area covered on foot by the wives would be different after each small move. Sometimes the family moved when the campsite became too muddy, the toilet areas over-used and when a longer stay would risk hostility from local Gorgios.

For such movements of relatively short distance within the region, and again and again to the same localities, amounting to a regular circuit familiar from childhood, work demands did not appear primary. Nor could Gorgio harassment be offered as an explanation. The Travellers had learnt to make themselves more acceptable to the different landowners, nearby residents, and parish authorities, so long as none of their sojourns risked being permanent. Those Gorgios who were affronted or disturbed by the Gypsies' periodic appearance, could console themselves that the people were 'here today and gone tomorrow'. The Gypsies did not remain a fixed mark on the landscape nor acquire squatters' rights. Families were tolerated more if they camped in small numbers and chose places less visible to the general public. This strategy of short stays in inconspicuous places, and the preference of some families for settlement on private land, were increasingly undermined by the authorities' post-1960 policy (see chapter 7).

Conflict with other Travellers

Departure by one of the parties in a dispute was often the preferred resolution to a conflict.

> Billy and Eileen left a permanent site because Billy had pinched someone else's tarmaccing job and feared a beating up. They moved onto a temporary site then had to move again only two weeks later. This family had five young children who seemed to annoy Travellers wherever they went. I had several experiences of their behaviour; for example they locked me in my trailer! The Travellers volunteered their comments:

> 'What they need is an iron collar, a long chain each – pegged down.'

> 'The local garage no longer gives us water. Eileen's children spoilt it 'cos they'd go there, in and out all day and leave the tap running.'

> 'They were always coming round asking for sugar, tea and jam. Eileen was sending them. It isn't as if they didn't have the money to pay for it. I stopped giving them anything.'

> 'Mrs Smith over there left the other site to get away from her. Then Eileen pulled on here the very next day. The woman's eyes nearly popped out!'

Billy and Eileen then had to leave the temporary site, after hostilities resulted in a fight and further threats.

Mr Smith: 'John went to Billy's trailer and just asked him to look after his children. He wasn't going to hit him, Billy hit him first. So John showed him what he was worth.'

Mrs Smith: 'Now if I came to you and asked you to look after you children you would say "All right, I will." But Billy didn't.'

Mr Smith: 'He found his match!'

Nine year old boy: 'Eileen saw Billy wasn't winning, so she started beating John with a broom, but Rose [another camp neighbour] took the broom off her, saying "He should do his own fighting – fight like a man."'

At the time, John had with him his wife's sister's teenage son, Dave, who had dark skin; his father being West Indian. 'Eileen and her kids called that boy Dave a "black b—". Well his mother [living in a house] sent a message saying she was going to come and beat up Eileen on Saturday. We're all equal, if you tell those people those things, they don't like it, do they?'

I had arrived unexpectedly at the site on the Thursday evening and was given details of the dispute. Eileen's china was packed away when I paid an amicable visit. They left on Friday afternoon. The motive was again confirmed by a young boy: 'I know the reason why that woman left, 'cos Dave's mother was gonna come and beat her up tomorrow. She was frit.'

Death

When the death of a Traveller occurs, kin and others travel to the camp where the body will eventually be brought from the morgue and displayed a day before the funeral. After the procession to the place of burial and destruction of the deceased's property, the occupants of the camp move off. Ideally the location should be avoided by close kin for a year or more (see chapter 12).

Ethnic image and political encounter

As in economic relations, the Travellers use any image and intellectual resource to acquire and retain access to land, all of which is controlled if not owned by Gorgios. For this purpose ethnicity may be exoticised.

disguised, degraded, or neutralised (cf. Okely 1979a). Health inspectors, or any policeman ready to listen, will be told by the offending family that they are 'real Romanies'. In the courts, the exotic image softens the magistrates and may be seen to justify an unorthodox life style. A Gypsy is invariably introduced by his solicitor as 'a member of a well known Romany family'.

> An Irish Traveller, housed, and attempting to pass as a Gorgio, faced prosecution for a driving offence. He told a Gorgio appearing as a character reference: 'I don't mind what you tell them. Say I'm a Gypsy, if it'll help.'

On their encampment and visible as caravan dwellers, the Travellers can less easily disguise and conceal their ethnic status. Occasionally, however, wealthy families with no traces of scrap metal, and owning a Range Rover rather than a lorry, convince officials that they are Gorgio housedwellers 'on holiday'. One such Traveller was permitted to park on a grass verge, while his acquaintances 100 yards on were summonsed and fined as Gypsies under the 1959 Highways Act.

The degraded image of the helpless illiterate defuses hostilities and is accompanied by earnest wishes to conform, to 'settle down' and send the children to school 'so they can 'ave a better life', thus reassuring the Gorgio of the superiority of his system. The few literate Gypsies conceal their ability, preferring to seem deprived. Their illiterate companions screw up or burn the official summonses, free from the intimidation of their texts. When Gorgios themselves first categorise and treat a Gypsy as degraded, it may be necessary to behave passively, however humiliating. A Traveller mother who, with her family, had lived most of her life either in a waggon or bender tent, recounted her experience:

> 'When the children were smaller, they were paddling in a stream. It was summer. A man came up to them and tried to talk to them. He offered them sweets. I've told my children to take no notice when strangers come. They came back to me. The man had been watching them playing for a long time. He spoke to me. "I'd like to see the children's hair." "Yes", I said. There were no lice. Sometimes you get little bits of white. See, look at Dolly's hair now. I've just washed it. It's clean. I let the man look. Then he asked to see the bedding. He looked in the bender. It was dry. The mattress was on proper waterproof sheeting. He said, "I could get you for this … I could have your children taken away, making them sleep like this." I said "It's dry. It's summer. The children won't come to harm." The man went away and I didn't see him again. You get plenty of people like that. It's best to be polite. You never know who it is. Yes, I had to let him look at the children and the bedding … It's best.'

Families seeking site places talk at length to the warden about their desires to give up travelling, 'for the childrens' sake'. Tales of hardship on the road are exaggerated. Weeks later, puzzled officials see the families depart, abandoning all the 'security' they appeared to want, and without having attempted to send their children to school.

The identity of the Gypsy may in some political contexts be known, but be less relevant, and exoticism, concealment or degradation be inexpedient. In relations with the police, site wardens and others in regular contact, a more personalised rapport develops. Families gain time if their faces are familiar and if they are names to the local policeman. Exchange of banalities reduces tension, avoids open conflict. A *modus vivendi* is found beneath the letter of Gorgio law, which indeed can never be enforced against all Gypsies, all of the time. This may assist the police in unexpected ways:

> A policeman informed a Gorgio that his force had no intention of moving certain families from their current stopping place. 'We like to know where they are. If one of them gets into trouble, we know where to go looking.' This group contained a Gypsy who had just returned from one of his numerous spells in prison.

The *modus vivendi* can be broken any time. When Gorgio liberals, concerned with 'legal rights', persuade Gypsies to defy the formal and informal pressures to move them on and to resist through due process of the law, their intervention may be counter-productive. The image of Gypsies as degraded and a 'public nuisance' is then brought to life by the Gorgio, not the Gypsy. The police and other officials retaliate with every weapon available in Gorgio law. The Gypsies, now unable to neutralise their image, arrested and exposed in court, discover that they may be punished by even greater fines or even prison.

> The husbands of two families, parked in a disused loop of road after it had been straightened, were arrested and fined under the 1959 Act. They were then encouraged by local Gorgio sympathisers to stay put, since they could only be fined once under that Act. They were arrested again, at dawn by police with alsations. Later, they were brought into court, unshaven and deprived of belts and bootlaces, and charged with 'obstruction' of the highway. Their request for legal aid meant delaying the case. A Gorgio woman stood them bail for several hundred pounds. Now obligated to her, they had to stay a week for the case. They were then fined for obstruction for each subsequent day as a separate offence. The magistrate ordered that these fines had to be paid immediately or the Travellers faced imprisonment. The Travellers were thus reminded by the authorities that it would have been better to

have left at the first sign of trouble, rather than rely on guidance from their Gorgio supporters.

Motorisation and technological adaptation

Motorisation among Gypsies in England and elsewhere is an important example of the continuing technological adaptation which they have made to the larger economy. It has not, as the sentimentalists would insist, modified the Gypsies' degree of independence from Gorgio society. Instead, modern technology has enhanced the Gypsies' nomadism. Greater distances can be covered in a shorter time. Larger, heavier homes, complete with calor gas for cooking and heating, can be transported. To some extent the families may choose to move their trailer less frequently, because motor transport now offers a wider radius in a day's work from a fixed base.

> One Traveller in his fifties said: 'Gypsies travelled further with horses.[3] You'd stay for maybe three weeks in the vicinity of a town. You went round it and through it, the women hawking. You'd get to know everything about it. You'd have to move on. For one thing you needed to let the grass grow again for horse grazing. Now the Travellers want to stay around London and take their iron there. They want to establish squatters' rights.' He did not imply that Travellers sought permanent settlement, for at another time he said: 'Some of the support people [Gorgios] tell Travellers to stay put and tell them they've got the *right* to stay. But Travellers don't want to stay too long. You need to travel for the work.'

Motorisation also affords the opportunity to travel greater distances in search of alternative camping places when others are closed (cf. Acton 1974:47). However, this would be unlikely to encourage families with a lucrative radius of work contacts to move beyond this radius in search merely of a 'safer' camping place. The petrol costs and labour time would be sufficient deterrents.[4] Motorisation has enabled families travelling to selected farms and areas for agricultural work to reach their destination in a shorter time. Again modern technology is exploited; the Travellers now telephone the farmer for the exact day when fruit picking is required.

In Humberside I encountered a number of Gypsies living in 'bow-top' waggons, whereas in the south east I saw only one horse-drawn waggon. Yorkshire and Humberside had the highest percentage of horse-drawn waggons: 28% in the 1965 census compared to 6% in the whole of England and Wales (M.H.L.G. 1967:12). The census indicated that 93% of all the families interviewed had trailers, and over three-quarters owned at least one vehicle (M.H.L.G.1967:19).

145

Three generations and a bow top waggon in the 1970s. *Evening Post-Echo Ltd*

Tables 10 and 11 indicate the type of transport available to the 73 families studied in the south-east in the early 1970s. Seven family units including one Gorgio unit had neither horses nor motor transport. Some depended on relatives to tow their trailer caravans at intervals. All lived in trailers except for two families who alternated during a two year period between a tent, a trailer and a house. One family, during their time in a tent, would travel on foot, pushing their possessions in a pram and a knife-grinding machine. They occasionally used a bicycle for daily trips. An elderly couple, with a horse and 'trolley' (i.e. open cart) for scrap metal and rag collection, lived in a trailer which other Travellers would tow when they moved between official sites in the locality.

The nine families with only a saloon car were unable either to tow

Table 10. *Types of transport available*

Horse and 'trolley' only	1	1%
Horse and 'trolley' plus motor vehicle	4	
Motor vehicle only (including 3 Gorgio units)	61	} 89%
None (including 1 Gorgio unit)	7	10%
Total	73	(100%)

Table 11. *Motor vehicle available*

Car only (including 1 Gorgio unit)	9	12%
Car plus 1 lorry/pick-up/van (including 1 Gorgio unit)	7	
Car plus 2 lorries/pick-ups/vans	2	77% with at least one lorry/ pick-up van
1 lorry/pick-up/van (including 1 Gorgio unit)	35	
2 lorries/pick-ups/vans	10	
3 lorries/pick-ups/vans	2	
None (including 1 Gorgio unit)	8	11%
Total	73	(100%)

their trailers or transport large items, such as scrap metal. A family with only a car was recognised by others as having little chance of earning a living in the Traveller economy:

'Look at that man, all he's got is that old car. How's he gonna make a living? What work does he do? All he uses it for is to go to the pubs at night. He's up to no good.'

The 1965 census also reported a low percentage (16%) of families who owned any car, with more than half of them owning additional vehicles,

A tent-dwelling family, twenty miles from London in 1970. *Evening Post-Echo Ltd*

147

and compared to nearly two-thirds of all families who had at least one lorry (M.H.L.G. 1967:19-20).

> Another woman who had worked for several months with her husband at tarmaccing and with the money she saved bought her own Land Rover, said she preferred that type of vehicle to saloon cars. 'Once I had a Cortina, it only lasted two weeks … cars don't last.'

More often when Travellers owned cars they were run-down vehicles soon to be broken up and prepared for the scrapyard. I was sometimes given hair-raising lifts in old 'bangers', with neither windscreen, lights, proper suspension, nor efficient brakes. One sported a disc advertising an amusement park where the tax disc should have been. Some families resorted temporarily to a car when seeking tarmac jobs, visiting relatives or for shopping errands from a fixed site, thereby saving petrol consumption. This practice had greatly increased by 1980, after rising fuel costs. Car ownership without a lorry was associated with Gorgios. A lorry was the preferred vehicle:

> A Gypsy woman talking to me about her car and lorry pointed to the lorry; 'That's the worker, we can't have anything go wrong with that.'

Since the lorry or pick-up was the major investment for work purposes and travelling, great care was devoted to its repair. The word 'lorry' was rarely used, instead 'motor'. It has supplanted the horse in many uses. The symbolism is carried over; the motor is also referred to as the 'iron horse' or, in Romany, *saster grai*. Travellers invariably took photographs of each other next to or alongside their 'iron horses'. Some painted scroll-work on the sides or placed transfers of horse motifs on the doors. The wings of the bonnet might be picked out in a different colour. Certain colours such as blue, or silver, were preferred. One woman told me 'blue is the Travellers' colour'. The extent of decoration was somewhat inhibited, as Travellers found themselves more conspicuous to the police, and the tarmaccers needed to disguise their Gypsy origins. An expensive lorry lent a businessman's respectability to their image.

Table 12 indicates the age of the best vehicle of 60 families. (Of the remaining families, eight had no vehicle and for four I could record no information.) Wherever possible, I had made a note of the letter of the alphabet at the end of the registration number which indicated the year. Notice the extreme contrasts between families with 28% owning vehicles, usually lorries, three years old or less. Some owned new 'T.K.' lorries as well as 'Range Rovers' which were replaced annually. By contrast, nearly 40% relied on a vehicle at least nine years old.

Ingenious techniques were used in acquiring and maintaining serviceable motors which rarely appeared on the open market, but instead

Table 12. *Age of best vehicle for 60 families (in 1971)*

(1968-1971) i.e. 0–3 years	17	(28%)
(1963-1967) i.e. 4–8 years	20	(33%) (including 1 Gorgio unit)
(pre-1963) i.e. at least 9 years	23	(39%) (including 2 Gorgio units)
Total	60	100%

were obtained through personal contacts, and which if necessary were cleverly patched-up to the minimum roadworthiness. Favourite sources of motors for poorer families were auctions of vehicles from the local council or electricity board. Boxed-in lorries were cut down, then new sides and floor boards inserted. Parts were replaced from other motors beyond repair and being dismantled for scrap. Contacts were established with employees at junk yards, garages and service stations from which odd parts were supplied at special rates. The main working vehicle of the less wealthy families had nearly always undergone major overhauls. When a vehicle required technically sophisticated repair work it was resold, or scrapped, or taken to a professional Gorgio mechanic.

Travelling and economic status

The wealthier families have been able to exploit most effectively the advantages of motorisation. Table 13 gives a breakdown of the travelling distances of families already indicated in table 7, according to economic status. The four Gorgio units are included: three of low economic status who did not travel and one of medium status who had travelled widely. (If excluded, the percentages for the lowest economic status become 13%, 65%, 22%, and those for the medium economic status become 30%, 35% and 35%.) With or without the Gorgio units, the same conclusions can be drawn (cf. Adams *et al.* 1975:151).

The greatest proportion of families of low economic status travelled only regionally whereas the greatest proportion of wealthy families travelled inter-regionally. Among families of medium economic status, roughly equal proportions travelled regionally and inter-regionally. A very low proportion of families of high economic status had not travelled in the twelve months. Among those of low economic status who travelled widely were several Irish families, with different and distinctive travelling patterns. Table 14 records travelling over time, in relation to economic status. Again the four Gorgio units are included; three of low status who did not travel and one of medium status who travelled part of the year. (If excluded, the percentages

Table 13. *Travelling distances and economic status (12 month period)*

| | Economic status | | | | | |
	Low		Medium		High	
Did not travel	6	(23%)	6	(29%)	2	(8%)
Travelled regionally	15	(58%)	7	(33%)	4	(15%)
Travelled inter-regionally	5	(19%)	8	(38%)	20	(77%)
Total	26		21		26	

Table 14. *Travelling over time and economic status (12 month period)*

| | Economic status | | | | | |
	Low		Medium		High	
Did not travel	6	(23%)	6	(29%)	2	(8%)
Travelled part of year	11	(42%)	12	(57%)	11	(42%)
Travelled all year	9	(35%)	3	(14%)	13	(50%)
Total	26		21		26	

for the lowest economic status become 13%, 48% and 39%, and those of medium economic status become 30%, 55% and 15%.) Again, with or without the Gorgio units, the same observations apply.

A significant proportion of families of high and medium status who travelled inter-regionally (see table 13) in fact travelled for only part of the year. They found it profitable to stay in one place for several months, especially in the winter. The wealthy families often belonged to powerful clusters able to monopolise the better, less conspicuous camping places and remain undisturbed for several weeks or months. They were also able to pay large sums to private landowners to stay on their land. Not dependent on car breaking, they aroused less hostility from the police and other authorities.

A comparison between tables 13 and 14 reveals that a significant proportion of families of low economic status travelled all the year, although not great distances, some being among those who travelled only regionally. Whereas the wealthier families chose the better stopping places and had the confidence and finances to withstand harassment and possible fines, the poorer families were more vulnerable. With little cash and diminished economic contacts beyond their locality, they could least afford to move long distances if faced with fines and possible imprisonment. Neither could they exploit as wide a daily work radius as the wealthy families who could afford large outlays on petrol. The poorer families moved shorter distances and more frequently.

Travelling

Thus geographical mobility and wealth are interdependent, given that the majority of wealthy families travelled great distances, while the majority of poorer families travelled only within one region or less. This did not preclude the wealthier families from staying in one place for several months at a time (nor even from settling more or less permanently, if they so chose). Investment in expensive and reliable vehicles gave greater opportunities both for the daily work radius and for inter-regional travel. A wider network of work contacts could be explored and maintained both at one time and over the year. Cash reserves facilitated journeys to new localities.

9 The trailer unit, spouses and children

Composition

The term 'household' is a misnomer for Travellers in caravans, given also their distaste for housedwelling. The domestic unit is best referred to by the Gypsies' word 'trailer' and in contrast to the Gorgio 'caravan'. (When talking to Gorgios, the Gypsies switch to the word 'caravan' thereby appearing to conform to the dominant ideology yet preserving their own).

The trailer is the moving home and shared sleeping, cooking and eating quarters for a family, whose members may collaborate in earning a living, budgeting, and the upbringing of children. It can also be an independent travelling unit. The great majority of these units consisted of a two generation nuclear family living in one or more trailer, tent or hut. Although families camped alongside each other and formed work partnerships, they continued to budget separately and owned no property in common.[1] The trailer unit, usually the nuclear family, is an important unit for production and consumption, but depends on cooperation with other Travellers. It is of course never self-sufficient, given the Gypsies' position within the wider economy.

Unless the nuclear family becomes 'fragmented' by the death or desertion of a spouse, it does not merge with another. (The term 'fragmented family' denotes a domestic unit which does not contain both a husband and wife.) Usually lone adults attach themselves to another nuclear family. A single adult, with or without children, is scarcely viable in an independent trailer unit. There were very few cases of trailer units containing only one adult. Adults without a spouse who remained in the travelling community tended to form variants of the nuclear family by joining with one or more adults in a trailer unit.

Table 15 reveals the composition of the 73 family trailer units encountered in fieldwork (see also Okely 1975e). These were included in the 125 families in Adams *et al.* (1975:58). Unmarried adults in their late twenties or older were offspring who had foregone marriage to look after an aged parent, or disabled dependents. Thus 59 family trailers contained no adults additional to spouses or unmarried offspring. Five trailer units contained additional adults from a fragmented family. Three trailer units formed variants of the nuclear family and only six trailer units contained only one adult, who either depended on Gorgio welfare, or closer cooperation with another trailer unit or they ceased to travel. As with the national census (M.H.L.G. 1967:9), each nuclear family contained a considerable number of offspring, so that in this study the majority of family trailer units contained at least six persons, and in some exceptional cases as many as twelve.

Marriage

Among Travellers, there are no large time spans between puberty and marriage. Their life style does not demand as prerequisites permanent rights in land and neither rented nor mortgaged housing. Gypsies from wealthier families do, however, expect to own expensive trailers and furnishings at marriage. A couple can marry young and be financially independent. Girls tended to marry at the age of 16-17 and boys at the age of 18-19. The vast majority had married by the age of 22. Greater details on some aspects of family and married life can be found in my 'The Family, Marriage and Kinship Groups' (Okely 1975b:ch.3) and in Okely 1977.

Table 15. *Composition of family trailers (total 73)*

Nuclear family	
Husband and wife, plus children own or adopted and unmarried offspring	52
Husband and wife, offspring now left	3
Husband and wife, no children	4
Subtotal	59
Nuclear family plus additional fragmented family	
Husband, wife, children; plus unmarried daughter and her child	1
Husband, wife, plus divorced daughter and her daughter	1
Husband, wife, child, plus wife's father	1
Husband, wife, child, plus husband's male cousin	1
Wife (husband imprisoned), son; plus married daughter, her husband and their children (all Gorgio; temporary arrangement in crisis)	1
Subtotal	5
Fragmented family	
Widow plus adult unmarried son	1
Widow plus adult unmarried son and daughter	1
Divorcé plus unmarried adult son and nephew	1
Units containing only one adult	
Divorcé	1
Widower plus children	1
Wife (husband imprisoned); plus children	2
Widow plus grandchild and young nephew	1
Widow	1
Subtotal	9

All the procedures by which Gypsies come to be considered married are marked by the spatial and temporal divisions of a *rite de passage*, and are given some lawful status. One is a type of 'elopement' without recourse to a registry office. Another may or may not combine a visit to a registry office with a convivial celebration by both sets of kin (see also Thompson 1927:116,119-20 and 158). Few undergo a church wedding ceremony. The Gypsies themselves use the English verb 'to marry'. The Romany words *romered* or *romado* mean 'married' (Wood 1973:128) but I rarely heard them. While using the English word, both among themselves and in communication with Gorgios, Travellers are aware of differences, for instance in the manner in which Gypsy or Gorgio marriages are established or broken, and in the rights and obligations associated with marriage. Since ideally a Gypsy should not marry a Gorgio, marriage regulations among Gypsies imply an opposition to those of the Gorgio.

Prohibited categories in choice of spouse

The Travellers were willing to volunteer a few statements about marriage prohibitions but were not forthcoming about marriage preferences. The general prohibitions among Travellers in this study were: (1) marriage to a Gorgio, (2) marriage to a first cousin (if not second cousin), (3) marriage to a person much older or younger, (4) marriage within the immediate family, including parents' siblings and siblings' offspring.

(1) Marriage with a Gorgio was considered to threaten the purity of the 'race' and 'blood'. In practice, as shown in chapter 5, children of such unions were usually accepted as Gypsies. Indeed the most prestigious and powerful group of siblings in the research area had a Gorgio mother who was given high status. Yet both they and some less powerful Gypsies stated that this group were *tatcho* Romanies (or 'real' Gypsies). Rules against Gypsy–Gorgio marriages were strengthened by pollution taboos and sexual stereotypes. Both Gorgio men and women were considered *mochadi* (polluted). Sexual and marital relations with Gorgio men carried the threat of pollution to Gypsy women (see Okely 1975d and chapter 11). Gorgio men were seen as sexually rapacious. To Gypsy men, Gorgio women were depicted as sexually uncontrollable, and therefore exciting as sexual partners, but dangerous as wives; fidelity could not be guaranteed. 'Every Gypsy man wants to lay with a Gorgio woman.' The same Gypsy man gave an alternative view of Gorgio women: 'They're like refrigerators, it's no good marrying one of them. You'd get more life from a bit of raw steak.' Both views affirm the dangers in forming a permanent relationship with a Gorgio woman.

In practice, as already indicated in chapter 5, a number of Gypsies do marry Gorgios and may continue to be accepted as full members of the community, although the status of the Gorgio spouse will always be ambiguous. From the information available on housed siblings, it seems that a Gypsy woman marrying a Gorgio man is more likely to drop her Gypsy connections, thus marrying out, whereas a Gypsy man marrying a Gorgio woman can more easily maintain Gypsy connections. Both among Gypsies and Gorgios, the husband is expected to demand from the wife submission and adaptation. Gorgio wives are easier to bring into a Gypsy community and less anomalous than Gorgio husbands.

Two of the four Gorgio husbands (one a West Indian) among the 15 Gypsy–Gorgio marriages remained permanently outside Gypsy male gatherings, and depended entirely on their wives for status. The third Gorgio husband Dick had been controlled and trained by his father-in-law, Joe, since the age of 15 and before marriage.

> 'Dick gets on with Joe 'cos Dick's a Gorgio and he listens to his father-in-law. Now Joe's other son-in-law [a Traveller] wouldn't stop alongside Joe. Joe used to take Dick out to work with him and show him everything about Calling, and making a chop [bargain].'

The fourth Gorgio husband self-consciously 'Gypsified' himself; he always wore a *dicklo* (a Gypsy kerchief), was respected for his ability with horses, wherever possible contended that his ancestors were Scottish Travellers, and adopted a prestigious name from that group.

The Gorgio wives who remained with the Traveller society could more easily be accepted, provided they endured ostracism and initial accusations of pollution. (Since fieldwork, three have left their husbands.) They could never lose the title 'Gorgio'. Some were never accepted by the husband's family:

> A middle aged Gorgio wife who married at 16 recalled: 'My mother-in-law insulted me, we didn't speak to each other and when she died I walked past the funeral in my brightest colours. My sister-in-law wouldn't speak to me either. The first time ever was at her husband's funeral two years ago. But I couldn't be friendly, not after all the things she said about me.'

This woman was respected among other Gypsies. Some Gorgio wives wielded considerable influence, especially when older. They exploited their literacy, at the same time observing every rule concerning dress, posture, washing and cooking, and proved themselves capable of earning a living in the Gypsy manner. If Gorgio wives could demonstrate they were better than Gypsies in this way, their husbands were considered justified in marrying them:

> 'He's married to a Gorgio woman. She lifts scrap and does

farm work. A good worker. I've seen her lifting a big sledge
hammer to a car. She's better than any Traveller.'

A minority of marriages with Gorgios is not merely a recent
phenomenon. Thompson found in the genealogical records of the
J.G.L.S. a number of Gypsy–Gorgio marriages before the 1920s: 6 out
of 50 in a Price genealogy, 8 out of 16 in a Wood genealogy (1926:11), 8
out of 44 in a Heron genealogy (1926:13). Unfortunately Thompson
was not concerned to discover whether the persons in these marriages
and their descendants continued to participate fully in a Gypsy community. More recently the Gypsy writer, Wood, has stated: 'The
Woods made a point of accepting the occasional Gorgio into the tribe –
but it had to be a very special type of Gorgio that fitted well into the
Romany way of life' (1973:2).

My evidence suggests that the general prohibition against marriage
with a Gorgio is a fundamental ideal, but unlike the Rom in Barvale,
California (Sutherland 1975:248), Gypsies in England permit a small
number of Gorgio–Gypsy marriages, provided the Gorgios repudiate
their origins and adopt Gypsy values.[2] Information on families in addition to those with whom I became closely acquainted also revealed a
preponderance of marriages between two Gypsies rather than between a Gorgio and a Gypsy. Thus ethnic endogamy was both the ideal
and the practice of the majority of travelling families who recognised
themselves as Gypsies.

(2) In so far as it is possible to demarcate groups of kin in a cognatic
system (see chapter 10), some exogamy is maintained where first
cousin marriage is prohibited. ('Cousin' refers to offspring of both
parents' siblings.) With a few exceptions in the research area this prohibition contrasts dramatically with information from Hall and Rivers
(1913) and that collected from the *J.G.L.S.* archives by Thompson
in the 1920s on Gypsies in Wales and some English regions. According
to Thompson, in the genealogies of earlier generations, more especially groups in Wales, on the Welsh border and in northern England,
in some cases first cousin marriages outnumbered others (1926:11).
One informant in Wales stated positively that first cousins were preferred to second (1926:10). Others stated that marriage with a 'name-
sake is specially desirable, or believe that it was once customary'
(1926:17). Thompson admits his material is inadequate on Gypsies in
three English counties, 'All of whom are said, or are vaguely known,
to have favoured first cousin unions' (1926:13). This preference cannot
be presumed, since a number may have married first cousins despite
the prohibition. Thompson reported that other groups, near my research area, 'do not seem to have favoured such unions', despite a few
examples (1926:16). It is impossible at this stage of research to make
generalisations about first cousin marriages beyond the area of this
field study.

Cases of first cousin marriage in the research area in the 1970s were disapproved of but, like the few Gorgio–Gypsy marriages, came to be tolerated in practice. In no case did it seem that first cousin marriage was a preferred category.

> 'You shouldn't because they're the same blood.'

> 'If you go to a priest and he finds out, he won't let first cousins marry.' (This is not true in Gorgio law.)

Criticism was made of a Gypsy group in another region: 'They nearly all marry their first cousins.' Comments were made about a couple in the research area,

> 'Nelly's frit 'cos she's married her first cousin. She lost one baby and she thinks the devils are gonna take the other ones away from her. She daren't be on her own.'

Nelly was very evasive to me in discussing why or whether first cousin marriage was prohibited, but spoke of the problems between her husband and his mother-in-law:

> 'My mother's always rowing with my husband. It's 'cos he speaks straight to her. He doesn't beat about like her other sons-in-law.'

Her husband was the son of her mother's sister who would normally be in the role of 'aunt', a more permissive role than mother-in-law.

Genealogical information could never be acquired in response to questioning and there was little discussion of ancestry. It was therefore difficult to confirm always whether or not certain spouses were in fact third if not second cousins, or in other ways distantly related, especially among the older couples. First cousin marriages were easier to discover both because of statements about parentage and because the Travellers were keen to express disapproval of such a match. Out of the 69 Gypsy families there were three first cousin marriages. A male offspring of one of the families has, since fieldwork, married his father's brother's daughter, to the disapproval of the group. First cousin marriage occurred least among the wealthier and mobile groups. The genealogy of other Gypsies related to those I encountered revealed the marriages of four sisters with four brothers who were their first cousins. These marriages were perhaps seen as more important for their sibling linkages than their cousin connections (see chapter 10). The brothers, in the example above, had been brought up in a house and their wives became housed after marriage. These families were no longer mobile and had reduced contact with other Gypsy groups. Similar examples among semi-sedentary families came to light after the main period of fieldwork.

(3) Marriage was also generally prohibited or disapproved between persons having a large age gap. This is consistent with Needham's observation that in cognatic systems, age is more important than category in marriage choices (1974:106). Marriage was permitted with a person technically of ego's parents' generation but of the same age range as the spouse. Gorgios were criticised for the practice of older men marrying younger women. Greater status was given to older men and women and this would be upset if their spouses were of a younger generation. When a marriage broke up, each spouse invariably sought another partner of a similar age. It was accepted that generally a man could be only slightly older than the woman.

(4) Sexual relations, as well as marriage, are predictably forbidden between members of the immediate family. Like Sutherland (1975:313), I found no word for 'incest'. Some Gorgio observers including social workers closely associated with Travellers remark that there is 'in-breeding' among Gypsies and that they all marry their 'relations'. Closer inspection reveals the contrary. Travellers refer to their cognates as 'my own', 'my relations' or 'delations': affines are not included, but referred to as 'my wife's/husband's relations'. Gorgios have mistakenly included cognates' affines in the term 'relations'. As already indicated by the paucity of first (and as likely second and third) cousin marriages, there were very few marriages between cognates. Many marriages among Travellers in this study were merely consistent with the prohibited categories. Nevertheless, as discussed in detail in chapter 10, a significant number of marriages were reinforcements of existing ties with the affines of ego's siblings or cousins.

The developmental cycle

After marriage a husband and wife form their separate trailer unit. Ideally and in practice, the couple may choose to ally themselves with either the wife's or the husband's kindred. The choice need never be permanent. However, some couples opted to reside regularly with only one set. Residence patterns were influenced also by the age of the parents and siblings. As more offspring from one family married and formed separate units and the parents became less mobile, married siblings would tend to travel and reside together, rather than with parents (see Okely 1975b:76 for examples).

The first child is usually born within a year or 18 months of marriage. Their absence is considered a great misfortune. Up to a certain point (e.g. six children under the age of 15), the number of children in a family did not seem to correspond with differences in wealth, occupations or travelling patterns. In later life at least, large families have positive advantages for both parents and offspring. Parents will have a greater number of close kin for assistance in old age. Adults will benefit from many siblings as potential allies, widely dispersed.

Since children are highly valued, they are never abandoned nor voluntarily handed over to Gorgios. Stories of Gypsy children forcibly taken into care in the past were recounted with great bitterness. Disapproval was directed towards people who voluntarily left their children to strangers, the practice being regarded as an attribute of Gorgios not Gypsies (for examples, see Okely 1975b:71). Children who lose their parents due to death or misfortune are fostered or adopted by kin or other Travellers who assume the title 'Mum' and 'Dad'. A few families were known to contain adopted children, separated from their original parents. Some of the adopted children came from Gorgio parents who had willingly handed them over to Gypsies; they were certainly not 'stolen' as in a popular belief about Gypsies. It seems that these children, if adopted very young, could be fully incorporated as Gypsies.

Separation and remarriage occur independently of Gorgio court processes, which are costly, delayed and specific about 'grounds for divorce', custody of children and division of property. Usually a Gypsy marriage ends precisely because one if not both spouses goes to live with someone else, who will be referred to as husband or wife. Children can go with either biological parent and be absorbed as the social offspring of the new parent. From his evidence in the 1920s Thompson also records that children resulting from unsuccessful marriages 'normally passed under the control of stepfathers; but they need not be pitied on that account, as there is no suggestion that they were treated less indulgently than their fellows' (1927:152-3).

Separation, sometimes referred to by Travellers as 'divorce' or 'revorce', was more frequent than suggested by the Ministry's claim that 'Desertion, separation and divorce are very rare: the traveller marries for life' (M.H.L.G. 1967:28). Already in the 1920s, Thompson had recorded evidence of temporary alliances (1927:152). Thompson also records: 'Among English Gypsies the dissolution of a marriage was a purely informal affair that left the parties free to wed again if they chose' (1927:157). In this study, out of 61 family trailer units, for whom evidence was available (and excluding the four Gorgio couples), 17 (28%) had at least one spouse who had experienced a previous marriage ending in divorce, while 44 (72%) contained no such spouse. Nevertheless, marriage as a permanent and monogamous union was the ideal (see also Thompson 1927:152).

Out of 73 trailer units (including four Gorgio couples), there were five widowed persons; one widower and four widows (table 15). Only three were living without the mutual support of another adult. There were others who lived as permanent residents on sites where Gorgio welfare was more easily obtainable. The proportion of widowed persons living alone seems to be considerably lower among Travellers in caravans than among the total housed population of England and Wales. It is likely that many other widowed Travellers moved into houses or became settled and less visible on non-Gypsy caravan sites or

159

on individual plots of land. Here offspring and other Travellers were expected to visit regularly and give assistance. Official Gypsy sites geared less to nomadic families and more to settlement may continue to attract the widowed and aged, as had occurred in the 1970s in the research area.

Education and childhood

The family or trailer unit is the primary means for the education of the next generation of Travellers and has many attributes which, for the wider society, are fulfilled by organisations external to the family; namely the school, college and place of work. No other group in the British Isles has maintained a similar independence. Only a minority of Gypsy adults in this study had ever attended school, and some of these for a few months only. The majority of Travellers were non-literate, as appears to be the case with Travellers elsewhere in the British Isles. Such facts continue to be a source of alarm and shame to Gorgios, though not necessarily to Travellers. The Plowden Report claimed that Gypsy children 'are probably the most severely deprived children in the country. Most of them do not even to go school and the potential abilities of those who do are stunted' (1967:59-60).

Fathers and daughters. *Evening Post-Echo Ltd.*

Although strategically useful in demands for assistance for Travellers, such a view is also extremely patronising, and devalues the Travellers' alternative skills and education. Later in the 1970s, a local authority official specialising in Gypsy education suggested that Gypsy children suffered from 'turbulence' because of their travelling life style. No social anthropologist nor a Traveller-Gypsy would make such a dangerous judgement of people with nomadic traditions.

Several national organisations were established in the late sixties and early seventies to encourage volunteers and local education authorities to arrange special teaching on the various sites or in schools. Some Travellers have made good use of some of these schemes. A number of children have attended school when living on a site but continuity was lost. One Traveller family in this study moved into a council house as their son approached school age because they wanted him to acquire basic literacy. This example shows that there is indeed a demand for schooling among some Travellers and especially if it does not entail major compromises with their mobile self-employed way of life.

It is not my concern here to discuss the Gypsy children's experience of schooling, nor to review the attempts to provide them with a more Gorgio education. There is a growing body of literature on this subject (e.g. Reiss 1975). I am more concerned with exploring a view of Gypsy children from within the group. Too often social workers, teachers and students have approached Gypsy children in a thoroughly ethnocentric way, and attempted to impose their own values. Even those who pay lip service to the notion of a Gypsy 'culture' presume that the ideal education for Gypsy children should be a preparation for wage-labour. One 'expert' suggested that a Gypsy girl should be given the opportunity to become an 'air hostess', as if this was a privileged position. Others have naively argued that Gypsies need literacy in order to read road signs, as if the nomadic group needs such directions! During fieldwork I observed how tolerant the Travellers were towards the Gorgio well-wishers who came to teach Gypsy children how to 'free play' with such materials as water, flour and plasticine. Some Travellers were healthily cynical about some of the people who called for more public intervention. Of one education officer who rarely visited the sites but presented himself as an expert it was said: 'It's like he's walking down a long dark tunnel. All he can see is a light at the end which says "O.B.E."'.'

Travellers recognised that a place on a site or the offer of a council house meant greater pressure to send their children to school. Resentment was sometimes voiced:

> 'They say that you've got to send the kids to school on these sites. I don't want my child going any more. I don't want her to have one of those jobs pushing a pen in an office, what's the good of that to my girl?'

161

One family where both spouses were illiterate and of the highest economic status refused to send their sons to school while staying on a temporary site for several months. They stated they did not want their children brought up in a way which risked losing them.

On sites some of the Travellers attempted to evade schooling. When I first met one mother camping on a by-pass she gave me the predictable statements about wanting her daughters in school, but that evening another Traveller said of her:

'Aunt Susy's kids were the worst when they were on the site. When the school bus arrived they'd be hiding up in the trailer or behind the wash house. They'd never go to school. That's a lot of talk.'

Those children who went to school sometimes had unfavourable experiences. Billy told me of his:

'I didn't like that school ... The boys pointed at my trousers and said "Look at that gypo with baggy trousers" ... my trousers weren't baggy 'cos I know me mam wouldn't buy me trousers what's baggy ... and they said we eat hedgehogs and cats.'

Even when Travellers express a desire for literacy and numeracy, few are interested in secondary education. Among those who had attended school almost none had attended after eleven or twelve. In commenting on university education most Travellers disliked the idea of their children being away from home: 'I wouldn't let my children live away from me.' Sometimes a completely negative attitude to literacy burst out. A 14 year old girl picked up a magazine in my trailer and without any apparent provocation tore it to shreds exclaiming 'Only Gorgios read!'

The Travellers recognise an alternative education both in form and content (see also chapter 4). Unlike the classroom where 20 or 30 children are isolated in a single age group and with one adult as teacher, the learning context for Traveller children is most often on the basis of one adult per child; a parent or relative. Alternatively, children learn from others of all ages on their changing encampments. Learning is by direct example and practice in circumstances similar to those they will experience as adults. From an early age boys and girls go out to work with their parents. A mother proudly described the progress of her eight-year old boy:

'I take Andrew with me *so he learns what to say*. He already knows. We called on a woman who had a couple of car batteries. She wouldn't part with them. She said she'd ask her husband when he got home; they always say that. But Andrew said, "I'm sure you don't want them messing up your garage.

It'd be better if we took them away." Then Andrew looked up at her, using his eyes. The woman said "Oh, I can't refuse the little boy when he looks at me with his lovely eyes." She gave him the batteries. When we got into the motor Andrew said "Never mind about me eyes Mum, you've got your batteries."'

Girls rather than boys go out hawking with their mothers and to watch fortune telling. Regular observation is a necessary part of the training, according to the Travellers, who say that if deprived of this experience as a child, an adult could never become skilled.

Young children soon learn to distinguish the different types of metal, for example, non-ferrous from ferrous. When outside the camp they retrieve scrap from ditches, dumps and rubbish skips. Since economic activities are carried on inside the camp, the children also learn at home, by assisting in scrap breaking, rag sorting or making wax flowers. Boys sit at the wheels of vehicles and master the elementary skills of driving at 12, before they can go out on the highway. Very young children are encouraged to handle and understand money. They have their own possessions, poultry or ponies which only they have the right to sell. They bargain and 'chop' (exchange) possessions and earn money independently.

In this context, the complaint by liberal educationalists (see Plowden 1967) that Gypsy children possess few 'toys' is meaningless. There is not the same division between work and play since children are directly involved with adult work where again there is not a rigid work–leisure distinction as in a wage-labour economy. In fact I did observe dolls, dinky cars, bikes and carts, but these did not long survive. Some were 'broken up' in imitation of their parents' scrap breaking. Moreover, like other nomads, Travellers learn to avoid accumulation of goods and chattels. Like their parents, the children made creative use of any available objects rather than things tailor-made. They had a variety of inventive games often connected with travelling and reflecting the pre-occupations of their society. But these activities have been largely missed by outsiders looking for replicas of their own educational priorities.

Any kind of participation is considered a learning process:

> A mother said of her four year old daughter: 'She's going to be a Traveller and marry one. You can tell. She likes messing around with the spanners and pieces when her father's mending the motors. She likes the dirt. I can't keep *her* clean.' The mother appeared pleased with her daughter's curiosity and made no attempt to thwart it.
>
> A Gorgio father living on the same encampment showed a contrasting attitude to his child's participation in adult work and mechanics: while examining a car engine with some Travellers, he was approached by his five year old son; 'Go

away Pete', the father said. 'You'll get dirty here.' The child obeyed.

Both inside and outside the camp, therefore, Traveller children are directly involved in the process of production; something usually denied to children in the larger society and condemned as 'exploitation'. Certainly Gypsy children are an important part of the labour force in farm work.

> When I went potato picking, wherever possible, families brought their children, gave them each a basket and carefully instructed them in the most efficient method. Of the families where I could discover details of the distribution of the earnings, children were given only a fraction which they could spend as they pleased. The remainder was retained by the adults.

Gorgios who marry into the community have more self-consciously to acquire the relatively unfamiliar Traveller craft at a later age. A 17 year old Gorgio was taken over by his Traveller wife's father, who said, 'I took him everywhere with me. I taught him all he knows.' Just as outsiders examining Travellers' skills in their terms describe them as 'unskilled', so Travellers assess Gorgios in that way.

Relations with outsiders

In some economic spheres the *chavies* (children) are especially advantageous. The presence of children for Calling at houses makes the Gypsy adult, male or female, less menacing to the potential Gorgio customer. Seen as harmless 'innocents' by Gorgios, Traveller children are also important in external political relations. Anyone approaching a Gypsy camp is first greeted by the *chavies* asking every question their parents cannot voice. During an exchange between Gorgio officials, children will listen in, and report details back to the parents. Well-meaning student teachers never find problems of access; their main concern is how not to be mobbed by the *chavies*, whose behaviour may have the desired effect of driving away unwanted visitors. The parents only intervene after desperate requests from the visitors and even then their reprimands are unconvincing. Children are told not to be 'brazen', but this is secretly a quality to be admired in dealing with Gorgios. Whether as public nuisances, 'disturbers of the peace', felons or accessories, the *chavies* are immune from Gorgio law. Whereas Gypsy adults, especially men, retreat from all cameras, children can be photographed without danger. They have no criminal identity. It is significant that the Ministry chose for the cover of its 1967 report a montage photograph of smiling and dishevelled Gypsy children.

The trailer unit, spouses and children

Traveller children are both immunised and politicised in their contact with Gorgios. Deemed innocent, in fact they perceive and learn their boundaries from infancy. The words 'Gorgio' and 'Gypsy' are learnt soon after 'dad' and 'mam'. A two and a half year old boy was asked by his mother, 'Who are you?' He replied 'I'm a Gypsy' to the delight of the Travellers present. Not kept in ignorance of public events, children are witnesses and actors. Evictions, police visits and arrests cannot be and are not shielded from children (see chapter 3).

> Louise aged eight made Sanie aged six lie down on a bunk-bed and covered her with a blanket. Louise acted her 'mum', and then got into bed with her. Suddenly she sits up startled: 'The *gavvers* (police) are coming!' She pretends to look at them through the curtains. 'They'll take us away ... I'd better go ... No, they won't take you my darling, they'll only take your mum.'

Social anthropologists have sometimes suggested that children are a valuable source of information. This was rarely the case with Gypsy children, who instead reported the outsiders' questions and anything else to their parents who had instructed them to conceal information from Gorgios and Gypsy neighbours. Predictably, such reticence has been interpreted by Gorgio educationalists as 'poor verbal ability' (M.H.L.G.1967:30). The following anecdote recorded by Borrow (1874) is recounted by Gypsies today (for example, Clifford Lee) as personal experience: 'We'd be in a crowd and my mother would say "Come away from the nice lady. Don't bother the dear lady. *Mong, chavo, mong!*" That was Romany and it meant "Beg boy, beg!"' (McDowell 1970:14). The child receives two conflicting orders and knows which to obey: the one in Romany. The child observes the mother's deception and acts as her accomplice. The implicit dualism in this behaviour is the opposite to the 'double bind' (Bateson 1973: 178-9).

Internal relations

In relations between Travellers, children are also witnesses and participants: few subjects and events are concealed from them. Parental quarrels, financial problems, disputes and fights with neighbours are played out before them. Armed with this information, children may assume an active role, for example, by playing one family against another where there is latent conflict.

> Ted, aged 11, was aware that his mother's brother's wife resented his mother's friendship with a Gorgio neighbour. He informed the Gorgio that his aunt had called her a 'Scotch bastard'. The Gorgio woman immediately walked over to

Ted's aunt and the two women beat each other up, watched by the whole camp, including Ted.

Lucie, aged 10, secretly telephoned some relatives of her father to report a series of insults allegedly made by her father. The relatives sent messages of equal venom via both Lucie and Travellers in the area. After several 'phone calls and growing threats of a big punch up, the two families discovered Lucie's role and the tension was diffused.

Older children assume adult responsibility for younger siblings when their parents leave the camp. It is then also their duty to look after the trailer. Girls assist in cleaning and cooking and, in emergencies, the boys assist, just as they will be expected to as men; for instance, Ted from the example above cooked meals for the family before and after his mother returned from hospital after childbirth. When inside the confined space of the trailer, children are expected to sit quietly, packed in rows listening to and participating in the adults' conversations. Delicate china, often within reach of tiny hands, is never broken, lace blinds and soft furnishings are untampered, and no finger-prints smudge the long mirrors. This contrasts with the more boisterous activities outside the trailer where the *chavies* are allowed to range within sight of the camp, but no further, unless with an adult. To this extent child–adult boundaries are expressed in space. So long as the child is in sight of a Gypsy adult he or she is allowed free run of Gorgio territory.

Activities presumed by Gorgios to be merely childish things may be a preparation for adulthood:

Several children had catapults and aimed shots at the council huts. A council worker appealed to the parents to discipline their offspring. All denied that *their* children even possessed such 'bad things'. Then Billy aged four was caught with his catapult by the Gorgio. He was punished, not for possession, but for being discovered. A few weeks later I watched the children's fathers practising with their giant catapults (which they normally use for killing pheasant).

Learning to fight is also part of learning to be a Gypsy both for girls and boys. I heard a mother repeatedly chant the following maxim to her seven year old daughter, after the girl had been hurt by another:

'Don't throw stones, stripe 'em up then they won't come back no more. If you can't hit 'em, kick 'em; if you can't kick 'em, pull their hair, if you can't pull their hair, pinch 'em, if you can't pinch 'em, bite 'em; if you can't do that you're bloody useless. You'd better lay down and take your punishment.'

She said her own mother used to tell her that.

Jimboy aged nine returned from school with blood on his nose and clothes. A boy had called him 'Gypsy' and Jimboy hit him so hard he reeled in the road. Any tentative suggestions by myself that he ignore the Gorgio was opposed by his father Raymond: 'He's got to learn to fight. If he didn't fight back the boys 'ud think he's a mug ... Did you win? ... you have a good fight with him. You finish him off.' The next morning Jimboy didn't want to go to school. His father showed him 20p which would be his if he fought the boy and won the fight. Jimboy didn't get his 20p because he said the boy wouldn't come out and fight.

The Traveller children's presence at funeral rites and acquaintance with death also illustrate their first hand involvement in adult society.

The dead man's sons and daughters aged between one and seven travelled in the funeral cars to the churchyard with their mother, grandfather, aunts and uncles, all sobbing and wailing as is customary. No attempt was made to quieten or comfort the children. They stood at the graveside as their father's coffin was lowered. Earlier they had seen his corpse laid out in the trailer. Other children peered into the grave and threw in pieces of earth.

Innocence a protection

The single topic from which Gypsy children are permanently excluded in adult conversation concerns sex and reproduction. Parents assert that their offspring remain ignorant of every aspect. An Irish Traveller writing about the Travellers' objection to lessons on sex and reproduction in schools recognised the ritual status of the public silence: 'It's like a religious saga' (Connors 1972:11). In practice children, including adolescents, exchange information among themselves They understand that such knowledge should never be brought into the public adult sphere. Innocence is widely if not universally associated with children, but its form varies in each society. Ideally children in the dominant Gorgio society are divorced from the wider economic and political process. By contrast, in Gorgio child-centred schools there is formal instruction in sex and reproduction. Whereas Gypsy children are encouraged from an early age to share the economic and political experience of adults, in sexual matters there is a formal ban on all such information.

The relationship between sexuality, pollution taboos and the ethnic boundary which is found in the case of Gypsy women (see chapter 11), can be contrasted with that of Gypsy children. Gypsy women are made aware of the dangers of their sexuality through pollution taboos which control their relations both with Gypsy and Gorgio men. They must protect the ethnic purity of their group. Gypsy children, however, should be made unaware of sex and their own sexuality. At the same time, after early infancy, they are incapable of polluting and are seemingly less vulnerable to pollution from Gorgios (see chapter 6). For example, Gypsy children can accept Gorgio cooked food more freely than adults, and are treated in hospital with less risk. Gypsy children are 'innocent' mediators between Gypsies and Gorgios, but they must not be in contact with Gorgios, unless within sight of Gypsy adults. (Some exception has been made for the controlled context of occasional schooling.) The absence of elaborate internalised pollution taboos for children is consistent with their attributed bodily innocence, and acts as a reminder to their parents of their vulnerability.

The reinforcement of children's innocence is not explicable solely as a need for protection in terms of relations within the family unit and trailer. The children's innocence requires protection from the far greater threat beyond the ethnic boundary where Gorgios are seen as part of 'nature' as opposed to Gypsy 'culture', and are attributed by Gypsies with all the crimes they consider most heinous and perverted. While the danger for Gypsy women is that they might conceive a Gorgio or 'half-caste' child, the danger for Gypsy parents is that their 'pure-blooded' children, the next generation already born, might be stolen by Gorgios before becoming fully Gypsy and able to defend themselves as such. The most frequent accusations made against Gorgios are that they kidnap, murder or 'interfere' with children. Gypsy children are not specifically told about assault, but are terrorised by stories of Gorgio child-thieves – strange men with 'long beards and brief cases'. Thus Gypsy children are kept within Gypsy space, and they learn to associate Gorgios with terrifying, predatory instincts. For the parents, the specifically sexual innocence and vulnerability of their children symbolises their children's total vulnerability to Gorgio violation and control from which they must be preserved.

On the other side of the ethnic boundary, Gorgios also see Gypsies as part of 'nature', and children as especially 'wild' and innocent. It is the Gypsy children who can most effectively appeal to the Gorgios' idea of common humanity, so energies and money are devoted to educating, 'taming', assimilating or taking Gypsy children 'into care', before they are lost to Gypsy adulthood. Hence the Travellers' very real fear of Gorgio authorities taking custody of their children. Since Gypsies are seen as part of 'nature' by Gorgios, Gypsies are also attributed with the crime of child stealing. The Gorgio fear is that Gorgio children in turn, innocent and vulnerable, might be stolen before being schooled and civilised into Gorgio culture, a fear recognised in the familiar verse:

> My mother said I never should
> Play with the Gypsies in the wood.

The trailer unit, spouses and children

Gypsies also see Gorgio children as innocent and, like the Gorgios in their attitude to Gypsy children, they respond to them favourably, precisely because they have not yet been lost to Gorgio adulthood.

10 Group relations and personal relatives

Nations and leaders

The basic ideological division between Gypsy and Gorgio has national political significance in limited spheres: the common observances at national fairs and the solidarity in a crisis when a cross section of families are directly threatened by Gorgio authorities. In a conflict over encampment and land use, for instance, Travellers are expected to unite against Gorgios. But both here and in other contexts, Travellers may also be in direct competition with each other.

As is admitted by the Gorgio members and others of the Gypsy Council founded in 1966 (Acton 1974:163-85, 235-40), Travellers in England have only a vague sense of national identity and do not attach this to a common territory. The Gypsies encountered in this study did not appear to see themselves as part of an international movement, although they were always interested to hear about Gypsies elsewhere in the world.

The former Secretary of the Gypsy Council, Gratton Puxon, a Gorgio, supported the idea of a Gypsy homeland called *Romanestan*, but given the Gypsies' special place in relation to a larger economy this seems unrealistic. When Puxon argued in *New Society* (6 Dec. 1973) for the rights of free entry into Britain of Gypsies from the E.E.C., the Gypsy Chairman and Gypsy General Secretary of the Romany Guild replied with strong objections (*New Society*, 13 Dec. 1973).[1]

There are no political units such as the three or four 'nations' (*natsyia*) of Rom found in North America (Sutherland 1975:180, 184-8) and elsewhere in Europe (Yoors 1967:134-5), i.e. the Kalderash, Machwaya, Churara and Lowara. The British Gypsies or Travellers are relatively isolated compared to Gypsies ranging over the potentially wider travelling area of either the American or European continent. In south-east England a number of families referred to themselves as 'Ludari'. Their parents had migrated to England between the wars, and some had married into English groups. In the 1970s the title referred only to a small cluster of kindred. This loss of identification with a *natsyia* category is likely to have been the case with any Rom who migrated to the British Isles. Alternative divisions among Gypsies or Travellers in the British Isles are associated with the four national boundaries of the larger Gorgio society: Ireland, Scotland, Wales and

England. When there is movement between these areas, national identity becomes more apparent.

Since the late 1960s, and especially after official site provision, the state and its representatives have sought Gypsy representatives and 'leaders' with whom they could negotiate, in order to minimise confrontations and to predict, if not control, the Gypsies' movements. In the 1970s a number of Gypsy organisations emerged in addition to the Gypsy Council: the Association of Travelling People, the Romany Guild, the Southern Gypsy Council, and the Association of Gypsy and Romany Organisations. All competed for national and local government recognition and assistance. Some have been very effective in arguing the Travellers' case on television and radio. Earlier, this somewhat bureaucratic development in Gypsy leadership was interpreted as part of a revolutionary uprising of Rom throughout Europe (Kenrick and Puxon 1972:214).

The Gypsy Council and Romany Guild had secretaries of Gypsy descent in the late 1970s and were recognised and grant-aided by the Department of the Environment. They acted as useful spokesmen and negotiators. Earlier, in 1972 representatives from the Gypsy Council, some Gorgio, some Gypsy, had agreed for the first time to designation under the 1968 Act in four areas. Their approval was given the appropriate publicity by the D.O.E. *(Guardian,* 3 June 1972). Months later the Gypsy Council decided to oppose designation in principle. But the political impact was lost.

Among Travellers in this study there appeared to be little or no formalised system of individual leadership, with neither hereditary offices nor a concentration of power in a single person. Deference was given to age, but did not guarantee authority. One or two persons, unrelated to the politically powerful families in the area, claimed the existence of 'elders' who allegedly held final authority among all groups, and also intimated 'there are things we can never tell you'. Wood refers to his grandmother as 'the elder of the tribe' (1973:26). But many denied the existence of such a formal office of 'elder'.

My evidence suggests that older persons, sometimes given the deferential title 'elder', are indeed consulted on occasions and may meet informally with similar persons in crises where a dispute is not resolved by force. Their statements may be advice not law. These discussions may be comparable to the *diwano* (a group of adults convened to discuss a matter publicly) recorded by Sutherland in California (1975:131). But there seems to be no equivalent formal organisation such as the *kris romani*, a formal trial by a council of elders who adjudicate and are given the authority to decide on specific fines and periods of banishment (Sutherland 1975:132).

More significant politically than 'elders' are those individuals who enjoy a degree of charismatic authority based on abilities like bargaining or fighting. Other individuals with technical skills were made use

171

of, but their authority not extended. The Gypsies' travelling patterns and economy neither demand nor facilitate concentration of power nor fixed leadership. If one individual attempted to dominate others beyond a certain limit, he would risk their departure to another locality and other allies. Charismatic leadership without sanctions can only be sustained by voluntary followers. One Traveller ridiculed the deference given by some Gorgios to a Gypsy 'leader':

> 'The only leader of the Gypsies is the man who takes his coat off at Stowe Fair. If any Traveller dared say he was leader, there'd be a line of men all the way to London ready to take him on. Before he said he was "King of the Gypsies", he'd have to get through that lot!'

In the research area, the authorities found no leaders nor representatives, even for small numbers of families in the locality. Travellers rarely vested authority in a few individuals to make agreements with outsiders on their behalf. Some local authorities have learnt this to their cost.

Cognatic kinship and political clusters

The Travellers in this study have a cognatic system of kinship whereby an individual can claim membership of both his or her father's and mother's kindred. Each Gypsy had ideally a core of close cognates forming exogamous limits for ego and to whom, after the members of his or her natal family, obligations are morally paramount, although not always politically expedient.

There is an additional range of options open to adults. After marriage, both spouses retain their original kin connections, so the couple can choose to associate with members of either the husband's or wife's kindred, often alternating between the two. Residence has been used by anthropologists as an important defining factor in kinship affiliation. This factor is more complex among Travellers in this study. Residence is neither virilocal nor uxorilocal. Each family may camp alongside the husband's parents and members of his kindred, then later alongside the wife's parents and/or members of her kindred. At other times, the family may camp alone or alongside other Travellers where there are neither cognatic nor affinal connections. A Gypsy couple do not have to make a once and for all decision. Each family retains a pool of kindred on both the husband's and wife's side from whom they can select neighbours, travelling companions, work partners or collaborators, helpers and allies.

There can be no fixed nor clearly demarcated groups formed from the interlocking kindreds of parents and spouses. But numbers of families tend to form political clusters with a history of association: regular visiting where possible, monopolies of camping land against rival Travellers, shared encampments, economic cooperation and mutual aid. These clusters may join together in disputes and offer assistance, possibly with physical force. The political units within the travelling society are not necessarily composed just of an extended family (contrary to Acton's claim, 1974:58), nor of close cognates, nor do they necessarily reflect the husband's cognatic links. A married couple may find it strategically preferable to associate either more frequently with or only with some of the wife's cognates. The word 'cluster' rather than 'extended family' better describes the political processes, as membership is flexible and depends on circumstances. Sometimes the cluster includes affines and cousins and excludes some siblings. By contrast, the exogamous unit for each person is not flexible. Close associations occasionally develop between families where there are only affinal links and no cognatic connection with either spouse. This may occur even when other cognates are travelling in the locality. A cluster of families may be formed therefore by individual choices which do not necessarily reflect the proximity of kindred to ego. Cognatic kinship, however, remains the fundamental means for association, followed by affinal links.

Naming

Travellers use 'surnames' to accentuate their associations with selective kindred. Contrary to the Gorgio legal practice, an individual does not automatically assume the surname of his or her father, nor does a wife necessarily assume the surname of her husband. A woman may use her mother's 'surname', rejecting both that of her father and husband, especially where there are political advantages. The name may also be changed, depending on which area the family is travelling in. The 'surnames' may be an indicator of political clusters, but ambiguous because a name might refer to all the close cognates of one or more prominent individuals or it may refer to a select number of cognates and associates in an active political cluster. One or two Travellers encountered in this study and Wood (1973:8) have used the word 'tribe' in connection with some of these 'surnames', but its referents are very flexible and cannot denote discrete groups. The word has been variously used to refer either to an extensive kindred, or to a select number of cognates who choose to associate with each other in, for instance, a major dispute. The word 'tribe' as used by these Travellers is possibly synonymous with a kindred which has flexible limits.

A particular name like Lee, Cooper or Smith may be found inter-regionally among several groups who trace neither actual nor mythical cognatic links. Other 'surnames' appear to be more regionally specific (see Okely 1977:166). In order to protect the identity of Travellers I have had to disguise or exclude from this study references to many names. If Travellers want to be more specific about a group of close cognates, e.g. extended families of three to four generations, they may use the first name, together sometimes with the 'surname' of an older male or female relative, or a prominent brother as follows: 'Ben's lot' or 'Dolly Smith's lot'. Theoretically, this can include the individual's offspring and spouses, grand-children and offspring, siblings and spouses, and nephews and nieces. In practice, it refers to the families from this potential pool who live up to their obligations as close cognates. But this means of grouping does not necessarily coincide with a political cluster, which may include more distant kindred and affines.

One important limit or edge to ego's kindred is his or her exogamous unit which includes: members of the nuclear family, parents' siblings, first if not second cousins, and siblings' offsprings. In practice, the total number of these close cognates rarely come together or act as a political unit; they merely provide the basic core from whom ideally a person can summon assistance, to whom obligations are paramount, and who one may not marry. All persons within this exogamous unit rarely assume the same 'surname'. When a Traveller talks of 'my relations' or 'delations', 'my own' or 'your own', he or she is usually referring to this exogamous core of cognates.

This grouping of persons is often reflected in the first names. Offspring, usually the eldest son and daughter of a couple, are given the first names of their parents. The names will continue through to grand-children, so there may be three if not four direct descendants with the same first name. These are distinguished in various ways, for example, by diminutives like 'Johna', for the son of 'John'. Names for the other offspring are usually drawn from the siblings of the parents. Again, ways must be found to discriminate between individuals. Thus a grandmother called Rosie is referred to as 'Granny Cooper', her daughter is referred to as 'Rosie', another daughter's daughter is referred to as 'Little Rosie', and the daughter of 'Little Rosie' is known as 'Little Rosie's Rosie'.[2] Other names may also be given, such as those of honoured affines, e.g. one man without brothers named his second son after his sister's husband. Obviously the same names may be found in several unrelated groups.

In addition to conventional first names, the Travellers use 'nicknames' to distinguish offspring from parents or parents' siblings, e.g. 'cross-eyed John' (see Okely 1977:168). These nicknames are sometimes duplicated or inherited, but when paired with a spouse, e.g. 'Spider and Brother', or associated with a parent, e.g. Mary's Cowie, there is no confusion. These first names, nicknames and couplings with spouse or parent indicate the continuity of identity within the cognatic system where 'surnames' are flexible. Identification without single, fixed surnames depends on an intimate knowledge of genealogies which Gorgios do not possess. The names which Travellers may offer for Gorgio birth, marriage and death certificates do not reflect their cognatic identity, nor do they reveal that an individual is merely one piece in a genealogical jigsaw. A surname may be selected at one time by a Gypsy either for internal political expediency to denote current allegiance, or to confuse Gorgios.

Some of the 'surnames' or 'tribal' names have a long tradition in Gorgio if not Gypsy history. Some have been taken up by Gorgios as an indication of 'real Romany blood', hence their use by Gypsy fortune tellers at the Derby and at seaside booths, e.g. 'Gypsy Rose Lee'. When first meeting Gorgios, Gypsies may indiscriminately adopt such names. I found little evidence of any internal political or ritual superiority among groups using the surnames popular in Gorgio folklore. I found both in this field study and in the *Journal of the Gypsy Lore Society* several Gypsy names rarely associated with the popular Gorgio stereotypes (see Thompson 1923b:114-26, Hoyland 1816:165, Smart and Crofton 1875:55 and Okely 1977:169-70). Some of these names may be found inter-regionally and in historical records, and have acquired currency in the Gorgio Gypsiologists' categories of 'real Romanies', which may in turn have stimulated greater sophistication in an individual's claim to authenticity. Some Travellers may have publicly adopted 'appropriate' surnames more for the benefit of Gorgios than as a mythical charter for political superiority recognised by contemporary Travellers, whose internal political reputation rests on other factors. Some families used names found neither in Gorgio records nor apparently in other regions. But they could just as easily attain local power and prestige, and were accepted as suitable marriage partners by others with more 'traditional' names. Immediate ancestry and cognatic and affinal connections with living persons seemed more important than links with the prestigious genealogies recorded by Gorgios of the Gypsy Lore Society.

Marriage links and patterns

In this study at least there were very few marriage links between persons cognatically related. Yet Acton has claimed: 'In England ... many Gypsies show ... an expressed preference for close-kin marriages' (1974:55). Instead, marriage is used to form alliances with persons where there is *no* cognatic connection. Thus the range of potential allies over a wide area is increased. Different clusters of cognates were linked by multiple ties of marriage.

Chapter 9 indicated certain prohibited categories for marriage. Although there were no prescriptions other than the ideal ethnic endogamy, a detailed examination in this study revealed some regular patterns, namely the practice of two or more brothers marrying two or more sisters. These links might also be cemented for instance by a first cousin of the brothers marrying one of the sisters (see figure 1). Such marriages were not seen as merely coincidental, but systematic. One Traveller said: 'The A—s used to marry the D—s; now they're

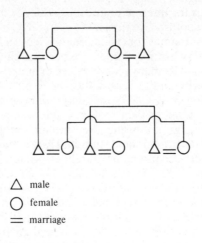

△ male
○ female
═ marriage

1   Types of marriage links.

marrying the C—s.' Two known links between the first groups were two brothers marrying two sisters. Figure 2a and 2b are examples of marriage links encountered in fieldwork. Since there was only a small number of cases of a brother and sister marrying a sister and brother, the more usual alliances could not be called sister exchange, but perhaps instead sibling exchange.

In the 1920s, Thompson also found many examples of sibling exchange, and again a greater number of brothers from one family marrying sisters from another, as opposed to a brother and sister from one family marrying a sister and brother from another. He finds 57 examples of marriage between two (or more) brothers to two (or more) sisters, or a brother and a sister to a sister and brother. Omitting 11 first cousins and 6 'remote' cousins, he finds 33 marriages between two (or more) brothers and two (or more) sisters as against 7 only of a brother and sister to a sister and a brother (1926:26). In California, Sutherland records 'frequent mentions in the literature and newspapers of double weddings between two families (sister exchange)' (1975:212). She does not discuss the alternative exchange of mixed siblings which is not sister exchange. Elsewhere, Maybury-Lewis' work on the Akwé-Shavante in South America records: 'The best marriages, from a Shavante point of view, are those which unite a group of brothers with a group of sisters. In this way patrilineages are not broken up through the rule of post-marital residence' (1974:88). By contrast obviously residence is flexible among the Gypsies, but mixed

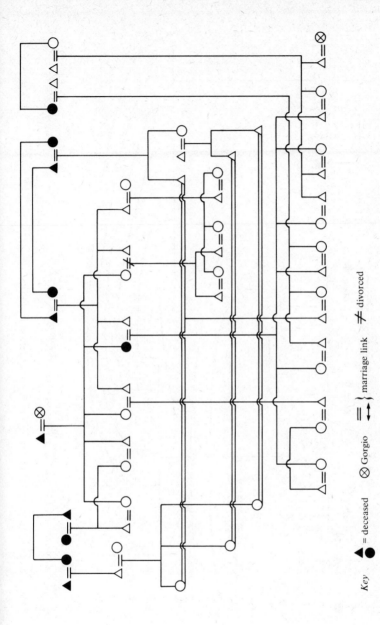

Key ▲● = deceased   ⊗ Gorgio $\substack{= \\ \longleftrightarrow}$ } marriage link   ≠ divorced

2a   Examples of marriage links.

177

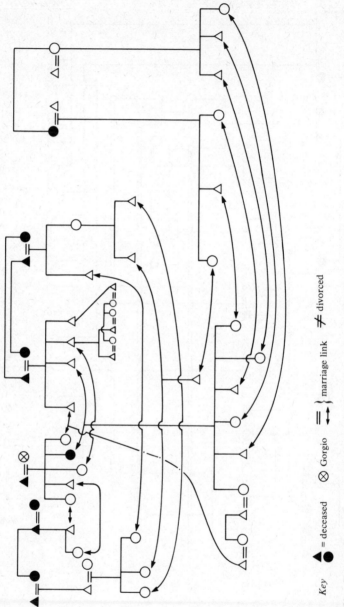

Key   ▲● = deceased   ⊗ Gorgio $\equiv \atop \longleftrightarrow$ } marriage link   ≠ divorced

2b   Example of marriage links, in a different representation from figure 2a.

sibling exchange may be seen to strengthen groups of brothers (as well as groups of sisters).

In the case where several brothers marry several sisters, cooperation between siblings is enhanced. Siblings are not separated by the conflicting and varied allegiances of their spouses, since these are all siblings, who in turn are not inevitably separated by marriage. Given the sexual division of labour, it might be supposed that the respective siblings would form regular work partnerships. This was not borne out in practice. The benefits of these marriage links, as well as those between sets of mixed siblings, emerged in less formal economic and financial assistance, and in a broader political context, which included the resolution of disputes and the choice of associates for the monopoly of camping land.

Conflict is neutralised between groups of families where there are affinal links; the more links the better. In confrontations with other groups where there was no inter-marriage, the affinally linked families would tend to align together. Similar advantages accrue where there might be only one marriage link, but cooperation could be more precarious. Sibling exchange not only expands links with non-cognates, but also tightens and draws boundaries within a seemingly unlimited choice for possible allies. One marriage is followed by others which reinforce the first. Then a potential group exists in a set of siblings united by the marriage ties they have in common. Thus within this cognatic system, sibling links (and sometimes first cousin links as 'honorary' siblings) were reinforced by spouses.

Marriage between sets of siblings cannot be described as sister exchange because, more often, the pattern was brothers from one family marrying sisters from another. In the next generation, the wife givers did not become wife receivers; the offspring would be first cousins, a prohibited category. Marriage was not necessary to create links with cognates. Marriage between cousins would reduce links with other potential allies. For a nomadic group, access to a wide territory, not land ownership, is essential and is assisted by marriage links with non-cognates, i.e. limited exogamy. This contrasts with a sedentary agricultural group dependent on specific land holdings and whose inheritance is often protected by close kin marriage, i.e. endogamy. For groups of Travellers, the dilemma is whether to create a new marriage link with strangers, or whether to consolidate ties with the existing affines of ego's siblings and other close cognates.

By contrast, marriage with a Gorgio rarely brought allies. The Gorgio spouse invariably severed links with his or her cognates who were usually housed. On the positive side for the Gypsy spouse, a Gorgio would be virtually incorporated and thus present no rival loyalties.

Marriage links also reflected and reinforced the different levels of wealth among families. Although they sometimes linked persons from families of lower economic status with those of medium economic status, or linked persons from families of the higher economic status to those of medium status, there were no examples of marriages linking persons of the lowest to the highest status. Where spouses came from families of differing wealth, however slight, their future circumstances depended partly on which cluster of cognates they chose to associate with.

Political clusters: some characteristics

Political clusters of Gypsy families from the wider interlocking kindreds were enhanced by a number of factors: (1) territorial proximity, (2) experiences of shared encampments at various times, and (3) economic cooperation. Some clusters were able to monopolise camping land to the exclusion of others. Clusters of families both depended on and expressed their mutual support in disputes with other Gypsies.

(1) Territorial proximity was one limiting factor. The limits of territory will vary according to the mobility and travelling patterns of each family trailer unit.[3] Links with kindred beyond the travelling area of a family will become dormant, but can be revived (see Okely 1977:171). Those families who travelled beyond several counties and inter-regionally were able to maintain contact with greater numbers. They were also able to spread their nets wider in marriage partners. On the other hand, families who travelled only within a limited number of counties might find their kindred more concentrated, due also to the latter's restricted travelling patterns. Territorial proximity facilitated contact and cooperation.

Families could also benefit from political solidarity against other Travellers by reserving and monopolising land. This was especially the case where harassment and evictions by Gorgios were least likely, where work opportunities in the vicinity most lucrative. The political clusters most successful in achieving this boasted superior fighters and fierce reputations, and were invariably among the wealthiest. They also had the resources to threaten or 'bribe' poorer families to leave, and the greater mobility. They could therefore more easily incur fines or escape Gorgio authorities by leaving the region. Other families who, either by misfortune or choice, lacked political standing, preferred to surrender territory to the stronger families. Invariably they were of lower or medium economic status, with fewer cash reserves, poor vehicles and a limited travelling range. For them, only a major crisis would compel flight from the region.

The stronger, wealthier families were more able to monopolise local authority sites if they so wished. When a Gorgio official tried to persuade some families without political muscle to move off the roadside onto a vacant council pitch, they often preferred police harassment to the greater threat from politically dominant families who might resent them occupying the site. Tenants learnt how to manipulate the Gorgio wardens, so that sites often contained clusters of allied families. Comparative strangers, whatever their wealth, were excluded where they lacked available allies:

> Nathan (who called himself a 'Welsh Romany') travelled intermittently through the area, accompanied by his aged parents and married son who would drive back and forth, towing his own and his grandparents' trailer. The three trailers were parked on a verge adjoining a site occupied by a cluster of families with no links with Nathan. A warden offered him a pitch on another site. Nathan said he would look first. Having discovered the tenants included two renowned fighters, he stayed put. The nearby tenants resented his presence even outside the site. That evening they contrived an argument in a pub. They challenged the authenticity of his gold ring and smashed windows as a warning of worse to follow. By the morning, Nathan and his party had left.

(2) Shared encampments both reflect and reinforce political clusters. Whereas day visits can be relatively formal and the privacy of the family trailer retained, living alongside others brings greater exposure. Each family observes the times people leave and return, the contents of their lorries, and the nature of their work. Each family overhears domestic quarrels, and converses day and evening with neighbours in and out of trailers. Children transmit information which eludes the adults. Camp neighbours must be united against the common enemies, Gorgio landowners and officials. Families must co-reside with those they can trust. Here cognatic and affinal ties offer security and continuity. Given the changes in place of residence, camp neighbours and choice of travelling companions, there are certain patterns over a period of time. Regularity in shared residence is therefore a major ingredient in the formation of political clusters. Figures 3-7 reveal the residence patterns of numbers of families and the links between camp members.

(3) Another characteristic of political clusters is general economic cooperation. The families in a specific locality are vulnerable to internal dissension in the competition for work. Cognatic or affinal links were used for some form of economic collaboration, for example temporary partnerships in tarmac jobs. These persons did not necessarily reside in the same camp, although they were in the same locality. Two male first cousins, or the husbands (not related as cognates) of two sisters, or other individuals connected affinally often worked together. It was rare for brothers to work together as partners; instead affinal ties were exploited and strengthened in partnerships. Associates in a political cluster might also exchange tips about work contacts and customers, or loan equipment and cash, or a man might do

181

a deal for another and take a percentage. Partnerships between affines were accepted more easily as temporary and where obligations had specific boundaries. Disagreement between close cognates working as 'partners' might conflict with the overriding and permanent obligations considered the ideal behaviour between such persons. Partners become as brothers, but brothers do not need to be partners.

Families tended to associate with and marry their offspring to those of a similar economic level. Thus similarity in economic status was a factor in political clusters. Little contact existed between families of low economic status and families of the highest economic status. Kindred links between such families were not activated except at funerals, and no marriage alliance was created. Travellers of extremes of wealth or poverty would often remain unacquainted with each other, even in the same locality:

> A Gypsy woman from a wealthy family showed a Gorgio acquaintance an article in a magazine: 'That's pictures of some people living in Ireland.' Unknown to the Gypsy, the easily identifiable photos were of tented Gypsies living only six miles away.

Links were activated between those families of medium and high status where persons were close cognates. For example, newly married offspring and aged parents, as yet too young or now too old to amass wealth, would receive special assistance from wealthy parents or offspring.

Such assistance would extend less frequently to distant cognates and kindred. Siblings might also be separated by their choice of spouse. There are several examples of siblings of the same or opposite sex who travelled within a region but did not associate, i.e. they never visited, never shared the same encampment, did not cooperate in work and offered no support in a dispute. Some adopted a policy of permanent avoidance after a major disagreement. Others had drifted to their spouses' kindred. The level of wealth of siblings and other close cognates was not always the same.

> Patty and Frank rarely associated with Frank's sister Dolly whom both considered had made a bad match in Henry. Patty and Frank were now very wealthy with a Vickers trailer and other accoutrements. Henry came from a very poor family some of whose kindred were referred to disparagingly as 'tent-dwellers'. Patty: 'I feel sorry for Dolly with that man, he's kind enough, but he's got no ambition. All he does is smash cars. She'll never have nice things.' Dolly in turn complained to me that Patty and her brother Frank rarely visited. They were stopping only two miles away.

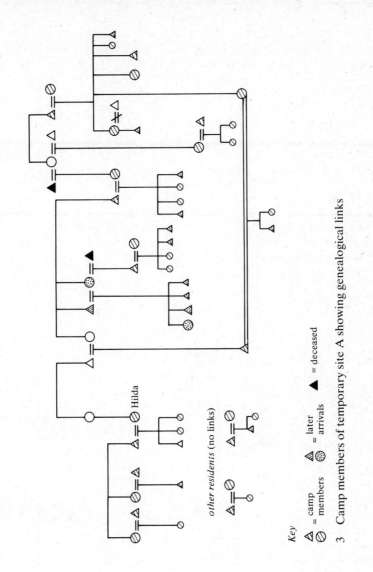

Hilda

other residents (no links)

Key

△ = camp
⊕ = members

△ = later
⊛ = arrivals

▲ = deceased

3   Camp members of temporary site A showing genealogical links

183

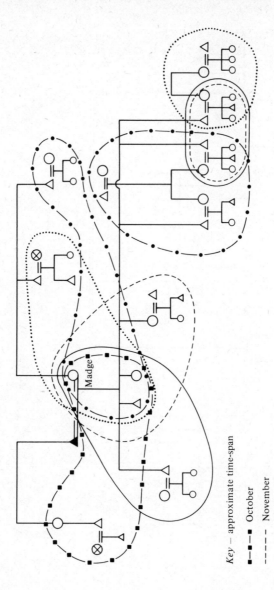

Madge

Key – approximate time-span

■—■ October

■--■ November

—— December

.... January

●—●—● February

4 Co-residence of Madge, a widow, her offspring and others, where known (5-6 months).

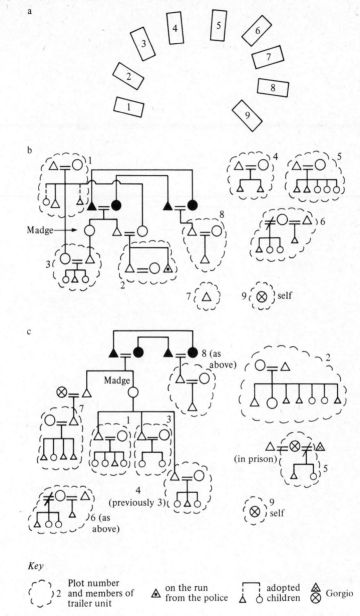

Key

⌐ ¬ Plot number
( )2 and members of   ⚠ on the run   ⌐ ¬ adopted   Gorgio
⌐ ¬ trailer unit   △ from the police   △ ○ children   ⊗

5   Temporary site B occupants: a - camp layout; b - February; c - June.

185

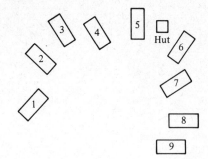

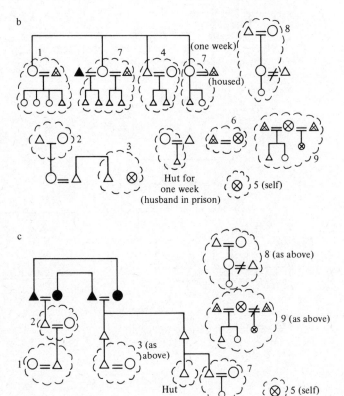

6 Temporary site C occupants: a - camp layout; b - August; c - February.

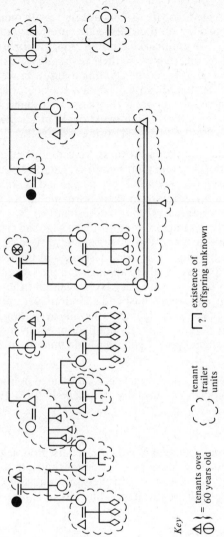

7 Tenants of permanent site (June).

The decision by a husband and wife to associate more with members of his or her kindred depended on their respective prestige, not merely their current location. The political clusterings of members of kindred and affines might be flexible, but less so their economic status. Wealth and political prestige (often based on fighting ability), however, did not necessarily coincide. Families might amass considerable wealth but be unable to risk physical combat with others. A husband and wife therefore would also weigh up the fighting strength of selected members of their respective kindred when choosing associates:

> Three of Lena's mother's brothers were renowned for their fighting ability. They and their families regularly associated in travelling, residence, economic exchanges and as allies in disputes. Lena more often used their 'surname' in referring to herself; neither her father's nor her husband's.
>
> When Wally beat up a Gorgio student who had frequently assisted Lena's husband Bill in writing letters etc., Lena got her mother's brother's son Tom, also a good fighter and of Wally's age, to force Wally to apologise to the Gorgio or else be beaten up by Tom who had never even met the Gorgio. Wally apologised. Lena's husband's kindred were not called upon, for he lacked such an impressive ally even though some of his kindred were wealthy. By not fighting Wally himself (in any case a younger man), Lena's husband minimised and contained his kindred's involvement.

As this example suggests, an additional characteristic of political clusters is (4) mutual support in disputes[4] (see Okely 1977:192-213).

Groups in contexts

The differing or overlapping demands of the Travellers' groupings are revealed according to context: whether as kin categories and moral units, or as politically expedient clusters, or as Travellers in contrast to Gorgios. The contexts to be examined are: weddings, funerals and fairs.

Weddings

Wedding feasts, celebrated among the wealthier and usually most powerful families and clusters, are not an indiscriminate get-together for all Travellers in the locality, regardless of kinship or affinal connections. They are a meeting of those most affected by the new alliance; namely close cognates of the bride and groom (among whom exogamy is required), and additional kindred and affines who form the major clusters associated with the family trailer units from which the new couple originate. Already other affinal links may have been forged between members of the bride and groom's exogamous units.

Figure 8 reveals the existing and subsequent links between the families most interested in the wedding of Terry and Claira and the genealogical positions of most of those present. Another of the bride's father's brothers, who was estranged from his siblings, did not attend. It was taken for granted long before the event that weddings are the

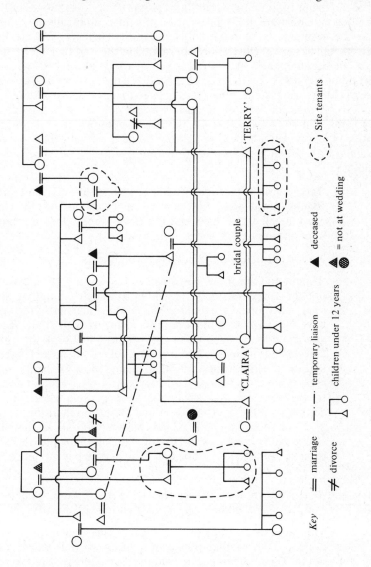

8   Genealogical links of some of those present at wedding party on a site.

occasion for conflict both between affines and between close cognates. This fighting both reflects the underlying rivalry between affines and affirms the kind of combat normally permitted between close cognates without wider repercussions.[5] Controlled fighting between new affines paradoxically expresses a new solidarity. Individuals are given the opportunity to demonstrate their pugilistic abilities. Some of the contests are no more than light-hearted sparrings, politically contained and between guests, united if only temporarily against rival Traveller clusters. These rival clusters are not invited to the wedding, since they are neither cognates nor affines, nor trusted associates. At one wedding a Gypsy man, in no way connected to the key families, arrived ready for a serious fight, but he was obliged to leave. The wedding was not to be an arena for a dispute which could not be easily contained. Several women, a week before another wedding, that of Tom and Rosina, expressed a hope that fighting would not occur, but were resigned to it. Even if there was no fighting, people were expected to 'let go'.

> 'I remember at Harriet's wedding, we had this mike and I was singing. I walked all between the chairs, in and out, the lead was tangled in the chair legs. The chairs were falling over but I kept on singing.'

Elisa described her behaviour at a Gypsy wedding:

> 'I spent an hour in the hairdressers' – it was all standing up. I bought a new suit and everything to match – handbag and shoes. My uncle's daughter was getting married. He must have spent £1000 on the reception, hiring tents and that. Well, you should have seen me. I enjoyed myself. I took the mike and started singing. I did the Hokee-cokee. My uncle laughed and liked it. I was drinking Babycham. I lost the heel of my shoe. There was beer spilt all down my skirt … I took the suit to the cleaners and asked for an expensive clean. They couldn't get the beer stains out, so I left the suit at the cleaners. You see, when us Travellers have a celebration we really like to enjoy ourselves and we say, "the more people, the better it is", otherwise it's no good. The people have to let go.'

Although Elisa says 'the more people the better', she is not referring to just any Travellers but close associates; the more of these the better. At Tom and Rosina's wedding, as feared, fighting began early:

> Men were threatening or even hitting each other with broken bottles. Tom's father was even fighting with his eldest son, Brian. When the police arrived the Travellers covered up for one opponent who had a suspended sentence hanging over him and made out he was innocent.

Case study of a wedding

At the wedding of Terry and Claira, Travellers in the locality lacking cognatic, affinal or other connections felt extremely vulnerable. Only a tiny minority of such persons were invited or dared attend, even if invited. It was to take place in a community hall next to an official site. Neither Terry's nor Claira's family trailer unit was a tenant – only two of the 15 tenant families were connected to them (see figure 8). Other tenants included three married siblings whose policy was never to risk confrontation with these wealthier, more powerful families. Although no direct threat was conveyed to them, all three siblings and families pulled their trailers off the site for several days until the wedding guests had dispersed. They feared that the light-hearted fighting between the guests (mainly cognates and affines) could become a serious confrontation if they turned their attention to outsiders.

Six other tenant families consisted of an older couple Joe and Lisa, their two married sons and three married daughters. They had recently established themselves here after Joe and Lisa had been evicted from another site. It was said that the warden had been put up to that eviction by a rival cluster of families some of whom would not be guests, including Claira's father's cognates. Joe, Lisa and offspring feared now that the fighting, normally contained and regulated within a marriage celebration, might spill over to them, the outsiders. Old rivalries could be revived and violence go beyond mere display. They were worried that their rivals planned to take over this site as well.

Accordingly Hilda, the wife in one of the two site tenant families related to the bridal couple, made some diplomatic overtures. As the daughter of the bride's father's sister, she approached Joe's eldest daughter Louise and invited her and siblings and parents to the wedding. These two women regularly negotiated when the potential friction between the rival families on the site became too threatening. But Louise, who had a reputation for violence which she felt compelled to exercise at the slightest provocation, left with her husband for a week, pulling their trailer off the site. Joe's two sons, having been repeatedly assured of their welcome, made brief appearances, together with Joe's two other daughters, and one son's wife. None of these women had cultivated a reputation for fighting. By contrast, none of Joe's three sons-in-law went near the wedding. Joe, once a great fighter, was now immune from any challenge; he was a cripple, thanks to an injury in the Second World War. Of his wife, Lisa, Joe said: 'She daren't come near 'em' (the wedding group), 'she's frit.' Unlike her husband, Lisa could claim no immunity if challenged, and she had shown the most violence when the family were evicted from the previous site. Joe talked to me of the bride's father and associates:

'They're all right so long as you leave them alone. Cor, we

wouldn't like to be up against *them*. Course none of them ever fought in the last war. Nobody could catch them.'

Joe, unlike his rivals, had not had a wide network of contacts and the resources to lie low in Ireland, for example, during the war.

The occasion of Terry and Claira's wedding reveals a strategy of evasion adopted by families in the vicinity of others who are more threatening, and with whom there are neither cognatic nor affinal links. The site tenants had every Gorgio 'legal' right to be there, but this became irrelevant. The wedding hosts and guests had made no overt moves to take over tenancies, many being content to stay temporarily and illegally in an adjoining field, but the tenants had everything to fear from the reaffirmed solidarity of the bride and groom's combined kin and associates.

Funerals

These can be contrasted with weddings by the different groupings of Travellers which take place. Weddings are restricted gatherings of mainly politically associated cognates and affines of the bride and groom and where some fighting is permitted. Funerals are the occasion for an unlimited gathering of Travellers who may or may not be cognatically or affinally related to the deceased. Close cognates, especially those who were once in a single trailer unit with the deceased, have a prominent role. Wider kindred of the deceased, regardless of political cluster or differing economic status, attend. Affines are present, but must keep at a distance in the ceremonial. Former camp neighbours and associates, indeed any Travellers in the vicinity, come to pay their respects. The ordering in ceremonial reflects the predominant moral obligations to close cognates, but the composition of the gathering emphasises the unity of all Travellers, transcending political clusters and rivals.

In contrast to weddings, there is a prohibition on all discord and fighting. Those who fear they might lose control and become embroiled in a dispute stay away. In one case the sister of a deceased man did not attend the funeral, as she did not want to risk a public confrontation with more distant kindred. Alternatively, past or potential rivalries between individuals and clusters are temporarily suspended. Quarrels with the deceased must be ended. A Traveller woman spoke of the suspension of animosities at funerals:

'You must never stop anyone seeing a dead person, even if that was the worst enemy. If he wants to follow him [join in the procession], you must let him.'

On a lesser scale the same rule applies at the birth of a baby: 'You must never stop a person seeing a new baby.'

The day before the funeral, the body is brought in an open coffin from the underakers' and placed in a trailer on the camp where the deceased and family were living before the death. Already cognates, affines and many others have travelled to the camp, some from across the country. Day and night they sit around a fire, the men around one, the women around another. A marquee and chairs may be hired from a Gorgio firm. Members of the deceased's trailer unit or close cognates provide snacks. People go at intervals to look at the corpse laid in the trailer.

The following day, and before the lid is finally closed, everyone must have a final look at the corpse. The hearse and hired funeral cars arrive. As the coffin is brought out, close cognates and some other Travellers form a circle around the trailer door. Further back stand distant kindred, affines, former neighbours and associates; the men in one group, the women in another – everyone in black. The hearse is followed by funeral cars containing the close cognates of the deceased, i.e. parent(s), spouse, offspring, siblings and then parents' siblings. In this context the unity of each family trailer of the siblings, parents' siblings and offspring is broken and the original family trailer unit of the deceased is reunited. The spouses of siblings, offspring or parents' siblings, since they are not cognates, do not travel in the hired funeral cars at the front of the procession. Throughout the ceremony they are in the background. The only affine of the deceased to be seen in the foreground is the widow or widower.

The prestige of the deceased is marked for this last time by the number of vehicles and persons who 'followed' the hearse to the graveyard and by the number of lorries piled high with expensive wreaths. Travellers say: 'there were a hundred motors at my father's funeral', or 'they had to stop the traffic for two hours, there were so many people following my mother', or 'If you stood at the beginning you'd never have seen the end of the motors, and there were six lorries with wreaths.' A man or woman is remembered not only by the number of kindred and affines asembled, but perhaps more by the number of Travellers assembled without such connections. These demonstrate the extent to which the individual inspired respect as a Gypsy, regardless of factional interests; indeed the extent to which he or she is a loss to the entire Gypsy group or community.

Dramatic expressions of grief are expected from close cognates and the spouse of the deceased. They wail and sob, and appear to have 'fits'. They tremble and fall to the ground, apparently unconscious, when the coffin is lowered into the ground. As each individual excels him or herself in public grief, the onlookers state the exact cognatic relationship to the deceased. When a chair was brought for an older man trembling from head to foot, the murmer went up, 'He's [the deceased's] brother's son.' When a woman was carried rigid from the graveside people said: 'She's his sister.'

Close cognates and the widowed spouse must show the greatest grief because they are most vulnerable to the *mulo* (ghost) of the deceased

193

(see Chapter 12). Others at the funeral, and standing further back, may carry on day to day conversations, even smile. People will be greeting each other after long absences. Close cognates and the widowed spouse must wear black mourning colours for a period, in some instances over a year after the burial. They must not return for many months, ideally never, to the camp from 'where he was took'.

Thus precedence is given at every stage of the funeral to close cognates: the exogamous unit, and neither to affines and cognates' affines, nor to specific political associates. Close cognates gather around the coffin as it is closed, walk first to the vehicles, travel immediately after the hearse in hired cars, walk nearest to the coffins, into the church and walk first in the procession to the grave, where again they stand nearest its edge. There is also an order among the close cognates, for example, the eldest son before others:

> 'Sam pushed himself forward and told the newspaper men, "I'm the eldest son, ask me the questions." But Luke was the eldest. He should have been first.'

One Traveller stated that when the old waggons were burnt at death, the eldest son inherited the iron base which he used to make a new waggon.

The wreaths of close cognates are placed nearest to the grave and some on the coffin. Before death it is the duty of close cognates to visit the dying as often as possible:

> When Bob was dying in hospital, he was visited almost daily by his widowed father and wife. When a social worker casually mentioned this to his mother's sisters they took offence and boasted that they had visited him more often. Other cognates also contested that they had visited the most. Detailed information on the man's latest condition was used as proof of a recent visit.

Close cognates should be present at the moment of death. Hospital rules on visiting hours and numbers permitted are vigorously broken:

> 'When our mother was dying, the nurses tried to stop us coming when we wanted. We soon put a stop to that. It's our way to visit our people.'
>
> In one case the nurses and matrons were overrun by visitors at all hours, day and night and in large numbers. Finally they had to put Bob in a private patient's room where other patients would no longer be disturbed by the constant chatter. Ten people or more witnessed the final moment of death, whereupon they let out great wails and shrieks.

The ultimate responsibility for the funeral cost lies with the close cognates and widowed spouse who are publicly shamed if the ceremony and burial plot are parsimonious:

> A widow died in poverty aged 78. Her daughter, also widowed, and married grandchildren in the locality had often been accused of neglect. A covering of artificial grass had been placed all around the grave hole. Before the coffin was lowered, a Traveller, not a close cognate, whipped away the green covering, claiming that the deceased was being buried cheap in a communal grave. It was said that the material covered other coffins. In fact this was unlikely, but people were looking for an excuse to shame the relatives. All week, Travellers commented on the disgraceful economy for a mother's funeral.

Close cognates must also pay for the gravestone, tend the grave and lay wreaths at Christmas and at anniversaries for years to come. If the widowed spouse, parents, or offspring travel out of the locality they send payment to the vicar or caretaker for the upkeep of the grave and wreaths. All affines, except the spouse of the deceased, although valued for their presence, are expected to keep a distance. They must not precede the deceased's cognates at any stage of the procession to the churchyard or graveside. This includes the spouses of the deceased's siblings:

> Violet complained about the behaviour of the son's wife (a Gorgio) at the funeral of Violet's brother. 'She pushed in front of me, she put herself forward. That's not right.'

Discord must be absent at funerals, which may be the occasion for the breaking of non-speaking or avoidance relationships without humiliation (see Okely 1977:194). Conflict, especially between close cognates and/or affines at the death and funeral of a Gypsy, are seen as a threat to the whole community. In the following case study, Travellers in no way related to the deceased intervened to resolve a dispute and ensure the reconciliation between close cognates and immediate affines and neighbours, the proper treatment for the deceased, and ultimately protection from the pollution of death (see chapter 12).

Case study of a funeral

When Carrie died, her widowed mother, siblings, nieces and nephews, her first cousins and their spouses, her more distant kindred, affines, neighbours and associates in the region, all donated money to her husband John who would be expected to put it towards a new trailer home for himself and his young unmarried offspring. At death, Travellers insist that the trailer formerly inhabited by the deceased and used for the display of the corpse before the funeral and now polluted must be broken up and burned a few days after the final burial (see chapter 12).

John, however, did not destroy the family trailer. Instead with the money donated by the Travellers, he bought a horse and flaunted his new acquisition. The Travellers were shocked, but no dramatic action was taken. Two and a half years later, Carrie and John's daughter Rose, in her mid-twenties, developed the same illness that had killed Carrie. Rose died, it was alleged, exactly three years after her mother. This was seen as Carrie's revenge, as Rose was her favourite daughter. Death occurred because the trailer had not been burnt. It was still being used as John's family home. The trailer, it was said, was polluted and haunted by Carrie's *mulo* (ghost).

This time, Carrie's siblings and other cognates, neighbours and associates refused to contribute money either to John or to Bill, the husband of Rose. Moreover, they insisted that both John's trailer and Bill and Rose's trailer should be burnt. Replacements for the two trailers and the cost of the funeral would be enormous. A major crisis could ensue. Both John and Bill had young offspring to care for. A permanent rift could develop between John, his cognates or associates and those of his widow. Due respect would not be paid to Rose, and there might now be two polluted trailers in the locality.

Accordingly, Ivy, unrelated to any individual in the crisis, chose to intervene, exploiting the political dominance and fighting prestige of two of her mother's brothers. Ivy visited every family on John's site and others in the locality, asking for a contribution towards the funeral and new trailers. She asked a Gorgio student to record on paper the names and sometimes the amount of money donated. Each request was preceded by a threat of force: 'My uncle [the toughest fighter] and his brother asked me to collect the money.' Carrie's close cognates could now pay up to Ivy, an outsider, without losing face in their rift with Carrie's widower. Some families, especially camp neighbours with neither cognatic nor affinal ties, were still very resentful and refused to pay. But later they sent their children down with money. The majority of Travellers in the locality, including Ivy's uncles, contributed.

The crisis which had threatened to spread beyond close cognates and affines was thus resolved by outside intervention. Two days after the funeral, both John's trailer (formerly inhabited by Carrie) and Bill's trailer (formerly inhabited by Rose) were ceremoniously broken up and burnt. As a sequel, Bill claimed that money for his new trailer had been stolen. The Travellers were sceptical, but made no complaints because Bill, seemingly destitute to the Gorgio local authority, was given a new trailer and a site place. No Travellers objected to this exploitation of Gorgios so long as proper observances had been made for the dead.

Fairs

In contrast to weddings and funerals, the great annual fairs at Appleby and Epsom are marked by an inter-regional character. Travellers, unacquainted with each other, can experience a common identity, overriding cognatic or affinal links and localised political clusters. This potential communal identity is modified by the opportunity which large gatherings offer for making or breaking the prestige of individuals, close cognates and political clusters. Disagreements, simmering for the previous year, can now be brought before the widest audience. There may be friendly interaction, but also major combat. Information on the outcome will be transmitted through an inter-regional network.

Some horse-dealing takes place at Epsom in the Derby week, but the most important event for this is at Appleby later in June. Horse-dealing (restricted to men) is not only a commercial activity, but also an affirmation of ethnic identity. Gypsies, possibly strangers to each other, without a history of competition for land, work or allies, can establish a relationship, albeit ambiguous, over a 'deal' or 'chop'. The two people exchange or buy and sell a horse, usually in front of witnesses who ensure that a common code is observed. The deal is publicly clinched when the two men slap their right hands together in a 'chop'. The exchange of horses in this context is especially significant to Gypsies, since the horse is their most prized possession (see chapter 6).

In contrast to economic exchanges between Gypsy and Gorgio, that between Gypsy and Gypsy is symmetrical in that both should be aware of each other's tricks and ruses (cf. Okely 1979a). If a Gypsy makes a poor deal with another, he cannot cry shame; it is shame on him. At a fair with hundreds of families in the vicinity, each transaction will affirm or undermine an individual's prestige more than any other occasion. While establishing contact with someone from a distant region, a Gypsy will also be protecting his status in terms of his own associates and region. The ability to make a good chop and display wealth in buying and selling will be observed and reported to people back home. Exchanges and acquisitions at fairs are recalled throughout the year.

The making of a deal can also be understood as an aggressive act, it being a humiliation to refuse because the person thereby admits his incompetence before the first round. Bargaining or having a chop is often the first overture between families, strangers or not, who meet up on the road. The husband from one family trailer approaches another saying: 'What do you have about you?' Some of the phrases used to introduce the article to be exchanged are: 'If I'm half a man for this'; or 'I'm a man for exchanging this.' The readiness to exchange is thus linked with manliness. It is no answer for a man merely to say he doesn't want to part with something:

> Albert told me he had been approached by Ned, a man of great fighting ability and political stature, to do a chop over Albert's black and white horse. Albert didn't want either to risk negotiating with Ned or to exchange it. So he told Ned it

197

wasn't his horse, but that of his son aged six. Ned accepted this
since children have independent property rights.

Fighting and chopping are parallel activities. Here a sexual division
is apparent. Women can and must fight. Women can bargain and
exchange most items, but not horses. They are excluded from this
exchange with ritual significance. In the horse-dealing field they are
conspicuously absent, except for one or two older women.[6] Otherwise
the women, infants and girls visit the fairgrounds and each other's trailers. Just as a Gypsy child must learn to fight, so he must learn to chop:

> Pete and Sylvia drove to a horse fair. Pete, recently housed,
> had taken his seven year old son from school having estab-
> lished these regular arrangements with the headmaster. 'My
> son's got to learn … Gypsies don't need to be educated like
> the Gorgios. A Gypsy has to learn to chop; what to say. Did
> you notice that old man with the waistcoat and gold watch-
> chains? He said; "Look at this horse, if you take her, you can
> have me wife for the night as well." Now you couldn't learn
> that in school. Can you see a Gorgio doing that? He wouldn't
> know how to start.'

Fairs are simultaneously an arena for communal identity and political rivalry. Families can contact close cognates now travelling in and
lost to other regions, as well as distant kindred, former associates and
neighbours.

> 'You meet all sorts of Travellers, people you haven't seen for
> years … My mother met her sister at Epsom and she hadn't
> seen her for twenty years.'

> 'I'm going to look for Jodie at Epsom. I haven't seen her since
> I was a young girl.'

In 1965 the Gorgio authorities tried unsuccessfully to close the
Appleby Fair (Boswell 1970:191), and in 1967 they tried to prevent
Travellers assembling at Epsom, just as they had tried in 1938 (Acton
1974:102, 170). Faced with this external threat, the Travellers displayed an overall unity in their defiance of Gorgio regulations. This
loose alliance when the fairs were in jeopardy was the nearest to an
organised demonstration of national solidarity.

Fairs are not just the scene for national unity. Political status can be
established by a display of violence, or ruined by public shame. Serious
disputes between political clusters and groups in competition during
inter-regional travels may be settled at fairs. Rivals will challenge each
other to fight or just steal up behind them.

'Bob was just walking past the pub at Barnet and the Walkers beat
him up. But he was nothing to do with it!' Travellers who were not witnesses to the confrontation will usually hear of the events. They usually

know in advance which past incidents and disputes will be brought up at the gathering and which individuals or groups will be preparing for a fight. Some families may choose to avoid certain pubs lest they be inadvertently drawn into the dispute. If a party to a dispute chooses not to come, the consequences may be worse when the confrontation occurs on more private ground without mediators.

Individuals and groups may not only be brought down in physical combat, but also by public shame when a 'law' common to all Travellers is broken. The annual fairs are the closest equivalent to the *kris* among Rom in California.[7] The methods of adjudication are not apparently formalised, but the consequences are as great. Distant groups, members of overlapping kindreds and political clusters are freely assembled. Anyone who has committed a shameful, *mochadi* act is most vulnerable, along with his or her close cognates and associates. The following case study concerns a shameful incident which occurred at a fair and which was dealt with at subsequent fairs.

Case study of conflict at a fair

Two young Traveller men, each from different wealthy and prestigious 'tribes' and who were neither cognates nor affines, were arrested and charged with a serious crime (in terms of both Gypsy and Gorgio 'law'). Immediately, the father of one, Elijah, who was greatly respected in several regions, pulled his trailer off the field near the fair and moved to another county, refusing all assistance to his son. The event could not have occurred in more embarrassing circumstances with so many Travellers assembled to hear of the arrest. The court case did not come up for a year, but the Travellers did not wait for the verdict in Gorgio law to shame the persons involved. Another Traveller at a smaller fair a few months later described the scene:

> 'Henry was there with his lot, the Y—s and the Z—s. All the big tribes were in a fight. The women were coming out saying, "She's his sister", "I'm his mother." You could tell something was up. [Notice that as in the case of funerals, the close cognates were picked out.] There was murders. Each was blaming the other tribe. It had to be the big ones, not the others like Billy's lot or the B—s or the D—s. Elijah says he can't put his head up now. He can't go to the pub.'

A Gorgio solicitor appealed to the Travellers to corroborate Elijah's son's claim that he was not present at the time of the crime. But no Travellers came forward. The men eventually went to prison.

The Travellers' use of the word 'tribe' referred here to an extended group of cognates who associated under a common name. Affines or distant kindred who might cluster politically with these persons would not suffer the same shame as close cognates to Elijah and son. In future they might disassociate themselves from the offending family. The Y—s, the Z—s and Elijah's group were inter-regional wealthy Travellers who had more to lose from a tarnished reputation than the poorer, less mobile B—s, D—s and close cognates of Billy.

In this chapter, I have examined the Travellers' internal political organisation. Although the Travellers do not form a separate society, they have developed strong sub-groupings which transcend the single trailer unit and nuclear family, and which offer some solidarity against or within the dominant non-Gypsy society.

11 Gypsy women[1]

In this chapter I shall discuss the extraordinary contrast between the outsider's stereotype of the Gypsy woman, and the ideal behaviour expected of her by the Gypsies themselves; the two are more closely connected than the conventional opposition between fact and fantasy, the real and the ideal. The relationship is reflected in the Travellers' beliefs in female pollution. This cannot be satisfactorily explained through the Travellers' internal organisation alone, but can be properly understood only when set in the context of the Travellers' external relations and of the more general pollution taboos between themselves and Gorgios.

Gorgio view of Gypsy women

Throughout Europe the Gypsy woman is presented as sensual, sexually provocative, and enticing. In England a stereotype of the Spanish Gypsy is often thought to be typical and is so depicted in popular paintings: a black-haired girl in décolletage, with flounced skirts and swaggering walk, hand on hip – every operatic Carmen walks this way. One of the *Oxford English Dictionary* definitions of Gypsy is, 'term for a woman, as being cunning, deceitful, fickle, or the like … In more recent use merely playful, and applied esp. to a brunette.' She is thought to be sexually available and promiscuous in her affections, although sexual consummation and prostitution are elusive in the image. Sometimes the suggestion is explicit: in the eighteenth century, Ellis, a farmer near the area where I later did fieldwork, referred to the local Gypsies as follows: 'These miscreants and their loose women, for no doubt all of them are so, as they lie and herd together in a promiscuous manner … a parcel of Rogues and Trollops' (Ellis 1956:78). Usually the image is more romantic. George Borrow wrote:

> The Gypsy women are by far more remarkable beings than the men. It is the Chi and not the Chal who has caused the name of Gypsy to be a sound awaking wonder, awe, and curiosity in every part of the civilised world … upon the whole the poetry, the sorcery, the devilry, if you please to call it so, are vastly on the side of the women. (1874:174-5)

201

Arthur Symon's poem 'To a Gitana Dancing', published at the turn of the century, carries in essence the Gorgio male view of the Gypsy female:

> You dance, and I know the desire of all flesh, and the pain
> Of all longing of body for body; you beckon, repel,
> Entreat, and entice, and bewilder, and build up the spell.
>
> (Sampson 1930:135)

Ultimately, possession of this 'witch of desire', as Symons called the Gitana, can never be achieved.

The Gypsy women especially have been the objects of the dominant society's exotic and erotic projections and disorders. Their image has been associated by non-Gypsies with sexual attributes beyond the bounds of Gorgio 'culture' and with certain animals. In Gypsy–Gorgio relations the men of each group project the image of uncontrolled female sexuality onto the women of the opposing group. The cat is associated with female sexuality both among Gorgios and Gypsies (see also Leach 1972:56), and Galsworthy reveals the common Gorgio stereotype of the Gypsy woman when he writes of Carmen: 'In her is sublimated as it were the Cat Force in human life' (1932:viii). Prosper Merimée, the creator of Carmen, several times compared her with a cat (1845:56). Such images obviously conflict directly with the Gypsies' own (see chapter 6). We also find analogies between Gypsy women and wild animals. Hindes Groome wrote of a Gypsy girl: 'Of a sudden her eyes blazed again and you were solely conscious of a beautiful wild creature' (Sampson 1930:128).

The Gypsy woman, from an alien culture, but not in a foreign land, is in dangerous and ambiguous proximity. She is placed by Gorgios in nature and in contradistinction to the sedentary 'culture'.[2] Non-Gypsies transfer to her their own suppressed desires and unvoiced fears. Nothing about her is ordinary; if pretty she is made outstandingly beautiful, if old she is considered a crone. The implication is that Gypsy women are beautiful despite or in contrast to the projected inferiority of their Gypsy males, who are victims of more derogatory stereotypes and negative projections in a dominant patriarchal ideology. Borrow revealed the same bias: 'How blank and inanimate is the countenance of the Gypsy man ... in comparison with that of the female Romany' (1874:175). Gypsy males are dubbed parasites, thieves, and unclean – menacing but belittled. One reason for the denigration is that the Gypsy male, rather than the Gypsy female, is seen as a potential 'home-breaker'. He may liberate a housedweller virgin *à la* D.H. Lawrence (1930), or abduct a woman to be his own in Gypsy society. This male fear is expressed in the popular ditty about a rich lady who goes 'Off with the Raggle Taggle Gypsies O'. The Gypsy woman does not offer the same threat to housedwelling society, partly because the Gorgio male is credited with greater control over his choice of partner, while the female is not. Unmarriageable but endowed with sexual attraction, the Gypsy woman is also credited with strange, supernatural powers: for instance, her presumed ability to foresee the future and tell of the past by the 'black' art of fortune telling. Also, depending on the outsiders' response, she can bring either bad luck by her curse, or good luck by her blessing.

Gypsy view of Gypsy women

The Gorgios' stereotype clashes with the Gypsies' own ideal for Gypsy women. The Travellers are aware that Gypsy women are attributed a special eroticism, and a tendency towards prostitution; they have in turn a derogatory view of Gorgio women, whom they contrast with their own. A male Traveller said to a Gorgio interviewer: 'We're not like Gorgios: Gorgios just take their women as they are. But our people have always been called whores and Christ knows what. Our women, when they get married, they're scrutinised, they're examined to make sure they've stayed a virgin' (Sandford 1973:81). The Traveller woman must remain a virgin until lawful marriage. Traditionally girls were inspected by married women. More recently, another procedure has been adopted, as I discovered:

> 'It's wrong to do it before you've married. When I was going with a boy, my mother, as soon as she heard, sent me straight down to the doctor's for an examination ... then I took a certificate back to my mother. She did that with all my sisters.'

After marriage, a wife must remain sexually faithful to her husband. To maintain her reputation she must even avoid being alone with another man or being seen in conversation with him on the camp, lest she risk the accusation of infidelity. I was present when a Gorgio man called at a Gypsy trailer for the husband, who was out. The unsuspecting visitor remained, so he was instructed to stay near the open door, as far away as possible from the wife and myself. Another Traveller woman soon appeared: 'What's going on here?' The wife replied, 'It's all right, she's here,' indicating my presence – another woman to safeguard her reputation. The presence of a child old enough to relate events was also considered a protection.

A woman should ideally remain with one husband for life, and is supposed to be subordinate to her husband's orders. In addition, her deportment and dress are dictated by certain restrictions. Far from being a flighty seductress, the Traveller woman is burdened with many domestic duties. A wife is expected to give birth to numerous children and has the main responsibility of their care. Food purchase, cooking, and cleaning are also the woman's domain. The Gypsy woman (perhaps more in the past than now, although the tradition is still the ideal among most families) is expected to work outside the camp earning a living. She is greatly valued for her ability to obtain goods and cash from the Gorgio:

> 'My aunt had loads of gold rings she'd got from Gorgios. When I was with her, she'd say, "Do you like that suit the lady's wearing? Well, you'll have it." The lady'd be talked into giving it. Some'd take their earrings off. They didn't dare tell their husbands. Auntie'd say, "See the ring she's wearing? Well, I'll have that." And next week I'd see her wearing it.'

Gypsy men may expose their women to certain risks and do not monopolise the external economic activities themselves because women are in some contexts more successful at Calling than men would be. Here the Gypsies can exploit the housedwellers' ideal or stereotyped woman, whether Gypsy or Gorgio. In the dominant society, financial support is usually considered primarily the male's duty, so the Gypsy woman out Calling conceals her role as major breadwinner and often poses as an abandoned, near-destitute wife and mother. By eliciting the pity of the Gorgio, she can extract a greater economic return.

It seems that in the past the woman was almost wholly responsible for obtaining food and other domestic requirements.

> 'In the old days the women earned the money. The men sat in the camp all day and the women went out.'

> 'Gorgio men give money to their wives. They don't make them work. Maybe it's not like it used to be, but in the old days a Traveller's wife *had* to work. Otherwise they'd beat them.'

The men had to provide the waggon and horse. More recently, in many cases, the man's contribution has increased relative to that of the woman. Some of his earnings are handed over for food and domestic expenses, yet it is still considered important that a woman should be able to earn a good living, if only in crises. 'I'd take my last pegs from the line, clean 'em, and sell 'em 'fore I let my kids starve.'

Thus traditionally the Gypsy women have been responsible for subsistence production with its consequent daily obligations and minimum opportunity for capital investment. They are also responsible for the bulk of domestic (unpaid) labour. The Gypsy men by contrast have invested earnings in capital goods like horses, hunting and racing dogs, waggons, trailers and motor vehicles. Woman have rarely, if ever, been permitted to deal in and own such items, although they may own small dogs like Yorkshire terriers, and jewellery.

Contradictions

There is a paradox embedded in the Gypsy woman's role. Within her own society she is hedged in by restrictions, expected to be subservient to her husband and cautious with other men. Yet nearly every day she is expected to go out to 'enemy' territory, knock on doors of unknown people, and establish contact with new customers, some of whom will be men. Success in obtaining money or goods will depend on her ability to be outgoing and persistent, and her readiness to take the initiative. She must be aggressive – quite the opposite to some of the behaviour required of her in the camp.

There do exist formal restrictions on the woman's activities outside the camp. Wood has claimed that in the past, at least, when a Traveller woman knocked at a door and a man answered, she was to ask for the mistress of the house, and if she did not appear the Traveller was expected to leave forthwith (1973:29). Such restrictions explain the apparent inconsistency in the husband's boasting of his wife's mechanical knowledge: 'She knows all about motors', while at the same time discouraging her from learning to drive a vehicle. The latter would give her considerable independence: 'I'm not having you running about; I want to know where you are.' Mechanical knowledge is acceptable so long as it is not used by the women for independent transportation. When out Calling, the woman is expected to travel on foot, or on the more constricting public transport. Nonetheless such controls over the woman's activities outside the camp are either trivial or unenforceable. When Calling with the women, I discovered that they frequently conducted business with men alone and stressed the advantage:

> 'If you get the men by themselves and keep them talking, you can sell quite a few flowers. Tell them to get a present for their wives. They don't know what their wives want.'

The Traveller or Gypsy woman also has an important political role as mediator. Men more than women are vulnerable to the superior force of Gorgio authority: husbands not wives are arrested, prosecuted, imprisoned, and taken for military service. At least one Gypsy man spent the whole of the war in women's clothing, thus eluding Gorgio control. His simple transformation assured him near-magical safety. The Gypsy woman is nonetheless well prepared for possible attack. 'I always keep some hot water boiling. All I need do is sling it at any man that tries anything.' Sometimes the women will act to defend their husbands:

> 'One day the *gavvers* [police] turned up. John had just come back from work and I was making his tea, he was tired. They said they'd have to take him to the station. I asked if he could have his tea first and they said no. This *gavver* was standing in the doorway and I said, "You can have your tea", and I picked up the kettle and threw the water. At the station the same *gavver* said, "Oh no, not her." He thought I was mad.'

The women deal with unwanted journalists and cameramen:

> 'Once they came with those things that go round [cine-cameras] and Elsie and I went for them, threw them up in the air … smashed them. They didn't come back.'

Gypsy women are considered by Gorgios to be physically less threatening than their men, since they are not credited with abilities to attack or defend, and they are thus able to make closer contact with Gorgios than their men can. The Gypsies are aware that, among many Gorgios, women are expected to be non-violent. When a Gorgio woman, who was married to a Gypsy, was involved in a fight with a Gypsy woman, she was complimented: 'You're not a Gorgio. You hit back.' While exploiting their presumed vulnerability, the Gypsy women actually cultivate fighting abilities.

As in her external economic role, so in her political relations with the Gorgio society, the Traveller woman is able to exploit the Gorgio ideal of women being the weaker sex. Regarded by Gorgios as non-violent and incapable of independent decision making, the women are left by their men to cope with visiting Gorgio authorities. The women can be suitably evasive and indecisive. When Travellers are threatened with eviction the men may usually disappear from early morning to night. The women have to offer excuses and plead. Safety for the family from prosecution or permission for a prolonged stay will depend partly on the women's success at diplomacy.

Pollution and Calling

Given the Gypsy women's frequent contact with outsiders, complete control over their activities can only be effected by supernatural beliefs, and ones fully internalised by the women. It is here that fears of ritual pollution have power. In addition to the pollution beliefs which the Gypsies use to erect and maintain boundaries between themselves and Gorgios, there are certain polluting powers attached to women which can be fully understood only in the context of Gypsy–Gorgio pollution, and the relationship between Gypsy and Gorgio. Here the woman's dual external and domestic role is important.

The Gypsy woman is a crucial intermediary since she has the main responsibility for acquiring or purchasing food from the Gorgio as well as its preparation or cooking. She goes between the unclean, alien, and, by implication, unsocialised or 'wild' Gorgio and the clean Gypsy group; she is the link between uncontrolled 'nature' outside the Gypsy system and controlled Gypsy 'culture' inside it.

Women must be careful about their method of obtaining food and the type acquired, as well as its preparation, which may involve cooking. One danger is that they might obtain unclean food. But another danger is that the women might trade sex for food and thereby threaten the ethnic inheritance of the group. The pollution beliefs associated with Gypsy women largely reflect these problems: the woman's need to control her sexuality in certain contexts; the separation between her external, unclean Calling role and her internal, clean culinary role; and the necessity for discrimination between Gorgio and Gypsy males.

Thompson recorded aspects of female pollution current among English and Welsh Gypsies of the time (1922, 1929). My own fieldwork revealed the continuation of some pollution beliefs, although it was often difficult to obtain distinctly positive or negative information on many occasions. Acton (1971) claims that the emphasis on the uncleanliness of women has virtually disappeared. However, his own material sometimes contradicts this. Moreover, he does not discuss the pollution associated with childbirth. If, indeed, female pollution taboos have become less important, this coincides with the relative decline in the women's external economic role; and thus my case that the two are interconnected is strengthened. The Gypsy woman's external contribution was still vital in the 1920s and the preceding years for which Thompson recorded his information. A meticulous ethnographer, he has noted the facts, but he can offer no explanation. I would summarise the power of the Gypsy female to pollute a Gypsy male in these three alternative ways, using both Thompson's and my own material:

1. Female sexuality is inherently polluting if mismanaged.
2. Menstruation is associated with pollution.
3. Childbirth is polluting.

Thompson finds greater emphasis on 1 and 3, a stress which was confirmed in my own fieldwork.

1. *Sexuality as inherently polluting if mismanaged*

The woman must be careful not to expose certain parts of her body nor to bring it into contact with a man (private sexual intercourse within marriage being the only permissible context in which this may occur). Both in the past and today this is exemplified in restrictions in the women's dress. During fieldwork I found that shorter skirts were permitted than before, but not mini-skirts. I found that blouses must cover the body up to the base of the neck.[3] Tight sweaters and 'hot pants' were banned. If trousers were worn by women, the hips and upper thighs had to be covered by a dress or smock. The woman has to be careful in her movements. According to Thompson, her legs must be held close together and she must not bend forward from a standing position, especially with her back turned to men. This was confirmed in my fieldwork:

'When that Gorgio woman first came on this site she didn't understand. She kept bending – in a skirt right up to here …

the men had to cover their eyes ... and she had a low neck, that was terrible.'

'Travellers don't like girls to sit with their legs apart ... even a girl of that age [six] would be told. It wouldn't be allowed.'

Thompson recorded that a woman had to take special precautions in her toilet habits and that a woman's underwear had to be washed separately from the men's clothing otherwise this could be polluted. It had to be dried out of sight. I never saw women's underwear on the crowded lines, except when hidden inside other clothing. Thompson also recorded how men could be polluted by touching women's clean linen or by walking under such a clothes-line. A woman's dress could also pollute men's underwear, according to Thompson. A woman had to wash her body in complete privacy and ideally from a special bowl reserved also for washing her underwear. Any man inadvertently seeing a woman relieving herself, i.e. exposing herself, was also liable to pollution. In my fieldwork, one of the major reasons given by Travellers against unsegregated toilet blocks was that a man might catch a woman by surprise. Breast-feeding, according to Thompson, was also to be done in private. I found that the vast majority of women avoided breast-feeding altogether and opted for bottle-feeding, despite the contrary advice of midwives and health visitors.

'I breast-fed only one of mine. But I locked myself in the trailer first and drew the curtain. We wouldn't let a man see. That's filthy.'

Thompson records that sometimes husband and wife, if not every member of the family, had to have separate crockery. I found cases where each member, whether adult or child, retained his or her own cup. Thompson's material indicates that food preparation and Calling require distinctly separate ritual procedures, thus, I suggest, reinforcing symbolically the separation between the woman's external and internal roles. The woman risks polluting a man via his food. Thompson records that food or water was polluted if a woman stepped over it, held it too close to her, or touched it inadvertently with her skirt. Traditionally, for cooking or food preparation, the woman had to wear a large white apron encompassing her lower body, front and back. Today these are smaller and patterned, but still considered the mark of a 'true Gypsy'. The apron for a Gorgio housewife has a diametrically opposed function which is to protect the dress from the 'dirt' of food and cooking. For the Gypsy, the apron is to protect the food and cooking from the 'dirt' of the dress, which is ritually contaminated by the outer body and specifically the sexual parts.

Thompson described the elaborate preparation required traditionally of a Gypsy woman going Calling:

After removing the ample white apron she wears in camp, she fastens the money-bags in position round her waist; puts on her hawking-apron, which is of black with an embroidered hem; fixes the *monging*-sheet [i.e. begging sheet] – a square damask cloth – behind her so that it is accessible from either side; re-ties the kerchief she is wearing on her head, and puts on over it her long-poked, lace-trimmed bonnet.

(1922:19)

Then she ties her shawl into a sling to hold her baby, puts on a red cloak, and takes up her basket. Notice how the money is placed beneath the hawking-apron which acts as the shield between the potentially polluting dress (and sexual parts) and the potentially pure *monging*-sheet which often contained food, and had thus to be protected from contamination. The hawking-apron (black) was never to be worn while cooking as it would in this other context be considered by some as *mochadi*. Some women still wear black embroidered pinafores for Calling or for funerals (see chapter 12). These pinafores are sometimes specially commissioned from local dressmakers and have no sleeves and cover the upper and lower body, front and back.

Although Thompson has recorded the polluting power of the female body, her clothing, her contact with food and Calling activities, he has not emphasised the more specific mismanagement of her sexuality. 'If a man marries an "unmarried mother", they say he's a fool because she isn't *pure*', I was told. Uncleanliness comes from illicit sex both before and after marriage.[4]

Defloration, also, even within the context of marriage, can be seen as an unclean act, a loss of purity. While Thompson has discussed at length the pollution associated with birth and death, he has not examined such possibilities in marriage, although his material elsewhere hints at this (1927:123).

The offspring from a casual sexual encounter between Gypsy and Gorgio is more likely to be born into the Gypsy group, if the mother rather than the father is Gypsy. Thus sexual infidelity with Gorgios by Gypsy women is more threatening to the group than that by Gypsy men. Possibly pollution via illicit sex may not occur between a Gypsy woman and Gypsy man.

2. Menstruation as polluting

Thompson's records and my fieldwork indicate a milder emphasis on this as a source of pollution. Only among some groups was the woman not supposed to cook during menses. Then, either her husband or other women took over this task. I was able to confirm this from only two such cases, but the occasional trips I noticed to fish-and-chip shops by husbands may have been to protect themselves from pollution. Specific mention of menstruation is not supposed to be made in front of men (cf. Thomspon 1922), so information is limited, especially for male fieldworkers.

Acton has suggested that the taboo has declined because of the invention of the sanitary towel. He inadvertently reveals ethnocentric bias by his assumption that a 'neater' and seemingly more 'hygienic' containment would solve the whole symbolic problem (1971). Moreover, even the technical problem is not solved by a modern invention: there remains the question of disposal, concerning which the women took great care, and often in contrast to the general attitude towards other rubbish thrown out of the trailer (see chapter 6).

3. *Childbirth as polluting*

Thompson considers that the Gypsy woman is the greatest potential source of danger to men during and following childbirth. Traditionally the woman retreated to a special tent on the edge of the camp during labour and for a time after the birth. She had her own crockery and was not allowed to prepare food for men for some weeks. Later the tent, bedding, and utensils were burnt. The newborn baby was also considered *mochadi* for a time and had to be washed in a special bowl, and so also its clothes.

Today the woman and baby are still regarded as temporarily *mochadi*, and cooking must be done by others. Moreover, the woman is forbidden to discuss her experience with any man or even to tell any man other than her husband (which she may do only reluctantly) the fact that she has entered labour and requires aid. A young woman was warned by the hospital to report immediately she had pains, as serious complications were expected. One evening, when she was in the company of an uncle as well as her husband and aunt, labour pains began:

> 'I was doubled up. My uncle asked what was the matter. I couldn't tell him, he was a man. You don't tell men those things … They went out for a drink and I had to wait till my husband came back. I walked up and down thinking, "If only there was a woman I could talk to."'

As in the past, men must not assist women in labour. The almost universal preference for childbirth in hospital has been misinterpreted as a conversion to Gorgio medicine and the welfare state. Yet women I encountered in fieldwork were reluctant to attend prenatal clinics and often jettisoned any prescriptions such as iron supplements. Any attendance at clinics indicated more a desire to ensure a hospital bed. The women usually discharged themselves early, to the consternation of the medical authorities.

> 'The nurses at the hospital said, "We're sick of the Gypsies. They never come to the appointments at the clinics." Mary wouldn't eat the food. She wouldn't let them wash her. She cried a lot.'

Many Travellers even complained of rough treatment and poor attention during the birth. Rather than being a safety measure for the women, hospitalisation is a convenient way of dealing with a polluting act. The Gorgios are given the task of supervising the process and disposing of polluted articles.

From the last two sections we can see that at menstruation and childbirth the women's ability to pollute is temporarily intensified because they are occasions for the outlet of bodily waste. In the light of the Gypsies' distinction between the inner and outer body, such rejected matter from the inner and lower body is especially polluting.[5] While, for some families, menstruation may not be considered especially polluting, childbirth seems always so. A certain shame is attached to pregnancy. Women must conceal their shape with coats or other very loose garments (coats are otherwise rarely worn). Conception is a dangerous affair and must not be misplaced, i.e. the father must be a Gypsy. The baby is ambiguous matter because it has been covered by the blood and waste of birth: the inside come outside. The baby remains polluting for a while, possibly because it has not been 'made' a Gypsy until some socialisation has taken place.

La Fontaine, in discussing women's *rites de passage* in relation to the mode of descent in a society, has suggested that the elaboration of ritual connected with the defloration of Gisu females reflects the importance of male control in a patrilineal society, whereas the greater elaboration of ritual at first menstruation among the Bemba is consistent with a matrilineal society. She does not 'know of a cognatic society in which *rites de passage* reach the scale and elaboration' of these two types (1972:184). For the Travellers, in this case a cognatic group, those *rites de passage* associated exclusively with one of the sexes are not 'elaborate' in La Fontaine's sense. There is little ritual attached to first menstruation as such, it is merely the point at which girls become capable of polluting men. Defloration is a dangerous and private transition, not so much a demonstration of male possession. Conception and childbirth are again dangerous but made private. The problem is not one of control by a particular descent group or kinship line, with name and property to transmit, but the protection of the ethnic group as a whole from the dominant society which is never far away.

It is notable that the women's ability to pollute men, while heightened at certain times, is also ever-present, and is not merely associated with certain events or *rites de passage*. The elaboration and public aspects of precautionary ritual lie in *continuing daily* observances. Since, in external relations, Gypsy women are always vulnerable to sexual contamination by the Gorgio, they must be taught that their ever-present sexuality and fertility are dangerous. The women's dress, deportment, and behaviour are matters for constant public scrutiny. They must shield their sexual parts, control their movements and misplaced desires. If women were distinctly polluting merely because of their unique bodily waste, then aprons would presumably be required only at childbirth and menstruation. However, women's sexuality is always potentially polluting to Gypsy men. The Traveller women must protect all Travellers from pollution by controlling every aspect of their sexuality; if indiscriminate and casual with Travellers, they could be so with Gorgios, thus endangering the group.

Gypsy view of Gorgio women

Travellers attribute to Gorgio women the inverse of behaviour expected of Gypsy women. Gorgio women are thought to show uncontrolled sexuality: 'show their arse', wear no knickers, strip-wash in front of men, and put on provocative make-up and revealing dress. For Gypsy men Gorgio women are fair game, if not actual prostitutes.

Prostitution appears more blatantly by projection in the Gypsies' stereotype of the Gorgio woman than in the stereotype held by Gorgios of Gypsy women. During the early part of my fieldwork three men joked with me. My naive response was repeated amidst uproarious laughter around the camp.

> *Male Gypsy*: 'If I gave you two hot pennies out of the fire, what would you do then?'
> *Female Gorgio:* 'I'd drop them.'

The joke partly said that the Gorgio girl would drop her knickers for the price of two pennies: a cheap prostitute indeed. I doubt whether this joke would ever be played on a Traveller woman. Joking behaviour of a sexual nature was the accepted form between Gypsy men and any Gorgio women visiting the camp. It was positively encouraged by their wives, perhaps as a defence measure: 'My husband would like to take you out in his motor. He'll take you to the pictures.' However, no such joking was permissible between a Traveller woman and a Gorgio male on the camp.

For Gypsy women if not men, the separation between the ideal and the fallen woman is reinforced by pollution beliefs. The few Gorgio women drifting into the travelling society as real or honorary prostitutes and conforming to the Gypsy stereotype of Gorgio women were treated as polluting. Their apparent ability to pollute other women was derived from their uncontrolled sexuality, not simply from their eating and washing habits. A Traveller woman described a Gorgio women:

> 'She was eating a meat pie and picking some of it out; "I don't like that jelly", she said. I told her "I reckon you like the jelly … you're dirty. I wouldn't have you drink tea with me, not let you touch my cups."'

When prostitution is resorted to deliberately as a way of life, by either the Gypsy or the Gorgio, then the ethnic stereotypes assume new significance. Any prostitutes of Traveller origin moved into Gorgio society and became housedwellers. They concealed their origins and dressed and behaved not as Gypsies, but as they pictured Gorgio prostitutes to be. For them, being a prostitute may be initially merely a fantasy. As the traditional control of their sexuality breaks down, they act out the opposite stereotype; the Gypsy view of the Gorgio woman. In order to consummate an illicit way of life, they cross the ethnic line.

Gorgio use of their Gypsy stereotypes

Some Gorgio women appear to exploit the Gorgio stereotypes of both Gypsy men and women to meet their needs. Escaping certain roles within their society, they go off with the 'raggle-taggle' Gypsies. I am referring specifically to women in transit, not those who assume the role of permanent wife with all its restrictions. I encountered several such drifters who, in breaking all the rules of dress and behaviour, invited anger and scorn from the Traveller women. It is only retrospectively that I understand their deliberate tactlessness and apparently irrational behaviour. They were fully aware of the correct code for Gypsy women, occasionally conformed to it, but usually flaunted it. Generally they were not aiming for honourable acceptance but were instead enacting their own fantasies. They seemed to be drawn towards the stereotype of the Gypsy male as exotic seducer. They also entertained images of themselves as peculiarly seductive, either as outsiders or as stereotyped Gypsy women. Although in their case not fictitious, their form of prostitution was freer and perhaps more amenable to fantasy than in Gorgio society.

This use of the Gypsies by Gorgios to soften and romanticise the Gorgio prostitute's harsh life and image reappears within Gorgio society. For example, there is the curious phenomenon of the Gorgio stripteaser without any Gypsy connections, who assumed the name of 'Gypsy Rose Lee', later celebrated in the film and musical, *Gypsy*. The stripteaser expressed most blatantly the Gorgio stereotype of the Gypsy woman who is sexually arousing but untouchable. This masquerade takes another perhaps more satisfying form: Clébert, in affirming the absence of prostitution by or among Gypsies, notes by contrast the existence of Gorgio prostitutes in Pigalle who dressed up as Gypsies (1967:208). Here the unobtainable is made obtainable through living fantasy.

To conclude: the boundary erected by both Gypsy and Gorgio between the two becomes a useful device for resolving powerful areas of inner conflict by compartmentalisation or 'splitting'. Different potentialities within persons are split between two groups. Just as men may be dissatisfied by the ideal woman they have created for themselves, so may women be troubled by alternative images and tendencies within themselves.[6] Both men and women protect themselves by projecting these tendencies, oversimplified, on to an alien people or on to strangers. Thus (as in figure 9) virginity, monogamy, and sexual abstinence, the ideals, are placed on ego's side of the ethnic boundary, while prostitution, promiscuity, or passive availability are placed on the other. Controlled sexuality is separated off from uncontrolled sexuality. Such a splitting process between 'good' and 'bad' is recognised in psychoanalysis as a fundamental way of organising a world view. In the case of Gypsies, sexuality, gender and ethnic divisions are all exploited in the splitting process, and by both groups.

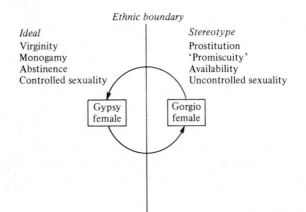

Ethnic boundary

Ideal	*Stereotype*
Virginity	Prostitution
Monogamy	'Promiscuity'
Abstinence	Availability
Controlled sexuality	Uncontrolled sexuality

Gypsy female

Gorgio female

9   The stereotyped and the idealised female.

This chapter has also indicated how the ideal of Gypsy women held by Gypsies, and the pollution taboos associated with women, are interdependent with the relationship between Gypsies and Gorgios, and also with the stereotype which Gorgios have of Gypsy women.[7]

12 Ghosts and Gorgios

Different explanations

Compared to other *rites de passage* there is an elaboration of ceremony in the Travellers' response to the death of one of their members. As with birth, death is associated with pollution. The Gypsies' funeral rites and their inordinate and continuing fear of ghosts or the *mulo* have attracted the attention of Gypsiologists. Leland compared the Gypsies with the positivists who 'seem to correct their irreligion through the influence of love' and whose 'real religion ... consists ... in devotion to the dead' (1893:48-9). Like others he saw the Gypsies' attitude as admirable piety. Thompson can provide no satisfactory explanation of 'origins or motives' (1924:8) for the Gypsies' death rites, which include the destruction of the deceased's property. Recently, Trigg has presumed a merely chronological explanation: 'The ancient origin of such a complete rite of disposal by destruction may very well have its origins in the funeral practices which many Indian Gypsies and Hindus have in common' (1975:129). In his unpublished doctoral thesis (1967), and in an article in the *J.G.L.S.*, Trigg deplores the evangelists' lack of interest in the Gypsies' beliefs which he considers could be exploited for Christian conversion: 'Magical beliefs, for intense, strongly based on the idea of death and ghost life might possibly, with proper application, be replaced with the religion based on death and resurrection' (1968:100). Elaboration of ceremonial and intense fear of the dead have been recorded among Gypsies elsewhere, for example in the U.S.A., France and Austria (Otter 1931:114-16). Sutherland notes the elaboration of ceremonial at the funerals of Californian Gypsies and fear of the *mulo* (1975:274, 283-5). Death, she concludes, is seen as a loss to the whole group (1975:98). Dollé asserts that for Gypsies in Alsace, elaborate funeral rites followed by the ban on mentioning the dead person's name are a form of psychological repression – 'scotomisation'. Death is a trauma with which the Judeo-Christian civilisation copes by an elaborate philosophy of death, whereas, the Gypsies' different response, Dollé patronisingly suggests, is because of their lack of such an elaborate philosophy (1970:15).

I hope to offer an alternative and more satisfactory explanation in this chapter. Although arising from information on English Gypsies, it may be more widely applicable to Gypsies elsewhere. The words of Lévi-Strauss direct us towards an explanation from social anthropology: 'the image a society evolves of the relationship between the living and the dead is, in the final analysis, an attempt, on the level of religious thought, to conceal, embellish or justify the actual relationships which prevail among the living' (1973:246). The 'final analysis' may exist at an unconscious level, to be made explicit by the social anthropologist. The Gypsies' death rites and beliefs must again be understood in terms of the relations between Gypsies and Gorgios, not merely the Gypsies' internal social system. These rites and beliefs are making statements about an ethnic boundary, consistent with the Travellers' eating and washing taboos, their concept of the body, and their animal categories (see chapter 6). Once it is recognised that the Gypsies' beliefs stand fundamentally in opposition to the Gorgio, Trigg's hope for a universalistic religious conversion and perhaps assimilation into the larger society fails completely.

When the Gypsies have explicitly adopted the Gorgio Christian rites and mythology, they have transformed their meaning and put them to their own use. For example, there are many Gypsy versions of the Crucifix story. A Gypsy in England gave me one:

> 'A Gypsy was asked to make four nails for the cross. After he'd made three, he found out what it was for and refused to make any more. If you look at the two feet on the cross, there's only one nail, 'cos the Gypsy wouldn't make the fourth.'

Thus the very sight or image of the Crucifix tells the Gypsy something about a specific Gypsy identity. Gordon Boswell gives a similar version which also explains Gorgio persecution:

> the Gypsy people found what these nails were for, and instead of giving them four nails they only gave them three – one of them managed to escape with one of these nails. And the Gentiles have been looking for that nail ever since. And it has been this search that has led to the persecution of the Gypsy.
>
> (1970:14)

Sutherland's version from California (1975:73) gives the Gypsies the right to steal; a right awarded by God in return for a Gypsy swallowing the nail for Jesus' heart. There are also Gorgio versions of these stories which accuse the Gypsies of unrepentant collaboration in the Crucifixion.

Recently, Gypsies in France and Belgium, for example, have interpreted and made use of Christianity in the form of the Pentecostal movement. It seems that their beliefs and practices, which include the emergence of Gypsy lay preachers, again affirm the Gypsies' separate identity as an oppressed minority, rather than their conversion to Gorgio ways.[1]

The ethnography of death

Having discussed funerals in the context of kinship and political clusters elsewhere (chapter 10), I am concerned in this chapter to examine the Gypsies' mortuary rites and beliefs as part of a total cosmology, including the implications for relations with non-Gypsies. There is historical continuity in the evidence both from the nineteenth and early twentieth centuries compiled by Thompson (1924 and 1930a) and that from my own fieldwork. It is of primary significance that for the Gypsies or Travellers death is seen as a polluting event.

Thompson has not investigated in depth the Gypsies' preference as to where death should take place, but makes several mentions of a special 'death tent' destroyed after burial (1924:8,10,14). For the Gypsies encountered in my fieldwork, death should occur ideally in a liminal place, outside the camp, and now in a Gorgio hospital, thanks to the National Health Service:

> When Billy's cancer was diagnosed, his relatives insisted on bringing him back to his trailer. Billy refused to undergo the operation suggested by the doctor. As symptoms developed and death seemed imminent, he was returned to hospital, but not in any expectation of cure. A new suit accompanied him, since the deceased must be buried in new or best clothing.

Once in hospital, the dying must be visited as often as possible, regardless of hospital rules, and death should be witnessed by kin and spouse. This contrasts with the obligatory privacy and sexual segregation at Gypsy birth (see Okely 1975d and chapter 11). In both cases, Gorgios are given the most polluting tasks in a location formerly not so easily available.

Thompson recorded the Gypsies' aversion to handling the corpse and the general preference for Gorgios to do the laying out (1924:15). The implication is, as it seemed from my fieldwork, that the dead body is polluting. Formerly the corpse was guarded night and day in the 'death tent' and sometimes on the edge of the camp (Thompson 1924:12). Today, according to my fieldwork, the corpse is brought back from hospital to the camp the day before the funeral and subjected to a similar vigil. Already cognates, associates and other Travellers will have assembled in the locality, and those closest to the deceased will sit up night and day around a fire (*yog*) which, like the lights in the deceased's trailer, is to ward off the *mulo*. Thompson noted: 'Afraid of the ghost, they said; that is why they sit in company round the fire' (1924:13). The corpse is today generally displayed in an open coffin and dressed in new clothing. The corpse must not be naked in a shroud (cf. Thompson 1924:16-18). A dead woman must be clothed in a suit of jacket and skirt, not a dress, I was informed. Perhaps this indicates top/bottom symbolism, although not as definite as among

217

Californian Gypsies (Sutherland 1975:264). More emphatic for English Travellers is the inside/outside symbolism; the clothing should be put on inside-out, I was told. Thompson noted this practice (1924:22-3) but offers no satisfactory explanation. His examples of Gypsies who, when lost at night, turned their clothes inside-out suggests merely that the living dress like a *mulo* to avoid being recognised and harmed.

The open coffin is placed in the deceased's trailer whose walls may be draped with white sheets. This is the last time the deceased, now inside the trailer, is permitted such access to Gypsy society. One Gypsy informed me: 'In the old days they put the person out on the shafts, not in the trailer.' As in the past (Thompson 1924:12), post-menopausal women have key roles as vigilators, with special powers to combat pollution. Several Gypsies informed me that they saw the ghost of the deceased during this period between death and burial.[2] An older woman declared: 'Its our religion to sit up with the dead.'

Mourners imitate the state of pollution of the deceased by refraining from washing. They abstain from sleep and cooked meals, especially meat (cf. Thompson 1924:11). Everyone should wear dark colours, preferably black, especially at the funeral. Women put on black or dark aprons and black scarves. Some dye their hair black. The Gypsy men wear black ties. At the funeral, handkerchiefs, polluted articles not used at other times, are conspicuous among both men and women.[3] Men who sometimes conceal baldness under trilby hats, both inside and outside a trailer, are now hatless.

Before the arrival of the funeral cars, the Travellers pay a last tribute to the dead (cf. Thompson 1924:8-9). One Traveller asserted 'You're not supposed to touch the dead, but you can talk to them.' This is consistent with the relegation to Gorgios of the laying out. I am uncertain whether this untouchability extends to the final parting where other Travellers stated that the corpse's face must be touched before the lid is closed: 'You must touch the face all over, otherwise you'll never forget it.' Note that the aim is to dispatch the dead fully from the minds of the living.

There is evidence that the cart used to take the coffin to the burial place was burnt afterwards (Thompson 1924:90). Today the Gypsies hire a hearse for the coffin and funeral cars for the chief mourners, so the pollution associated with these vehicles remains with Gorgios, just as with the marquee and chairs often hired from Gorgios for the vigil. One Gypsy encountered in this study was treated to a funeral with black plumed horses and open carriage.

To the Travellers the most memorable stage of the death rite is the journey to the churchyard (see also chapter 10). Thompson records large processions (1924:29) but does not explore their significance. This procession is the last time that the deceased travels. One Gypsy told me that when the corpse was placed on the shafts 'in the old days,

The procession to the grave. *Herts Advertiser*

the feet were facing out'. 'Why?' I asked, and was told: 'Thats because he's *going out.*'

The floral wreaths take many forms – an imitation cushion, a miniature horse and waggon, a replica lorry, a horseshoe, a miniature chair, even the deceased's own chair swathed in flowers, a floral television set or the motif of 'the gates of heaven'. Some are replicas of the things most liked by the dead person: 'everything he liked to handle', I was told. A young boy, fond of pepsi-cola, had a giant floral pepsi bottle at his funeral. The *J.G.L.S.* notes many funerals with elaborate wreaths. One that took place in Flintshire in 1955 was for a Mrs Fox (her surname may explain the main wreath):

> a wreath representing a dog was placed on top of the coffin, and a bird-cage covered with flowers on the hearse. Other reports mention that among the wreaths there was one in the shape of a box of matches and cigarettes (which Mrs Fox always kept at her bedside), and others shaped like a chair, a cooking-tripod, a boar's head and a horse-collar.
>
> (Leach 1956)

Thompson (1924) has ample evidence for the practice of placing the favourite possessions of the deceased inside the coffin. A Gypsy informed him these were 'things what the dead person was more fonder on than others and might find want of' (1924:24). Leland also records this practice (1893:58-9). It ensures that the dead person will

219

Chair wreaths and mourners. *Herts Advertiser*

not come looking for these possessions among his/her family or former *atchen tans* (stopping places). Thompson (1924) and Leland (1893) both record that coins were placed in the coffin. I found little evidence for this. One case was described to me of a gold sovereign placed in a young girl's coffin. I also learnt that each witness placed a coin in a bag, tied to the hospital bed-post, at the moment of death of one Traveller.

As already indicated in chapter 10, the length of the procession of hearse, funeral cars and lorries, often bringing local traffic to a standstill, and with a police escort, is a measure of the prestige of the deceased. Travellers show their respect by what they call 'following' a person. When the procession arrives at the church, the service is the least significant rite for the Gypsies. It appears to be Gorgio mumbo-jumbo which ensures the Gypsy's right to burial in a churchyard where the body is safest. The majority of Travellers do not attempt to enter the church, but stand outside chatting. The close cognates accompany the coffin, which is sometimes carried by Gypsy men, other times by Gorgio bearers. Inside the church the Travellers sit bolt upright throughout the service ignoring all requests to kneel or stand at the allotted moments. Hymns, in any case, cannot be read from books. No attempt is made to mouth or memorise them. But the Gorgio parson is confronted by the extraordinary and seemingly hysterical displays of sobbing and wailing (see chapter 10). After a funeral I attended, the parson gave his reaction to a journalist: 'It was very sad.' By contrast, the Gorgio wife of a Gypsy informed me: 'They say people have to cry out of pity for the dead. They've got to put on a show, even if they don't feel it.'[4]

The coffin is carried out of the church followed now by everyone to the graveside. After the coffin is lowered, and the close cognates have left first (some have to be carried out), the others gradually disperse. The wreaths are examined and heaped around the grave. It was at this juncture that I once heard a Gypsy remark: 'There's nothing more we can do for him now.'

In the past, relatives kept watch over the grave, when grave rifling and body snatching were a regular threat. Removal of the whole or parts of the body is dangerous as the *mulo* will not rest. The pre-burial

Children throw earth on the grave of a dead Gypsy. *Herts Advertiser*

vigil also ensures against this. James Crabb records the Gypsies' aversion to medical dissection in the nineteenth century:

> A Gypsy man, who was noted for his height and muscular strength, died of consumption. A medical gentleman, who knew not the Gypsy character, applied to them for the corpse; when, astonished and filled with indignation at his request, they would have done him a serious injury had he not speedily galloped from the camp. (1832:28-30)

Today the main threat is not theft for dissection in medical schools, but removal of organs for transplants, before or at death:

> A doctor and matron took Terry's father and wife aside. Would they consent to the removal of his kidneys at death? They said it seemed a pity to let these organs from an otherwise healthy young man go to waste and they would save another's life. The Gypsies were horrified and kept returning unexpectedly to examine Terry, hours after he died. They asked a social worker to talk to the hospital authorities.

Formerly, the Gypsies tried where possible to obtain interment not merely in a churchyard, but inside the church. Again it seems that the concern was that the body be safe from theft or tampering. In one case given by Thompson, it was specifically stated that interment in the church was 'not on account of any notion of sanctity of the place, but for its security' (1924:62). 'From the sixteenth century onwards records of Gypsy interments occur in plenty in parish registers' (Thompson 1924:66). (Thompson (1924) noted, incidentally, three Gypsy burials at the end of the eighteenth century within my fieldwork area). Burial on unsanctified ground was apparently very rare. Since the early nineteenth century, interment in churches has been difficult to obtain, but Travellers continue to prefer burial in churchyards. They reject cremation: 'We don't believe in it.' Presumably it would imply that the *mulo* had no proper resting place.

The funeral over, the personal possessions of the deceased must be destroyed as they are both polluted and a magnate for the *mulo*. Clothing, bedding, personal crockery, work tools, are broken up and burned on the perimeters of the camp. Parts may be buried or dropped into deep water. In theory, antique china should be destroyed and jewellery buried with the deceased. Thompson offers many examples of destruction of property (1924:23-4, 76-81). Both his information (1924:87) and mine reveal that money is not destroyed. The pattern of distribution of cash among descendants and spouse is variable. In practice the valuables are not always destroyed. Antique china and jewellery may be quietly sold, usually to Gorgio dealers. The deceased's animals, horses and dogs should also be killed (cf. Thompson 1924:77, 85-6). Alternatively they are sold to Gorgios or given to vets to destroy.

The consequences of retaining a dead person's property were vividly described by a Gypsy to Thompson. The retainer would suffer bad luck, disease, insanity and ostracism by other Gypsies, including close kin who would consider the wrongdoer under a curse (1924:87). The dead person's possessions will, it is feared, attract the *mulo* who will behave in odd ways. This was confirmed by Travellers during my fieldwork:

> Eileen described how her dead father-in-law's shaving brush, which was accidentally overlooked after his death, started hopping along a shelf.

As important as the personal effects of the deceased is the destruction of his or her former home, the trailer where the body was laid for the final vigil and to which the *mulo* is most likely to return. Failure to dispose of the trailer will bring bad luck, disease, continuing pollution and possibly a further death. The destruction of the home, formerly the horse-drawn waggon, is recorded also in the nineteenth century (Thompson 1924:77-81). The case study in chapter 10 reveals the problems when the deceased's trailer is not burnt. A Gypsy had retained the trailer after his wife's death. When their daughter died three years later it was said: 'There must have been something in the trailer, in the boards and walls.' The trailer was polluted, but also haunted by the revengeful *mulo*. I was directly involved in another example:

> On one encampment, the only available council trailer for me had formerly been rented out to an elderly Gypsy woman. At her death the council reclaimed it. The Travellers were extremely upset, insisting it should be burnt. Curiously no one tried, possibly because they feared to approach it. I was not at first sensitive to the full implications of living in this trailer. It had advantages, as I was guaranteed privacy especially after dark. Whereas Gypsy adults visited me in my previous trailer, virtually no one but children would enter this one. Some adults feared standing talking to me at the door because they had 'known her'. I was asked if I had been visited by the old lady's ghost. One neighbour said she had heard the ghost crying and banging the door. Another told everyone I had seen the ghost. One night a Traveller woman slept in the trailer with me, after being driven out by her sister and brother-in-law who were tired of sheltering her. She was frightened, so her sister lit a fire in the trailer to keep the *mulo* away. It was midsummer. My companion also insisted the light be kept on all night.

When the trailer is destroyed, the metal not consumed by the fire is weighed into the Gorgio scrapyard.[5] In one case a Gorgio student

223

making a waggon asked a Traveller couple for the aluminium sides of the trailer they were breaking up after the death of their child. They refused, saying that the material should never be used for another home. This family, to the disapproval of the Gypsy community, did not break up the trailer until a year after the death. The mother confided that she wanted to see her dead child 'just once'. Also, she could not so rapidly part with her memories of his presence in the trailer.

Some families possess extremely valuable trailers which are rarely destroyed after a death. The corpse is laid in a cheaper trailer, later destroyed, or a hired marquee. The main trailer is transported out of the region and sold, usually to Gorgio dealers who may be able to resell them to a Traveller, who will not be publicly confronted by its history and in any case will not have known the dead owner. The *mulo* is most likely to trouble those whom he or she knew in life. 'The buyer wouldn't ask too many questions', I was told. Here again the Gorgio is used to solve the Gypsy problem of pollution and to the Gypsies' financial advantage. There is evidence that at least fifty years ago Gypsies with costly waggons often refrained from burning them and instead sold them to Gorgio dealers (Thompson 1924:82). This may account for the survival in Gorgio hands, for example in the Bristol Museum, of a few ornate and 'traditional' Gypsy waggons. No Gypsy would live in them. Today the wealthy families may lay the body in a cheaper trailer or tent which is later destroyed while the main trailer is sold. Trigg claims that trailers are no longer destroyed or disposed of, allegedly because of their new high cost and the restrictions of living on official sites (1975:132). Clearly my evidence from fieldwork contradicts this. The Gypsies have adapted to new circumstances in a way which ensures the continuity of their attitude to their dead.

After the disposal of the trailer and property of the deceased, ideally all camp members should leave, if only for a while. The surest way to avoid the *mulo* is to travel. The close family are most likely to be haunted, so on an official site they may be the only ones to leave. They may return after some months or maybe never (cf. Thompson 1924:92). It is important whether the death actually occurred on the Gypsy camp or in hospital. If the former, the camp is especially polluted and dangerous:

> When Ivy was found dead in her trailer on a permanent site, the older Traveller woman who first discovered her and called the ambulance insisted that Ivy was not fully dead; 'she was still warm'. If it could be shown that Ivy died in the Gorgio ambulance and not on the site, the other tenants would be less threatened.

On another site where a man died *in situ*, the widow left only briefly as she was well placed for welfare benefits and had no close associates on any other site. One Traveller informed me: 'It's bad to stop at a place

where Travellers have died. It don't matter if Gorgios have died there.'
Many feared the sight of any ghosts, be they Gypsy or Gorgio, but they
were most likely to be haunted by the *mulo* of those with whom they
were closely associated in life. I was told sometimes I need not fear the
mulo of the previous inhabitant of my trailer: 'The dead only come to
those that knew them.'

Mourning is obligatory for the widowed spouse and close cognates,
for a year or more. The women continue to wear black clothing and
dark scarves and the men sombre colours, and occasionally black
armbands. The favourite food or hobby of the deceased may be
abstained from (cf. Leland 1893:49-55; Thompson 1924:92), again to
appease the *mulo*. The name of the deceased must never be uttered as
this is equivalent to 'calling up' the *mulo* (cf. Leland 1893:56-8). After
death, a person may for example be referred to as 'Jane's mother' or
'that old man that used to stop at Mill Pond Lane'. Someone with the
same name will generally be referred to by an alternative name, a deri-
vation or a nickname. This practice may well have psychological implications (see Dollé 1970:15 and his remarks on 'scotomisation' above),
but it should also be asked why the group fears the very specific practice of 'calling up' the *mulo*.

Neither the name nor the image of the dead should be given status
inside Gypsy society. Photographs should be destroyed, or at least not
publicly displayed inside the trailer.

> 'Betty's got her mother's photos all around her trailer. That's
> not right. It'd make me *trashed*' (frightened). (The speaker
> possessed one small photo of her mother which she kept with
> other family photos in a bag.)

A Gypsy will be known to be telling the truth if he or she takes the following oath:

> 'May my dead mother [or father etc.] who is lying in the grave
> rise up and take me or my children if what I say ain't true.'

Leland (1893:55-6) records a similar practice.

The mulo needs a fixed abode

Here I come to the central focus in the Gypsies' response to their dead.
The *mulo* is always a potential threat to the living, at least for the generations who knew him or her. The dead must be appeased in every
way possible. There seems to be no eventual re-integration nor benign
acceptance of the Gypsies' dead. Mythical ancestors of some generations' distance and immediate ancestors may feature in Traveller
stories, but do not assume an enviable status as honoured dead in a
higher or better realm.

It has been suggested[6] that the Gypsies use their bodies as the crucial

225

arena for expressing boundary maintenance because as nomads their bodies are the only things they always take with them. My interpretation of the evidence suggests that the dead must be made to cease travelling and that the *mulo* must become sedentarised. Significantly the dead person's name is written clearly on the grave. In a non-literate community this is the only context when writing (sometimes dismissed as a Gorgio attribute) is freely chosen to mark identity. A Gypsy would not utter to Hindes Groome his father's name, but instead produced a photograph of the grave with the name of the headstone (quoted by Thompson 1924:91). Hindes Groome learnt that Gypsies considered it bad luck to be drawn or sketched because blood was thus stolen from the face, and those portrayed might waste away and die (1880:337-8). Similarly, Travellers of today resent being photographed by Gorgios; there they are captured and frozen in time (and of course more vulnerable to Gorgio control). They are as cautious about giving away their names to Gorgios. By contrast, on the gravestone in Gorgio churchyards the Gypsies' names are finally exposed. In this way, the *mulo* must be laid to rest with the body and with its last image and name. Identification by naming is paralleled by the marking of the wreaths of floral lorries with the correct number plates of the deceased's last vehicle, so identified and brought to a halt. This again contrasts with the measures taken by Travellers to prevent Gorgios photographing their vehicles with number plates in view, and contrasts with their regular turnover of vehicles, chopped and changed through life.

For a sedentary society the place of birth is the primary marker. For Gypsies the grave is the ultimate marker. Among sedentary peoples a frequent question is: 'Where do you come from?' For travelling Gypsies this question offers no answer. It is best to ask where the person will be buried. Irish Travellers in England, with few exceptions, return their dead for burial in Ireland[7] thus affirming their national allegiance. The English Gypsies encountered in fieldwork chose to bury their dead near the graves of close cognates. Such graveyards, containing a number of Traveller graves, are important features of the Travellers' landscape.

The Travellers' mortuary rites can be seen as attempts to ensure the dispatch of the dead, who are dangerous if without a single, fixed location. The *mulo* needs a fixed abode. Thus great attention is paid to the grave. Costly headstones and vases are selected and jointly purchased by close cognates and associates. Wreaths must be regularly laid. Many of the wreaths laid at the funeral have, alongside the theme of travelling (as in the floral lorry), the theme of sedentarisation; of being rested and seated, as suggested by the floral chairs, cushions, pillows and televisions. Another popular wreath in the form of 'the gates of heaven' marks the final threshold. These gates indicate not necessarily the optimism of 'they've gone before', but that the dead have gone where there must be no return. The gates must stay closed behind them. The dead must be locked away from living Travellers.

Ghosts and Gorgios

In dramatic contrast to the camping ground, the grave must be kept scrupulously tidy. I accompanied a family to the grave of their young son. The father that very day had said: 'I like living in a dust bowl', in defiance of a television programme deploring the 'squalor' of Gypsy camps. In the churchyard I watched him making four separate journeys from the grave to the rubbish bin with last week's withered flowers, leaves and scraps of paper. In addition to weekly visits or more, the parents, like many other Travellers, paid the keeper to tend the grave. For the dead Gypsy's sake, the grave is a focus of cleanliness and order, just like the inside of the trailer, but outside Gypsy society. Graves must be regularly tended and visited lest perhaps their inhabitants return to the Gypsy camp. In addition to anniversaries, wreaths are laid at Christmas time and sometimes before the fairs to appease the *mulo* which might be attracted by the festive gatherings of the living.

Interpretation

In referring to one aspect of the Gypsies' mortuary rites, Thompson suggests: 'Fear, then, would seem to lie at the root of English Gypsy funeral sacrifice' (1924:89). But this is no explanation for the fear in the first place. Such an argument is tautologous. We should ask why the fear is so extreme among the Travellers. Although it might be argued by some that it is 'natural' for all peoples to feel frightened by the death of others, this does not explain why the Gypsies' beliefs and actions take these specific public forms. The Travellers' beliefs and actions cannot be explained away as 'common sense'. In some respects, they are markedly different from those of the surrounding Gorgios. Given that the Travellers regard themselves as different from Gorgios, it is also important to understand in what ways and why some of the Travellers' mortuary rites may be similar to those of the Gorgios.

First, at a Gypsy's death, the body is polluting and we see that attempts are made to place the dead in sanctified Gorgio territory. The outward appearance of the grave is kept orderly, although this attention cannot render the corpse clean and unpolluted.[8] Recalling the vital separation for the Gypsies between the inner and outer body discussed in chapter 6, we see that in death the corpse and the *mulo* are *mochadi*. This is because boundaries have been broken. At a Gypsy's death, I suggest, the separation between inner and outer body is no longer distinct; the inside has come outside. The corpse's clothes placed inside-out are a symbolic expression of this exposure. The bodily boundary is broken, so also is the boundary between Gypsy and Gorgio. It seems that the Travellers' tidying of the graves of their dead is in conformity with the Gorgios' emphasis on outer appearance, and in contrast to their priorities on their camp sites.

Secondly, there are also themes of settlement and appeasement in the Travellers' treatment of their dead. The Gorgio church service is treated as a *rite de passage* from the living and from the Gypsy group to an identity and place more Gorgio and settled. The grave in Gorgio hallowed ground is the necessary placing of the *mulo*, ideally sedentarised. It must not travel. Neither the polluted corpse nor parts of it must be allowed indecisive location. Hence the measures to prevent body snatching, dissection and transplants. Transplants would be doubly confusing as the organ would live on in another body. The dead body must be pinned down in space, just as Gorgios would pin down Gypsies on their sites.

The threat from the *mulo* is elaborate.[9] It is not merely that it is polluted, it is also malevolent. What characteristics does the *mulo* possess? Its intentions cannot be known, it is unpredictable, it may hurt out of caprice. It may suddenly appear to the Gypsies and may as suddenly disappear. The *mulo* brings diseases and may try to lure Travellers to their death. It can sometimes be kept away if given its possessions and maybe food. Gypsies can more successfully outrun the *mulo* by travelling and avoiding places liked and frequented by it (cf. Sutherland 1975:285).

I conclude that the *mulo* of a dead Gypsy has become like a Gorgio. Death is equivalent to assimilation. When the Travellers express their fear of the *mulo* they are reaffirming symbolically their fear of the Gorgio. Like the *mulo*, the Gorgio is unpredictable and may suddenly enter a camp site and as quickly disappear. The Gorgio may hurt or prosecute out of caprice. The Gorgio is *mochadi*, brings diseases and lures Gypsies to their death. The Gorgio in a sedentary society has a permanent interest in property. Just as the Travellers must avoid the favourite camp sites of their dead, so the Travellers must avoid land which Gorgios have regularly frequented. To escape Gorgio control, the Gypsies appear to give Gorgios what they want. To appease the *mulo*, the Gypsies give wreaths and attention, and abandon claims to its property. Gorgios must be discouraged from entering the trailer, and as with the *mulo*, elaborate devices are used to keep them out. If the Gorgio, like the *mulo*, cannot be kept at a distance by discouraging intimacy, the Gypsies keep travelling.

In some discussions the Travellers consciously associate banishment or assimilation with death. When a Traveller is banished from the group, the father and family pronounce the Traveller dead. His or her name is never mentioned again and is seen as polluting. This may happen when a Gypsy 'marries out' and to a Gorgio specifically disapproved of by the Gypsies, or when the Gypsy has committed an outrageous act.

> When a Gypsy woman ran off with a married Gypsy man she left her children, whom her deserted husband put into a Gorgio home as revenge. The woman's father was informed and, to his humiliation, had to collect them. The father threatened

to 'cry dead' his daughter. 'That'd been a terrible thing. He would never 've talked of her again. He wouldn't have gone to her funeral 'cos she'd be already dead. But he took pity on the grandchildren.'

In these circumstances the Gypsy is obliged to move into Gorgio society, and banishment is equated with death. Other forms of assimilation are associated with death: after the new 'permanent' and Gorgio controlled sites were opened, the Travellers' anxiety was indicated by their comments on the number of deaths which had occurred among tenants. 'There's several Travellers who 'ave died since these sites were opened. Something's wrong.' In fact the more elaborate sites tended to attract the aged and infirm, but this explanation for one or two deaths on sites was not suggested. Instead, the sites were seen as inherently threatening.

In the cases above, assimilation is equated with death, but I am also arguing the inverse: that death is less explicitly equated with assimilation or even sedentarisation, given the Gypsies' ideology of travelling. When the Gypsies destroy a dead person's property they are reminding themselves that complex inheritance laws and accumulated property are associated with sedentarisation. Extra special observances are required of close kin in laying the *mulo* to rest, to show that they do not benefit, through inheritance, by their cognate's death. They also demonstrate to the rest of the community that they have disassociated themselves from the dead.

Funerals, however, are not merely the concern of close cognates, as we saw in chapter 10. Any Travellers acquainted with the deceased gather together to dispatch the dead Gypsy from the living. The unity of Gypsies at funerals, transcending internal rivalry, is both a political and religious statement. All Travellers must combine against the greater threat of death within the group and against the Gorgio, whose likeness Gypsies assume after death. The Gorgio pursues the Gypsies to the grave and at the grave.

> I saw how the police provided an escort for a Gypsy funeral procession: not, the Gypsies stated, for traffic control, but to trap a man on the run, who must surely attend. He did, and everyone knew. The Gypsies rejoiced that he came and went free.

Thus there seems no joyful beyond, no Gypsy survival after death, only a blank space; a nothingness to be filled by Gorgios. The ultimate truth is that Gypsies are not separated from Gorgios in death. For Travellers, their children are their regeneration; the continuous thread of existence. Their dead ancestors are not the focus of continuity. As a revengeful and unpredictable *mulo*, the dead individual loses Gypsy or Traveller identity and his or her name is written in a Gorgio medium on

229

the gravestone. The dead Traveller is no longer classified as a member of the Gypsy group which continues elsewhere, in another place. In the celebrated 'Wind on the Heath' dialogue the Gypsy Jasper Petulengro says: 'When a man dies, he is cast into the earth, and there is an end of the matter.' Petulengro argues with Borrow:

> 'Life is very sweet, brother; who would wish to die?'
> 'I would wish to die...'
> 'You talk like a gorgio – which is the same as talking like a fool – were you a Romany Chal you would talk wiser. Wish to die, indeed!... A Romany Chal would wish to live for ever!'
>
> (Borrow 1851:325-6)

Acceptance of death is thus treated as a Gorgio characteristic.

Thus we see that so-called 'resurrectionism' and the Travellers' use of Gorgio church and graveyards are neither raw material for nor evidence of conversion to the Gorgio brand of Christianity. The Gypsies' mortuary rites are neither merely 'magical beliefs' as has been patronisingly suggested (Trigg 1968:100), nor admirable piety. As in many mortuary rites, the identity, social organisation and ideology of the living are disguised and inverted. That which pleases the Gorgio observer is ironically a rejection of his or her kind. The boundary between life and death is used to make symbolic statements about another ethnic boundary. The loss of a Gypsy through death is not seen merely as a loss of another human being and member of an amorphous society, but the loss of a member of a specific minority group, always vulnerable within the larger society. The Gypsy dead have crossed the ethnic boundary. The mortuary rites affirm the living Gypsies' separation from Gorgios, and their fear of becoming one of them.

Concluding remarks

The ending cannot be a conclusion as if I began with a hypothesis to be tested, in accord with the methods of positivism. Nor has this study been cast as 'problem-oriented'. In so far as there is a problem to be confronted, it is one which has been created largely by the dominant non-Gypsy order. The Gypsies have been classed as problematic because they have refused to be proletarianised, and have instead chosen to exploit self-employment and occupational and geographical flexibility. Within the larger economy they provide a variety of goods and services, many of which other persons or groups cannot or do not wish to provide. Using kinship and descent to restrict entry into the group, Gypsies express and maintain their separateness through ideas of purity and pollution.

The separation between Gypsy and Gorgio is socially constructed and can never be absolute. The Gypsy economy is interdependent with that of the larger economy, and the Travellers have always had to negotiate with Gorgio authorities for intermittent access to land. A 'modernisation' theoretical approach is to be rejected. It is a misrepresentation to suggest that the Gypsies were once self-sufficient and that they have inevitably been threatened by industrialisation and urbanisation. New problems have emerged for them, but these have not necessarily been those of economic redundancy. New occupations have been exploited. The Travellers' main difficulties in Britain have been the increased restrictions placed on their access to camping land. This does not mean that Gypsies were once tolerated in some golden past and in rural settings, as has so often been claimed.

The threat which the Gypsies, as a minority, appear to represent to the larger society is largely ideological. They are seen to defy the dominant system of wage-labour and its demand for a fixed abode. Not surprisingly, from the first appearance of persons called or calling themselves Gypsies in Britain in the sixteenth century, the state has attempted to control, disperse, deport, convert or destroy them. This study has outlined the repressive measures used against Gypsies, and charted some of the ways in which Gypsies have attempted to deal with and survive others' plans for them. History has demonstrated the Gypsies' survival as an ethnic group, despite attempts even at their extermination. The use of force by the dominant order against Gypsies has in the long run proved ineffective and only of expressive worth. The liberal integrationist view has also been misguided. Neither force nor charity have succeeded in making the Traveller-Gypsies disappear. It would seem better to recognise the Gypsies' continuing existence as an ethnic group which has chosen to reject assimilation. One answer for the majority is to seek ways in which confrontation can be minimised. For example, legal access to land rather than the monolithic construction of residential sites, designed and controlled by Gorgio authorities, should be an immediate priority. There is land enough.

Parallel to the various forms of control to which they have been subject, the Gypsies have also been exoticised by their allies and opponents. Outsiders have projected on to Gypsies their own repressed fantasies and longings for disorder. They have credited Gypsies with the inverse of all that they consider normal. Thus the Gypsies have been represented as lawless, amoral, unclean, and part of nature in opposition to others' notion of culture. This study has confronted such fantasies.

Although I had some initial associations with policy-oriented research, I did not keep to that preordained path. Policy questions are invariably set by those in power, and restrict what needs to be learned. Even research with the most democratic and benevolent intentions will fail, if the questions of relevance are devised by the uninformed. In this study, there are indeed some answers and lessons for Gorgio decision makers. However, my approach has been independent. Here the holistic and open ended approach of anthropology has authority.

The view from within and below[1] gives voice to those who are not represented in the social circles of the state. Ultimately the representation here of Traveller-Gypsies remains that of a non-member, despite the years of participant observation. As a Gorgio and outsider anthropologist, I cannot lay claim to any position as spokesperson. I lived and worked with the Travellers. They extended me their protection and friendship. They imparted to me their knowledge and wisdom. I was a witness. I mingled with Gorgio officials and supporters and observed their encounters with Gypsies. I listened to their accounts and read their reports and files. I have lived with those times long since. This book is in part a testimony of that experience.

Some Travellers, especially those with positions in national organisations, might object to any intrusive research. Yet they know that the Travellers' existence is affected by the way Gorgios represent them. Travellers cannot escape the gaze of the Gorgio. There are many naive or malicious misrepresentations to be countered. My aim has been to provide as far as possible an inside perspective which has been analysed in a form developed outside the non-literate group. I have translated and interpreted. Another aim has been to return part of the Travellers' history to them. I hope that the Travellers can make use of it.

Extract from *The Scholar Gipsy*

And near me on the grass lies Glanvil's book -
Come, let me read the oft-read tale again,
The story of that Oxford scholar poor,
Of pregnant parts and quick inventive brain,
Who, tir'd of knocking at Preferment's door,
One summer morn forsook
His friends, and went to learn the Gipsy lore,
And roam'd the world with that wild brotherhood,
And came, as most men deem'd, to little good,
But came to Oxford and his friends no more.

But once, years after, in the country lanes,
Two scholars, whom at College erst he knew,
Met him, and of his way of life inquir'd.
Whereat he answer'd that the Gipsy crew,
His mates, had arts to rule as they desir'd
The workings of men's brains;
And they can bind them to what thoughts they will:
'And I', he said, 'the secret of their art,
When fully learn'd, will to the world impart:
But it needs heaven-sent moments for this skill!'

This said, he left them, and return'd no more,
But rumours hung about the country side,
That the lost Scholar long was seen to stray,
Seen by rare glimpses, pensive and tongue-tied,
In hat of antique shape, and cloak of grey,
The same the Gipsies wore.
Shepherds had met him on the Hurst in spring;
At some lone alehouse in the Berkshire moors,
On the warm ingle bench, the smock-frock'd boors
Had found him seated at their entering.

...

And once, in winter, on the causeway chill
Where home through flooded fields foot-travellers go,
Have I not pass'd thee on the wooden bridge
Wrapt in thy cloak and battling with the snow,

Thy face towards Hinksey and its wintry ridge?
And thou hast climb'd the hill
And gain'd the white brow of the Cumner range;
Turn'd once to watch, while thick the snowflakes fall,
The line of festal light in Christ-Church hall;
Then sought thy straw in some sequester'd grange.

But what – I dream! Two hundred years are flown
Since first thy story ran through Oxford halls,
And the grave Glanvil did the tale inscribe
That thou wert wander'd from the studious walls
To learn strange arts, and join a Gipsy tribe:
…

Matthew Arnold (1853)

Notes

1. Historical categories and representations

1 The terms Gypsy or Traveller are used interchangeably and in no way indicate any hierarchy in ethnic identity (see chapter 5).
2 See chapter 5 for discussion of the definition of an ethnic group.
3 Anthropologists have found many similar practices among different societies around the world. They do not conclude that these all have a common spatial origin.
4 See Okely 1980, for an over-view of some of the literature on Gypsies in Europe.

2. Modern misrepresentations

1 This chapter is addressed to some of the themes suggested in the 'Changing Culture' series; see p. ii.

3. Methods of approach

1 Gypsies or their equivalents have been recorded currently in the Soviet Union and as far east as Thailand; in India, Iran, Afghanistan, North Africa, North and South America, Australia, and throughout western and eastern Europe.
2 I have made some suggestions as to how this could be explored in 'The Self and Scientism' (Okely 1975f).
3 On discovering that research on Gypsies was to be conducted at the Centre for Environmental Studies, a senior civil servant appealed to the Director and Governors to prevent any such research being done outside the Ministry. Fortunately a charitable trust had already supplied the grant.
4 All examples and case studies, unless otherwise stated, are from my own notes and fieldwork.

4. Economic niche

1 This chapter is an abbreviated and amended version of my 'Work and Travel' in Adams et al. 1975.
2 See later section in this chapter, 'Economic status and expenditure', for a discussion of economic status (pp. 63-4).
3 In this study it was unfortunately not possible to make a detailed economic analysis of the organisation of the trailer unit. Its composition is described in chapter 9. The wife's major subsistence contribution in

contrast to the husband's virtual monopoly of capital goods is referred to in chapter 11. Only a few observations can be made here, e.g. the internal divisions.

4   Bender tents are made from branches curved to an igloo shape after each branch end is driven into the ground, then covered with tarpaulin, sacking or polythene. See p. 147.

5   See Okely 1975c: 304-6 for examples.

6   See Okely 1975c: 149-51 for the figures from the total Centre for Environmental Studies sample indicating the different emphasis in occupations according to economic status.

7   The government census of Travellers in Eire, for example, asked of individuals: 'Has he/she *a* trade or craft? If so, what?' and 'Would he/she like to learn *a* trade or craft?' The recorded answers indicated only those specialised trades or crafts recognised in the larger society, with a marked division of labour. Positive answers were given to both questions by only a third of all adults. The questions precluded the recognition of generalised skills (*Report of the Commission on Itinerancy* 1963).

5. Self-ascription

1   This chapter is an abbreviated and amended version of my 'Gypsy Identity' in Adams *et al.* 1975.

2   By contrast, Acton applies the word 'Traveller' which 'gives the key to their ethnic separateness' (1974:64) to *either* of the following: first 'any person ... living on the road; following one of the modes of self employment ... perceived as the "Gypsy trades"...' Second, 'any person whose parents or other ancestors were 'Travellers' (1974:65). Only the second gives priority to descent.

3   This contrasts with the example of Heathcliff in Brontë's *Wuthering Heights* (pp. 64-5 in the Collins 1953 edition), a foundling of alleged Gypsy origins taken into a non-Gypsy household, who was 'wild', vengeful, but not inherently evil as the Gorgio foundling in the Gypsy story.

6. Symbolic boundaries

1   It will be obvious to the reader that in my discussion on pollution, boundaries and the symbolism of the body, I have been greatly influenced by the work of Mary Douglas, and more specifically her *Purity and Danger* (1966).

2   Personal communication, B. Adams.

3   Sharon and George Gmelch, when I questioned them about Irish Travellers, revealed a similar preference among them for wrapped food and a fear of poisoning. However, the Gmelches denied the existence of pollution taboos.

4   Sutherland (1975:275) has more systematic information on Californian Gypsy attitudes to health and illness. Health is associated with luck (*baxt*). The English Gypsies also have the notion of luck; the expression *kushti bok* (good luck) is very important.

I am grateful to Sutherland for the stimulus of her paper at Oxford in

1972 and to Acton (1971). They raised questions I then had to answer in my own fieldwork. Sutherland acknowledges her debt to Miller. My chapters on pollution were virtually complete before I could read Miller (1968 and 1975). I now find great similarities in our independent findings among the different groups.

5 My analysis of animal categories has been influenced by the articles of Leach (1972) and Tambiah (1973). I am grateful to Dr Tambiah for his inspiring lectures on many aspects of social anthropology at Cambridge 1969-70.

6 Thompson notes: 'after the meal Lavinia handed a plate of potatoes to Starkey to give to the dogs. Starkey began fooling about as usual, so she shouted out: "Mind what yous is doing … Mind that dog there doesn't touch that plate with its dirty snout." Then turning to me, she added, "We never lets a dog lick off'n a plate; that would make it *moxadi*, and honfit for Christians to heat off'n"' (1910:320).

W.A. Dutt, after reading Thompson above, recalled Gilbert Boswell saying that 'if a dog happened to drink from a pail of drinking-water carried behind his van, his father, Algar Boswell, would drive a stake through the bottom of the pail to ensure its not being used again' (Dutt 1910:156). A study of Viennese Gypsies between the wars reveal the following phrase, 'If a cat or dog licks a plate, we break it' (Otter 1931:126).

7 Wood writes: 'Dogs you could handle as much as you liked but you were never allowed to let them lick your face, or to touch your face with your hands if they had been in contact with your dog until you have [*sic*] washed them' (1973:70).

8 Again Wood writes, 'Dogs were never considered as dirty as cats – you handled them all the time – but they were not allowed inside a waggon or tent' (1973:70).

9 Sampson records the Romany word for hedgehog among Welsh Gypsies as *urcos* (1926:IV, 387), apparently from the English urchin; which in the *Oxford English Dictionary* also means hedgehog.

10 Earlier drafts of this chapter have prompted my Gorgio audience to become informants of their own ethnography. One anthropologist asserted that dogs were more of a domestic symbol than cats for housedwellers, so my case could not rest on Gorgio classification. However, I am concerned not so much empirically with how (by opinion polls) the 'majority' of Gorgios classify animals but how Gypsies believe Gorgios classify animals. There will be some overlap, but not necessarily.

11 Defecating on an object is in psychoanalytic explanations commonly considered a display of destructive aggression towards the object. In this example the Gypsy administered an especially forceful punishment on the cat which cleans itself by licking.

12 Whereas Leland records that black cats were considered by Gypsies to be unlucky, and 'things of the devil', white cats were considered good; like the white ghosts of ladies (virgins) (1893:135-6).

13 A former college servant at All Souls, Oxford once described to me how his own fighting cock was stolen by Gypsies. He recognised it on the back of their waggon as he fortuitously drove behind them in the High Street. But he dared not take time off to pursue them as he was due to serve at a formal dinner in college.

14 Personal communication, M. Kaminski, 1975.
15 Personal communication, A. Sutherland, 1975.

8. Travelling

1 The data in table 6 are not based on answers to a questionnaire. Wherever possible I asked questions. Often information was more usefully volunteered and then recorded in my diary. The data was then separated out for each family. This method afforded greater reliability than a single answer to a question. The period of 12 months overlapped for the majority but not all families, since I got to know them at different times during my 18 months' extended fieldwork period. Some families gave the most detailed information concerning months prior to my first acquaintance. So I backdated this. There is a fixed variable – a continuous time space of 12 months for each family, thus covering the seasonal variations.

2 The 1967 Report indicated that 'more than half the families had been on their site for less than six months, and just over a third for less than a month' (M.H.L.G. 1967:14).

3 A reduction in short-term stays when motorised is possibly the explanation in the 1965 census for the broad differences in travelling habits between Yorkshire/Humberside, with the highest percentage of horse-drawn waggons (28%), and other regions. Gypsies were asked if they had travelled in the previous year; Yorkshire and Humberside revealed the highest percentage – 86% of families, compared for example with 62% in the south-east (M.H.L.G. 1967:14). Short stops were also more frequently reported from the northern region, although this may be explained by other factors such as the wider dispersal of work opportunities in less populated areas.

4 The massive increase in the price of petrol occurred after my main period of fieldwork and it may be that poorer Travellers have reduced their daily work radius, choosing instead to move their trailers and home-base each time into a new smaller daily radius. However, the price for iron and steel also increased in the mid 1970s, thus bringing greater rewards for the scrap dealers, until the collapse of the steel industry by 1980. Some Travellers continued to find lucrative outlets for the export of iron and steel to Spain (personal communication, A. Rowe).

9. The trailer unit, spouses and children

1 Wood, in his description of his pre-war adolescence (1973:26-7), indicated that his grandmother held a 'common purse' to which several related families had to contribute all their farm work earnings and from which they could borrow. This practice was not confirmed in my own fieldwork.

2 Sutherland found that Gorgio–Gypsy marriages were unacceptable, but quotes Tompkins (1967) who says these marriages work if the *Gaje* wife is willing to 'become completely absorbed in Gypsy culture' (1975:250).

10. Group relations and personal relatives

1 The letter from the representatives of the Romany Guild contained the

following: 'It is an insult to the Gypsy and to the non-Gypsy communities of England and Wales to suggest, as the article appears to suggest, that the totally inadequate site provision contemplated by local authorities ... should be available in the foreseeable future to the hundreds of European Gypsies who hold EEC passports' (*New Society*, 13 December 1973).

2   These names are fictitious for the protection of individual Travellers.

3   Territorial proximity appears to have no label equivalent to the Rom category *kumpania* in California (Sutherland 1975:32).

4   The way in which Travellers settle disputes cannot be dealt with in this book. A useful study of this among Gypsies in Finland is provided by Grönfors (1977). Some preliminary observations are in Okely 1977.

5   Unfortunately I was unable to witness these fights, and had to rely on descriptions from several individuals, thus enabling some cross-checking to be done.

6   When I tried to observe horse-dealing at Barnet Fair there was only one older woman standing at a distance. Suddenly the horse was sent charging in my direction, pinning me against a trailer. I do not think this was an accident, but a warning to a female intruder.

7   Thompson does have some detailed evidence of trials, or the equivalent of a *kris* (1930b). Women were often excluded. This may account for my not having found clear confirmation of such an institution. Thompson also discusses the Gypsies' obligations to each other concerning financial loans.

11. Gypsy women

1   This chapter is an amended version of Okely 1975d.

2   By suggesting that Gypsy women are placed in 'nature' as opposed to Gorgio 'culture' (cf. Ardener 1972), I am in no way suggesting that women are universally seen as part of 'nature', nor that men are always associated with 'culture'.

3   The restriction on public exposure of the breasts is in marked contrast to the Gypsies in California (Sutherland 1975), and Gypsies in France (Clébert 1967:218). Sutherland records that a woman could, however, pollute a man by lifting her skirt and exposing the lower part of her body.

4   It was said that a husband once had the right to throw his wife on the fire for a transgression.

5   Presumably semen is clean because of its fertilising qualities. It is not waste by definition, although it may be wasted.

6   In this chapter I have concentrated on views of women. There is also the need to explore Gypsy and Gorgio views of men. I have hinted at this in Okely 1975d:75.

7   In Okely 1975d, which this chapter is amended from, as a feminist, I also examined how women experienced and attempted to subvert, consciously or unconsciously, their subordination to men. I included some of the women's responses to the libidinal restrictions placed upon them, and their apparent exploitation of the Gorgio stereotype.

12. Ghosts and Gorgios

1   My evidence comes from fieldwork and discussions with those acquainted

with Gypsies in Belgium and France, especially in Toulouse (July and September 1980).

2   There is some evidence that the deceased must be buried three days after death. I did not check this in the field, but later read of it in the *Blackpool Evening Gazette*. A Gypsy fortune teller was said to have hanged herself after the death of her sister-in-law. Her son stated that: 'She was also upset because the date of his aunt's burial had extended to six days from the date of her death which was contrary to their religious beliefs – it was usually three days among Romany people' (7 April 1977).

3   Hindes Groome quotes an account from *Truth* (28 August 1879) how at the funeral of an unmarried girl her coffin was covered by white pocket-handkerchiefs. Each Gypsy also required one. These were 'borrowed' from Gorgio villagers and returned, washed and bleached, after the funeral (1880:119).

4   Dora Yates, by contrast, notes that Welsh Gypsies 'hold the belief that excessive lamentation is an offence to the dead, and that tears disturb their rest' (1930:26). Loud lamentation at a wake and funeral, however, seems more widespread among Gypsies, e.g. Walter Starkie gives a vivid description of such behaviour at a Gypsy funeral in Hungary (1933:138,142).

5   One Traveller informed me that formerly the eldest son retained the iron frame of the waggon to make a new one. Thompson also records a Gypsy retaining the hub caps and some hooks from his father's trailer (1924:79).

6   Personal communication, A. Sutherland and D. Brooks. Sutherland also states that *mulo* 'finally go to "heaven" or simply disappear' (1975:285).

7   Personal communication, Father Daley, Oxford.

8   Dora Yates who has documented the Gypsies' taboos on washing and eating (1953:32-3) also notes an old Gypsy who 'placed a broken teapot on the grave of his 3-year-old son Horace "so as he'll never be thirsty in Heaven, poor lamb"' (1953:27). She does not record whether the teapot was once used by the son. But it is significant that the vessel is broken and therefore unusable and *mochadi* for the living.

9   For *mulo*, Fred Wood records in his word list: 'ghost of Romany man or woman in possession of a corpse at certain hours of the day and night; the devil in possession of a corpse' (1973:126-7). Further research and enquiry might clarify the full meaning. Perhaps also some ghosts may be benevolent.

Concluding remarks

1   See G. Huizer's introduction in Huizer and Mannheim 1979.

References

The following abbreviations are used in the references.
J.G.L.S. *Journal of the Gypsy Lore Society*
M.H.L.G. Ministry of Housing and Local Government (now part of the Department of the Environment)

Acton, T. 1971. The Functions of the Avoidance of Moxadi Kovels. *J.G.L.S.*, third series, vol.I (3-4): 108-36.
Acton, T. 1974. *Gypsy Politics and Social Change*. London: Routledge and Kegan Paul.
Adams, B., Okely, J.M., Morgan, D., and Smith, D. 1975. *Gypsies and Government Policy in England*. London: Heinemann.
Adams, J. 1952. (See Kent County Council 1952.)
Ardener, E. 1972. Belief and the Problem of Women. In La Fontaine, J. (ed.), 1972. *The Interpretation of Ritual*. London: Tavistock.
De Baraclai Levy, J. 1958. *Wanderers in the New Forest*. London.
Barnes, B. 1975. Irish Travelling People. In Rehfisch 1975.
Barth, F. 1955. The Social Organisation of a Pariah Group in Norway. *Norveg* (Oslo). Reprinted in Rehfisch 1975.
Barth, F. 1969. Introduction to *Ethnic Groups and Boundaries*. London: Allen and Unwin.
Bates, D.G. 1972. Differential Access to Pasture in a Nomadic Society: The Yoruk of South-Eastern Turkey. In Irons, W. and Dyson-Hudson, N. (eds.), 1972. *Perspectives on Nomadism*. Leiden: Brill.
Bateson, G. 1973. *Steps to an Ecology of the Mind*. London: Paladin.
Beck, S., and Gheorghe, N. 1981. From Slavery to Coinhabiting Nationality: The Political Economy of Romanian Gypsies. Paper presented to the Symposium on the Social Anthropology of Europe. I.U.A.E.S. Intercongress, Amsterdam.
Bohannan, P. 1963. *Social Anthropology*. London: Holt, Rinehart and Winston.
Borde, A. 1547. *The Fyrst Boke of the Introduction of Knowledge*. Reproduced in Crofton 1907.
Borrow, G. 1841 . *The Zincali: (Gypsies in Spain)*. London: Murray.
Borrow, G. 1851. *Lavengro*. London: Murray.
Borrow, G. 1857. *The Romany Rye*. London: Dent (1969 edn).
Borrow, G. 1874 *Romano Lavo-Lil*. London: Murray (1919 edn).
Boswell, S.G. 1970. *The Book of Boswell* (ed. J. Seymour). London: Gollancz.
Brown, I. 1928. Roms are Doms. *J.G.L.S.*, third series, vol.VII (3-4): 170-7.
Clébert, J.P. 1967. *The Gypsies* (trans. C. Duff). Harmondsworth: Penguin.
Connors, J.P. 1972. An Essay on the Education of Travelling Children. In

Wallbridge, J. (ed.), 1972. *The Shadow on the Cheese – Some Light on Gypsy Education*. London: National Gypsy Education Council.

Connors, J.P. 1973. Seven Weeks of Childhood - An Autobiography. In Sandford 1973.

Cotten, R.M. 1954. An Anthropologist Looks at Gypsiology. *J.G.L.S.*, third series, vol.XXXIII (3-4): 107-20.

Cotten, R.M. 1955. An Anthropologist Looks at Gypsiology. *J.G.L.S.*, third series, vol.XXXIV (1-2): 20-37.

Crabb, J. 1830. In A Summary Account of the Proceedings of a Provisional Committee Associated at Southampton. Bodleian Library (unpublished).

Crabb, J. 1832. *The Gipsies' Advocate*. 3rd edn. London.

Cripps, J. 1976. *Accommodation for Gypsies*. Department of the Environment. London: H.M.S.O.

Croft-Cooke, R. 1948. *The Moon in my Pocket; Life with the Romanies*. London: Low.

Croft-Cooke, R. 1955. *A Few Gypsies*. London: Putnam.

Crofton, H.T. 1907. Borde's Egipt Speche. *J.G.L.S.*, new series, vol.I (2): 156-168.

Dallas, D. 1971. *The Travelling People*. London: Macmillan.

De Vaux de Foletier, F. 1970. *Mille ans d'histoire des Tsiganes*. Paris: Fayard.

Department of the Environment, 1977a. *Gypsy Caravan Sites. Notes for guidance of local authorities in the implementation of Part II of the Caravan Sites Act 1968*. Appendix to Circular 28/77. April. London: D.O.E.

Department of the Environment, 1977b. *A Guide to Gypsy Caravan Sites provided by local authorities in England and Wales*. August. London: D.O.E.

Department of the Environment. 1979. *Gypsy Sites Design Guide*. London: D.O.E.

Dodds, N. 1966. *Gypsies, Didikois and Other Travellers*. London: Johnson.

Dollé, M.P. 1970. Symbolique de la mort en milieu Tsigane. *Études Tsiganes*, 16 (4): 4-15.

Douglas, M. 1966. *Purity and Danger*. London: Routledge and Kegan Paul (1969 edn).

Duff, C. 1963. Supplementary notes on British and American Gypsies. Reprinted in Clébert 1967.

Dutt, W.A. 1910. Moxadi. (Notes and Queries), *J.G.L.S.*, new series, vol.IV (2): 156.

Dyson-Hudson, N. 1972. Introduction to Irons, W. and Dyson-Hudson, N. (ed.), 1972. *Perspectives on Nomadism*. Leiden: Brill.

Ellis, W. 1956. *The Nuisance and Prejudice of the Gypsy Vagrant to the Farmer*. Cited in Bell, V. *To Meet Mr Ellis*. London: Faber and Faber.

Études Tsiganes, 1980. *Populations nomades et pauvreté*. Paris. (Reprinted in *Études Tsiganes* 27(3), 1981).

Foucault, M. 1971. *Madness and Civilisation*. London: Tavistock.

Gallichan, W.M. 1908. The State Versus the Gypsy. *J.G.L.S.*, new series, vol.I. (4): 350-8.

Galsworthy, J. and A. 1932 (trans.). Introduction to *Carmen*. London: Elkin Matthews and Marrab.

References

Geertz, C. 1975. Deep Play: Notes on the Balinese Cock Fight. In *The Interpretation of Cultures*. London: Hutchinson, ch. 15.

Gentleman, H. and Swift, S. 1971. *Scotland's Travelling People*. Edinburgh: Scottish Development Department, H.M.S.O.

Gmelch, G. 1974. Change and Adaptation among Irish Travellers. Unpublished Ph.D. thesis. University of California at Santa Barbara.

Gmelch, G. 1977. *The Irish Tinkers: The Urbanisation of an Itinerant People*. Menlo Park, California: Cummings.

Gmelch, S. 1974. The Emergence and Persistence of an Ethnic Group: The Irish Travellers. Unpublished Ph.D. thesis. University of California at Santa Barbara.

Gmelch, S. 1975. *Tinkers and Travellers*. Dublin: O'Brien.

Goulet, D. and Walshok, M. 1971. Values among Underdeveloped Marginals: The Case of Spanish Gypsies. *Comparative Studies in Society and History*, vol.XIII (4): 451-72.

Grellmann, H.M.G. 1787. *Die Zigeuner* (transl.M.Raper). London.

Grönfors, M. 1977. Blood Feuding among Finnish Gypsies. *Tutkimuksia Research Reports* (University of Helsinki), no. 213.

Gropper, R. 1975. *Gypsies in the City*. Princeton: Darwin Press.

Guy, W. 1975. Ways of Looking at Rom: The Case of Czechoslovakia. Rehfisch 1975.

Guy, W. 1978. The Attempt of Socialist Czechoslovakia to Assimilate its Gypsy Population. Unpublished Ph.D. thesis. University of Bristol.

Gypsy Council, 1967. Memorandum (unpublished).

Hall, G. and Rivers, W.H.R. 1913. A Gypsy Pedigree and its Lessons. *Transactions of the British Association for the Advancement of Science*. Section H (3).

Hampshire Association of Parish Councils, 1961. Report on Gypsies and Travellers in Hampshire (unpublished).

Hancock, I. 1970. Is Anglo-Romanes a Creole? *J.G.L.S.*, third series, vol.XLIX (1-2): 41-4.

Harrison Matthews, L. 1968. *British Mammals*. London: Collins.

Harvey, D. 1979. *The Gypsies. Waggon-time and After*. London: Batsford.

Heymowski, A. 1969. *Swedish 'Travellers' and their Ancestry: A Social Isolate or an Ethnic Minority?* Uppsala: Almqvist and Wiksell.

Hindes Groome, F. 1880. *In Gypsy Tents*. Edinburgh: Nimmo. (Reprinted Wakefield: E.P.Publishing, 1973).

Hindes Groome, F. 1930 *Kriesgspiel*. Cited in Sampson 1930.

Hoyland, J. 1816. *A Historical Survey of the Customs, Habits and Present State of the Gypsies; designed to develope the Origin of this Singular People, and to Promote the Amelioration of their Condition*. London.

Huizer, G. and Mannheim, B. 1979. *The Politics of Anthropology*. The Hague: Mouton.

Jusserand, J. 1889. *English Wayfaring Life in the Middle Ages*, London: Methuen (1961 edn).

Kaminski, I.M. 1977. Identity Conflicts:Gypsy–Romany. *Working Paper, Institute of Social Anthropology*, no. 14. University of Gothenburg.

Kaminski, I.M. 1980. *The State of Ambiguity:Studies of Gypsy Refugees*. Gothenburg: Anthropological Research.

Kenrick, D. and Puxon, G. 1972. *The Destiny of Europe's Gypsies*. London: Heinemann.

References

Kent County Council 1952 (Adams, J.). Gypsies and other Travellers in Kent (unpublished).

La Fontaine, J. 1972. The Ritualisation of Women's Life-Crises in Bugisu. In La Fontaine, J. (ed.), 1972. *The Interpretation of Ritual*. London: Tavistock.

Lawrence, D.H., 1930. *The Virgin and the Gypsy*. London: Martin Secker.

Leach, E. 1972. Anthropological Aspects of Language: Animal Categories and Verbal Abuse. In Maranda, P. (ed.), *Mythology*. London: Penguin.

Leach, E. 1979. Summary and Discussion. In Burnham, B. and Kingsbury, J. (eds.), *Space, Hierarchy and Society*. BAR International Series 59. Oxford, pp. 119-24.

Leach, G.B. 1956. A Gypsy Funeral at Bagillt. *J.G.L.S.*, third series, vol. XXXV (1-2): 88-9.

Leland, C.G. 1882. *The Gypsies*. Boston.

Leland, C.G. 1891. *Gypsy Sorcery and Gypsy Fortune-telling*. London.

Leland, C.G. 1893. *The English Gipsies and Their Language*. 4th edn. London: Kegan Paul, Trench and Trubner.

Lévi-Strauss, C. 1966. *The Savage Mind* (transl.). London: Weidenfeld and Nicolson.

Lévi-Strauss, C. 1970. *The Raw and the Cooked* (transl. J. and D. Weightman). New York: Harper Torchbooks.

Lévi-Strauss, C. 1973. *Tristes Tropiques* (transl. J. and D. Weightman). London: Cape.

Liégeois, J.P. 1971a. The Cave Dwellers of Andalusia. *J.G.L.S.*, vol.L (1-2).

Liégeois, J.P. 1971b. *Les Tsiganes*. Paris: Editions du Seuil.

Liégeois, J.P. 1976. *Mutation tsigane*. Brussels: Editions Complexes, and Paris: Presses Universitaires de France.

Liégeois, J.P. 1977. *Ideologie et pratique du travail social de prévention*, Toulouse: privately published.

Liégeois, J.P. 1978a. Tsiganes et nomades. *Hommes et Migrations* (Paris), no. 24.

Liégeois, J.P. 1978b. Bohémiens et pouvoirs publics en France du XVème au XIXème siècles. *Études Tsiganes*, no. 4.

Lineton, M. 1976. The Situation of 'Travellers' in Scotland and the Republic of Ireland. Final Report to S.S.R.C. (unpublished).

Liszt, F. 1863. *Die Zigeuner und ihre Musik in Ungarn*. Cited in Sampson 1930.

McCormick, A. 1907. *The Tinkler-Gypsies*. Edinburgh:Dumfries.

McDowell, B. 1970. *Gypsies: Wanderers of the World*. Washington D.C.: National Geographic.

McKnight, D. 1975. Men, Women and other Animals: Taboo and Purification among the Wik-mungkan. In Willis, R. (ed.), *The Interpretation of Symbolism*. London: Malaby.

Mandel, E. 1969. *Introduction to Marxist Economic Theory*. New York: Pathfinder (1979 edn).

Marta, C. 1979. *The Acculturation of the Lovara*. 2 vols. Imfo-Gruppen, Stockholm University.

Marx, K. 1887. *Capital*. Vol.I. Moscow:Foreign Languages Publishing House (1961 edn).

Maybury-Lewis, D. 1974. *Akwé-Shavante Society*. London: Oxford University Press.

References

Merimée, P. 1845. *Carmen.* France: Bordas. (1966 edn).
M.H.L.G. 1966. Circulars. Reprinted in M.H.L.G. 1967, pp. 70,77.
M.H.L.G. 1967. *Gypsies and other Travellers.* London: H.M.S.O.
Miller, C. 1968. Macwya Gypsy Marimé. Unpublished M.A. thesis. University of Washington.
Miller, C. 1975. American Rom and the Ideology of Defilement. In Rehfisch 1975.
National Gypsy Education Council. 1973. *Handbook for Voluntary Teachers in Summer and other Schools.* London.
Needham, R. 1974. *Remarks and Inventions: Sceptical Essays about Kinship.* London: Tavistock.
Okely, J.M. 1972. The History of Local Council Policy towards Gypsies. Paper presented to the Centre for Environmental Studies seminar (unpublished).
Okely, J.M. 1975a. Gypsy Identity. In Adams *et al.* 1975: ch.2.
Okely, J.M. 1975b. The Family, Marriage, and Kinship Groups. In Adams *et al.* 1975: ch.3.
Okely, J.M. 1975c. Work and Travel. In Adams *et al.* 1975: ch.5.
Okely, J.M. 1975d. Gypsy Women: Models in Conflict. In Ardener, S.(ed.) *Perceiving Women.* London: Malaby (paperback edn London: Dent).
Okely, J.M. 1975e. Gypsies Travelling in Southern England. In Rehfisch 1975.
Okely, J.M. 1975f. The Self and Scientism. *Journal of the Anthropology Society of Oxford.* Trinity.
Okely, J.M. 1975g. Review of Sutherland's *Gypsies: the Hidden Americans. Journal of the Anthropology Society of Oxford.* Trinity.
Okely, J.M. 1976. Time for a Better Deal for the Gypsies. *The Times,* guest column. 16 June, p.6.
Okely, J.M. 1977. The Travellers: a Field Study of Gypsies in England. Unpublished D. Phil. thesis. Oxford University.
Okely. J.M. 1979a. Trading Stereotypes: the Case of English Gypsies. In Wallman, S. 1979. *Ethnicity at Work.* London: Macmillan.
Okely, J.M. 1979b. An Anthropological Contribution to the History and Archaeology of an Ethnic Group. In Burnham, B. and Kingsbury, J. (eds.), *Space, Hierarchy and Society.* BAR International Series 59. Oxford.
Okely, J.M. 1980. Poverty in Nomad Populations. In *Europe against Poverty: Evaluation Report of the European Programme of Pilot Schemes and Studies to Combat Poverty.* Espoir Ltd presented to the Commission of the European Communities, ch.7.
Okely, J.M. 1981a. Nature–Culture as Used against and by Gypsies. Paper presented to the Conference on 'The Nature–Culture Debate'. University of Essex.
Okely, J.M. 1981b. Paper presented to the Symposium on the Social Anthropology of Europe. I.U.A.E.S. Intercongress, Amsterdam.
Otter, K. 1931. Viennese Gypsies. *J.G.L.S.,* third series, vol.X (3): 105-30.
Petulengro, Gipsy. 1935. *A Romany Life.* London: Methuen.
Plowden, Lady B. 1967. *Children and their Primary Schools.* Report for the Central Advisory Council for Education, vol.II, appendix 12. London: H.M.S.O.

References

Plowden, Lady B. 1972. Foreword to Wallbridge, J. 1972. *The Shadow on the Cheese – Some Light on Gypsy Education*. London: National Gypsy Education Council.
Puxon, G. 1973. *Rom: Europe's Gypsies*. London: Minority Rights Group.
Rao, A. 1975. Some Manus Conceptions and Attitudes. In Rehfisch 1975.
Reeve, D. 1958. *Smoke in the Lanes*. London: Phoenix House.
Reeve, D. 1960. *No Place Like Home*. London: Phoenix House.
Rehfisch, F. 1958. The Tinkers of Perthshire and Aberdeenshire. School of Scottish Studies. Edinburgh (unpublished).
Rehfisch, F. 1975. *Gypsies, Tinkers and other Travellers*. London: Academic.
Reiss, C. 1975. *The Education of Travelling Children*. London: Macmillan (Schools Council).
Report of the Commission on Itinerancy. 1963. Dublin: Stationery Office.
Reyniers, A. and Gilain, F. 1979. *Tsiganes de Belgique, Tsiganes du monde*. Documentation d'Anthropologie, no.15. Institut des Sciences Politiques et Sociales, Université Catholique de Louvain.
Sampson, J. 1923. On the Origin and Early Migrations of the Gypsies. *J.G.L.S.*, third series, vol.II (4): 156-69.
Sampson, J. 1926. *The Dialect of the Gypsies of Wales*. Oxford: Clarendon.
Sampson, J. 1930. *The Wind on the Heath. A Gypsy Anthology*. London: Chatto and Windus.
Sandford, J. 1973. *Gypsies*. London: Secker and Warburg.
San Roman, T. 1975. Kinship, Marriage, Law and Leadership in Two Urban Gypsy Settlements in Spain. In Rehfisch 1975.
Sartre, J.P. 1973. *Anti-Semite and Jew* (transl. G.J. Becker). New York: Schocken.
Seymour, J. 1970. Notes to Boswell 1970.
Sibley, D. 1981. *Outsiders in Urban Societies*. Oxford: Blackwell.
Sijes, B.A. 1979. *Vervolging van Zigeuners in Nederland 1940-1945*. The Hague: Martinus Nijhoff.
Smart, B.C. and Crofton, H.T. 1875. *The Dialect of the English Gypsies*. London: Asher and Co.
Smith, G. 1880. *Gypsy Life; or Our Gipsies and their Children*. London: Haughton and Co.
Smith, G. 1901. *His Life and Work by Himself*. London: Thomas Law.
Starkie, W. 1933. *Raggle-Taggle*. London: Murray.
Sutherland, A. 1975. *Gypsies: the Hidden Americans*. London: Tavistock.
Tambiah, S.J. 1973. Classification of Animals in Thailand. In Douglas, M. (ed.), *Rules and Meanings*. Harmondsworth: Penguin.
Thompson, T.W. 1910. Defilement by a Dog's Tongue. *J.G.L.S.*, new series, vol.III (4): 320.
Thompson, T.W. 1913. Gypsy Taboos and Funeral Rites. *Transactions of the British Association for the Advancement of Science*. Section H (4).
Thompson, T.W. 1922. The Uncleanness of Women among English Gypsies. *J.G.L.S.*, third series, vol.I (1-2): 15-43.
Thompson, T.W. 1923a. Consorting with and Counterfeiting Egyptians. *J.G.L.S.*, third series, vol.II (2): 81-93.
Thompson, T.W. 1923b. The Social Polity of the English Gypsies. *J.G.L.S.*, third series, vol.II (3): 113-39.
Thompson, T.W. 1924. English Gypsy Death and Burial Customs. *J.G.L.S.*, third series, vol.III (1-2): 5-38, 60-93.

References

Thompson, T.W. 1926. Gypsy Marriage in England. *J.G.L.S.*, third series, vol. V (1): 9-37.

Thompson, T.W. 1927. Gypsy Marriage in England. *J.G.L.S.*, third series, vol.VI (4): 101-29, 151-82.

Thompson, T.W. 1928. Gleanings from Constables' Accounts and other Sources. *J.G.L.S.*, third series, vol.VII (1): 30-47.

Thompson, T.W. 1929. Additional Notes on English Gypsy Women Taboos. *J.G.L.S.*, third series, vol.VIII (1): 33-9.

Thompson, T.W. 1930a. Additional Notes on English Gypsy Death and Burial Customs. *J.G.L.S.*, third series, vol.IX (1): 34-8.

Thompson, T.W. 1930b. Illustrations of English Gypsy Law. *J.G.L.S.*, third series, vol.IX (4): 152-70.

Tompkins, J. 1967. Gypsies. Report to the Welfare Department. California (unpublished). Cited in Sutherland 1975.

Trigg, E.B. 1967. Magic and Religion among the Gypsies of Great Britain. Unpublished D. Phil. thesis. Oxford University.

Trigg, E.B. 1968. Religion and Social Reform among the Gypsies of Britain. *J.G.L.S.*, third series, vol.XLVII (3-4): 82-109.

Trigg, E.B. 1975. *Gypsy Demons and Divinities: The Magical and Supernatural Practices of the Gypsies.* London: Sheldon.

Van den Brink, F.H. 1974. *A Field Guide to the Mammals in Europe.* London: Collins.

Vesey-Fitzgerald, B. 1973. *Gypsies of Britain.* New enlarged edn (1st edn 1944). Newton Abbot: David and Charles.

Viljanen Saira, A.M. 1978. Les Symboles culturels chez les Tsiganes de Finlande. In Liégeois 1978a.

Wade, R.A.R. 1967. Devils, Ghosts and Fairies. *J.G.L.S.*, third series, vol. XLVI (3-4): 123-32.

Wade, R.A.R. 1968. A Conference of Public Health Inspectors on Gypsies. *J.G.L.S.*, third series, vol.XLVII (3-4): 116-33.

Ward-Jackson, C.H. and Harvey, D.E. 1972. *The English Gypsy Caravan.* Newton Abbot: David and Charles.

Whyte, B. 1979. *The Yellow on the Broom.* Edinburgh: Chambers.

Windstedt, E.O. 1908. Gypsy Civilisation. *J.G.L.S.*, new series, vol.I (4): 319-49.

Wood, M.F. 1973. *In the Life of a Romany Gypsy.* London: Routledge and Kegan Paul.

Worcester County Council. 1966. Report of the Working Party of Gypsies. Worcester (unpublished).

Yates, D. 1930. Lamentation for the Dead. *J.G.L.S.*, third series, vol.IX (1): 26-8.

Yates, D. 1953. *My Gypsy Days.* London: Phoenix House.

Yoors, J. 1967. *The Gypsies.* London: George Allen and Unwin.

Glossary

(including non-Romany terms)

atchen tan	stopping place
baulo	pig, policeman
bender	tent
beng	devil
bok, bak, baxt	luck
bor	hedge
Calling	working by Calling at houses
chal	fellow
chavo	child
chi	girl
chik	dust, soil
chikli	dusty, dirty
chop	to exchange, an exchange sealed by the two individuals banging hands
chor	to steal
chovihanni	witch
dicklo	Gypsy neckerchief
didikois	allegedly half-bred Gypsies (see Smart and Crofton 1875:51)
dinlo	fool
divi	mad
diwano	a group of adults convened to discuss a matter publicly
drab	poison
drabengro	doctor
drom	road
dukkering	fortune telling
gavver	policeman
Gorgio	non-Gypsy, stranger, outsider
grai	horse
hotchi-witchi	hedgehog
jook	dog
kanni	chicken
kenna	house
kennick	Gypsy now a housedweller
kris	Gypsy council
kushti	pretty, good
lubbeny	prostitute
mace	swindle, obtain by confidence trick
matchka	cat

Glossary

mochadi, mokada, moxadi	ritually unclean, polluted
mong	to beg
mongri	begging
moosh	man
mulo	ghost
mumper, mumpli	hedge crawler, tramp
muskra	policeman
nak	nose
natsyia	nation
pal	brother
posh	half
praster	to run
rai, rye	gentleman
rat	blood
rauni, rawni	lady
Rom	Romany man
romado, romered	married
Romané	Romany
sap	snake
saster	iron
shoshi	rabbit
stirapen	prison
stived in	stifled
tatcho	real, true
totting	rag and bone dealing
trailer	caravan
trashed	frightened
Traveller	person of Gypsy or Tinker descent
trolley	open cart
vardo	Gypsy horse-drawn waggon
yog	fire

Index

251